Bold Plans
for
School Restructuring

The New American Schools Designs

Bold Plans
for
School Restructuring

The New American Schools Designs

Sam Stringfield
Johns Hopkins University
and
Steven M. Ross and Lana Smith
University of Memphis

LEA LAWRENCE ERLBAUM ASSOCIATES, PUBLISHERS

1996   Mahwah, New Jersey

Lawrence Erlbaum Associates, Inc. Publishers
10 Industrial Avenue
Mahwah, New Jersey 07430-2262

Cover design by Deborah Branner

Book design by Lyndell D. Smith

Library of Congress Cataloging-in-Publication Data

Bold plans for school restructuring: the New American Schools designs / [edited by] Sam Stringfield and Steven M. Ross and Lana Smith.
       p. cm.
Includes bibliographical references and index.
ISBN 0-8058-2340-9 (cloth) 0-8058-2341-7 (paper)
1. New American Schools. 2. New American Schools Development Corporation. 3. School improvement programs—United States. 4. Educational change—United States. I. Stringfield, Sam. II. Ross, Steven M. III. Smith, Lana.

LB2822.82.B65 1996
371.2'00973—dc20 96-18769
      CIP

Books published by Lawrence Erlbaum Associates are printed on acid-free paper, and their bindings are chosen for strength and durability.

Printed in the United States of America
10 9 8 7 6 5 4 3 2 1

In memory of three American educational reformers—
Audrey Cohen, Elsbeth Kehl, and Joseph Miller

Contents

Acknowledgments

Bold Plans for School Restructuring has always been a team effort. The editors are thankful to a highly skilled group of professionals, many working independently, yet all willing to contribute so that this book could be produced in a timely fashion.

John Anderson, president of New American Schools, encouraged the development of *Bold Plans* from the beginning, and co-authored a lively overview. He and his staff at New American Schools provided thoughtful suggestions as the project progressed.

The nine design teams produced their chapters during the very busy scale-up phase of their development efforts. While working with schools, fine tuning, and occasionally making major alterations in their designs, each team contributed a chapter. Each team wrote clearly, displaying the logic of their design and the power of their design team's convictions as to how to best improve America's schools.

Lyndell Smith shepherded countless practical and aesthetic decisions regarding the book's design. Decisions ranging from the selection of typefaces through the final camera-ready layout were safe in her hands. As the volume went through three rounds of refinement, she clarified and smoothed the writing of eleven teams of authors into a cohesive whole.

Cary Berkeley and Sam Kim coordinated with authors, made copy edits, and cajoled the editors into clear editorial decisions.

Naomi Silverman, senior editor at Lawrence Erlbaum Associates, has provided sage advice, frank assessments, steady encouragement, and dozens of technical clarifications. We could not ask for more.

All of the editors' work on *Bold Plans* was done in addition to their regular professional duties. Once again, each of us found work intruding into family time. We are deeply grateful to our spouses, Kathleen, Susan, and Dennie, for tolerating and even facilitating our efforts. As in so many aspects of our lives, we couldn't have done it without you.

Preparation of this volume was supported by a grant from the Office of Educational Research and Improvement, U.S. Department of Education, to the Center for Research on the Education of Students Placed at Risk at Johns Hopkins and Howard Universities (Grant No. R117D–40005). However, any opinions expressed by the editors or the chapter authors are their own, and do not represent the policies or positions of the U.S. Department of Education.

—*Sam Stringfield*
—*Steve Ross*
—*Lana Smith*
June 26, 1996

Introduction

Bold Plans for School Restructuring
Nine Designs from New American Schools

Sam Stringfield, Johns Hopkins University
Steven Ross, University of Memphis
Lana Smith, University of Memphis

Two powerful forces are driving America's demands for better schools. The first force, more traditionally recurring, is idealistic. A proud call for substantially more and better schooling for all of our citizens runs from Ben Franklin and Thomas Jefferson through George Bush and Bill Clinton.

The second force is new and economic. The current group of young Americans is in danger of being the first full generation to consistently make less money and enjoy fewer worldly rewards than its parents. From 1973 to 1992 the median income of young male high school graduates in the United States dropped by a third. For high school dropouts the decline was fully 50 percent and shows no sign of improving (Stringfield, 1995). A combination of technological advances and industries moving off shore has resulted in a dramatic drop in demand for unskilled labor in America. At some point, individual misfortune threatens to become a national calamity. Who will, or can, pay taxes to support roads, police and schools? Not someone who is working for minimum wages with no benefits, or is on unemployment, or in prison.

The intersection of idealistic and pragmatic forces has produced a period unparalleled in its calls for reform in U.S. education. The current calls are exceptional, not for their now familiar theme of urgency, but for the length of time they have been sustained. Following the publication of *A Nation At Risk* (National Commission on Excellence in Education, 1983), America has experienced 13 years of continuous calls for educational reform.[1]

The sustained calls for school reform are not driven by the fact that schools are failing more people. Schools are not. The percentages of students graduating from high school are, at worst, stable and appear to be gradually rising. The National Assessment of Educational Progress (Educational Testing Service, 1994) indicated that young people's reading skills were stable over the last 25 years and that their knowledge of math and science has been slowly improving. Rather, the costs of maintaining the success-to-failure ratios of the last quarter century have risen dramatically. There is a considerable fear in many policy circles that although our schools have maintained their quality, or even improved a little during the same period, the overall quality of education in many other countries, especially Asian countries, has risen dramatically.

Justified or not, an implicit parallel is being drawn between education and diverse industries. In this analogy, the issue for General Motors today is not whether the cars they are making now are as good as the cars they made 40 years ago when GM was the world leader in the field of automobile production. By a variety of objective measures, GM's current models are more efficient, more reliable, and offer many more options. Rather, the concern about General Motors is whether their rate of progress in the areas of efficiency, reliability, and ultimately, profitability is matching or can match that of several other automobile manufacturers around the world. At the end of World War II, U.S. public schools were the envy of the world, and the American work force was widely regarded as the best educated on earth. It is no longer clear that America's young people are graduating as the best educated and prepared of any group on earth for an information age economy. Parents and policymakers are understandably concerned.

In this environment, President George Bush called for an education summit. A first ever for the United States, the summit was held in September 1989. Along with 49 other governors, then-governor Bill Clinton actively participated. One of several concrete proposals emerging from those meetings was the creation of a private, nonprofit corporation charged with creating new, break-the-mold school designs for the 21st century.

---

[1] It is interesting to note that America's one previous systematic development and research effort on whole school change, the "Eight Year Study" (Aikin, 1942), was conceived and conducted during the Great Depression.

This book highlights the path traveled by New American Schools (NAS), and the first three years' work of nine development teams. As the chapter authors make clear, none of the paths has always been smooth. Yet striking new images, often accompanied by eye-opening techniques, are conveyed in the pages that follow.

Moving Through the Chapters

A few notes may help the reader move through the chapters. From its inception, New American Schools focused on whole school restructuring designs. Pullout programs, however effective, were to be nested within larger designs. School reforms were to help create and be supported by systemic reforms (Smith & O'Day, 1990). The reforms could involve novel combinations of public and private-sector know-how. The emphasis was to be on getting the job done, not on ideology.

The design selection process (described in chapter 1) was intense. Were potentially valuable ideas left unfunded? Surely, yes. The unfortunate reality was that the organization was working with finite resources. Are the remaining models worthy of serious consideration by the practical and academic educational communities, by parents and policy analysts? Even more surely, yes. Are other practical models of school restructuring alive and worthy of consideration in America today? Absolutely. The developers of some of those other models are involved in the NAS designs. For example, Theodore Sizer and James Comer have been key figures in the ATLAS design, and Robert Slavin leads the Roots and Wings program. We encourage readers to study such alternative restructuring programs as Paideia Schools (Adler, 1982, 1984) and Accelerated Schools (Hopfenberg & Levin, 1993; Levin, 1987), in addition to the options described here by the New American Schools teams.

Careful consideration of the broadest practical array of options can be an important component of school restructuring. On the one hand, examining many designs logically would increase the probability that a school choosing to implement a national design would choose a good fit for the particular school's context. On the other hand, examining multiple options should help schools that are committed to "home brewing" designs to consider the richest possible array of components before settling on a specific set of locally integrated reforms.

As an outgrowth of the nation's long-term demands for better schooling for all students, and of the leadership of New American Schools, we have reached a new level of sophistication in educational reform. Today, the products of bold new school restructuring designs and systemic reform can be melded, implemented, and examined by diverse audiences of practitioners and researchers.

As several of the design-specific chapters and the RAND Phase 2 evaluation in the final chapter make clear, research on the effects of these diverse programs has begun. Early indications from several programs are promising. Considering that many of the design concepts are built on previous research, and that some of the designs are themselves expansions of previously well-studied designs, this should not be surprising. No definitive outcome evaluation of the current efforts has yet been completed. However, in contrast to several previous reform efforts, a most encouraging sign is that early in the lives of these restructuring efforts, the gathering of hard data in multiple locations has begun.

Making the Information Useful

Having read each of these chapters in several drafts, and having considered several options for the order of presentation of the designs, the editors were unable to find a single, linear design dimension along which the designs varied. We then chose to present the designs in two groups, each group ordered alphabetically. Chapters 2–8 present the seven NAS designs funded through three full phases. Chapters 9 and 10 present two designs that were funded in phases one and two but not phase three. We do have some suggestions for readers of this volume.

1. Two related assumptions of the original proposers of the New American Schools were that (a) no single improvement plan can be best for all schools, and (b) by putting many thoughtfully developed plans forward at once, supporters of educational improvement could allow the marketplace of public schools and districts to determine what types of reforms could best work with the many contextual variables that define reform options at a given school.

A medical analogy may be useful. Even though penicillin and chemotherapy are both superb modern treatments, one is much better if the problem facing a patient is pneumonia, and the other is better for some types of cancer. There is an assumed context-reform design interaction that stands in contrast to centralized *One Best System* (Tyack, 1974) approaches. It is probably more frustrating than productive to try to determine which of these designs is "best" in an absolute sense. Rather, we believe it is more productive to imagine conditions under which a particular design might be a particularly strong, or weak, fit.[2]

2. A person reading these design descriptions as an academic exercise is obviously free of immediate concerns regarding the necessary processes for implementation. Persons searching for possible reform strategies for a particular school should be aware that years of hard work will be required to fully implement any of these, or any other school restructuring design or process. Reformers have an understandable interest in encouraging schools to give their design a good try. Practitioners need to be aware that if there were a long-term, hard-work-free route to dramatically improved schooling, most schools and school systems would already have taken it. In particular, successful implementation of any of these designs inevitably will require years of focused professional development for everyone at the school.

Given that these or any other reforms will be hard work, practitioners need to read with one eye focused on the potential of any one reform, and the other firmly trained on the long-term human and fiscal costs. We do not say this to discourage moving forward; indeed we regard reform as both desirable and inevitable. Rather, we advocate a sober choice among diverse paths.

3. We suggest that readers treat this book as a hypertext. Move around in it. Among other rewards, a certain enjoyment can be derived from reading a design chapter while hypothesizing rewards and problems that would be incurred implementing the strategy, and then reading the final chapter for design-specific events during the first two phases of New American Schools' funding.

However, after a few cycles of moving from program to process evaluation, the reader will have come to know the final chapter so well that the task becomes more like reading crossword puzzle clues while looking at a completed puzzle. If this back-and-forth strategy is appealing, readers may wish to pick a couple of models that strike them as particularly interesting as beginning places.

4. Be assured there are additional resources for learning about any of these designs. This volume provides overviews of nine designs. Each team will gladly provide additional information about

---

[2] We are aware that there would be a powerful temptation to consider comparisons among these and other designs as a "horse race." We believe that such a metaphor would be ill chosen. If readers were determined to take such a metaphor seriously, we would remind them of a fact known to all successful pony players: "There are horses for courses."

its particular design. Some have published entire volumes; most have videos available. Helpful information including addresses and telephone numbers for New American Schools and the Design Teams may be found in the appendix.

In addition, interested persons or teams might consider visiting one of the New American Schools "scaleup" jurisdictions. In these jurisdictions, interested persons may have the opportunity to visit multiple implementations of diverse designs. Presently these jurisdictions include Cincinnati, Los Angeles, Memphis, Dade County (Miami), Philadelphia, Pittsburgh, San Diego, the State of Maryland, and a Washington state alliance of districts in the Seattle area.

Organized visits to schools implementing six of the New American Schools designs, plus Accelerated Schools and Paideia schools, will be offered at the International Congress for School Effectiveness and Improvement, to be held in January 1997 in Memphis, Tennessee.

5. Remember that all of these designs are continuing to evolve. Between the time this volume goes to press and is published, virtually all the designs will have refined portions of their models or added new components. Indeed, it may be this ability to revise and refine the New American Schools designs based on experience in multiple sites that offers the greatest hope for the evolution of not just newer, but better, American schools.

Organization of Chapters

Chapter 1, by Kearns and Anderson, presents a fascinating history of the New American Schools Development Corporation and a strikingly energized vision for American educational reform. It repays reading from the perspectives of school reform strategy, policy, and politics. For example, the Kearns and Anderson chapter takes on different shadings, depending on whether it is read before or after the concluding RAND evaluation chapter.

The second through tenth chapters, each providing an in-depth picture of a different restructuring design, present wide-ranging visions of and experiences in school improvement. Each has clear areas of strength, and perhaps unavoidably, each leaves potentially important areas of school reform untouched.

We have sequenced the designs alphabetically in these chapters. Readers may find conceptual assistance in an additional grouping scheme. In chapter 11, RAND evaluators group the designs into three broad types:

Core Designs emphasize restructuring in seven elements associated with the "core" of schooling: curriculum, instruction, standards, assessments, student groupings, community involvement, and professional development. Because the locus of these changes is the school building, with direct and immediate influences on curriculum, RAND concluded that these designs are typically the fastest starting. Included in this category are the following:

- Audrey Cohen College (chapter 2),

- Co-NECT (chapter 4),

- Expeditionary Learning (chapter 5), and

- Roots and Wings (chapter 8).

Comprehensive Designs extend the core designs by including the elements of integrated social services, governance changes, and organization and staffing changes. In comprehensive designs, a major emphasis is establishing connections with external groups (e.g., social service agencies) to achieve restructuring goals. RAND has found that, to date, these additional components and the associated operational challenges generally reduce the speed of implementation relative to core designs. However, the extensive within-school focus of the comprehensive designs does allow substantial, tangible changes to be realized in early years. The comprehensive design category includes the following:

- ATLAS Schools (chapter 3),

- Modern Red Schoolhouse (chapter 6).

- Community Learning Centers (chapter 9),

- Los Angeles Learning Centers (chapter 10), and

Systemic designs operate primarily outside the individual school by attempting to change the external systems that have impact on educational policies and programs. Such systems include the central office, the state legislature, professional development providers, social service providers, and the community. Obviously, such a broad focus results in systemic designs becoming the most challenging to implement, and thus they are likely to be the slowest in demonstrating school-level changes. On the other hand, by influencing external policies and governance, systemic designs have great potential to readily impact large numbers of schools within a district or state. One New American Schools design fits within the systemic category:

• National Alliance for Restructuring Education (chapter 7).

The final chapter provides an important and evenhanded analysis of the programs' progress through the first three years of funding. Reading chapter eleven, and then moving between specific design chapters and back through the evaluation chapter is probably a good strategy for considering dreams and visions as shadowed by the first two years of implementation experiences.

References

Adler, M. (1982). *The Paideia proposal: An educational manifesto.* New York: Macmillan.

Adler, M. (1984). *The Paideia program: An educational syllabus.* New York: Macmillan.

Aikin, W. (1942). *The story of the Eight-Year Study.* New York: Harper & Brothers.

Educational Testing Service (1994). *NAEP 1992 trends in academic progress.* Washington, DC: National Center for Educational Statistics.

Hopfenberg, W., & Levin, H. (1993). *The Accelerated Schools resource guide.* San Francisco: Jossey-Bass.

Levin, H. (1987). Accelerated schools for disadvantaged students. *Educational Leadership, 44*(6), 19–21.

National Commission on Excellence in Education (1983). *A nation at risk.* Washington, DC: U.S. Department of Education.

Stringfield, S. (1995). Attempts to enhance students' learning: A search for valid programs and highly reliable implementation techniques. *School Effectiveness and School Improvement, 6(1),* 67–96.

Smith, M., & O'Day, J. (1990). Systemic school reform. In S. Fuhrman & B. Malen (Eds.), *The politics of curriculum and testing* (pp. 233–267). Philadelphia: Falmer.

Tyack, D. (1974). *The one best system.* Cambridge, MA: Harvard University Press.

1

Sharing the Vision
Creating New American Schools

David T. Kearns
John L. Anderson
New American Schools

We have a vision for our nation's schools. We see schools that enable all of America's young people to develop the skills they need for productive lives as citizens and workers. We see schools that challenge all students, recognize and build their strengths, help them realize their goals, and reward their efforts. We see schools that value and respect all individuals. We see schools that command the respect of their communities and involve parents, business people, social service providers, and policymakers in education. In short, we see New American Schools, schools that provide today's children with the academic and social skills they need for tomorrow's world.

In these New American Schools, all children have the opportunity to learn at high levels, and all children are held to high standards and given the means to achieve them—at a cost comparable to the cost of today's schools. The founders of the New American Schools Development Corporation—leaders in the corporate and foundation communities—set out to create schools that embody this vision. The founders cast aside conventional assumptions about schools and replaced them with an innovative and forward-thinking strategy for educating tomorrow's citizens.

These "new" schools do not need to be created from the ground up. Years of experience with school reform have generated valuable lessons about what works and what does not work. Successful reform efforts should not aim to bypass existing schools, but to "transform" them—revitalize the teaching and learning processes by incorporating high standards and inspiring high performance.

The New American Schools mission is to reinvigorate schools and education systems through the following broad tasks:

- Create high-quality, comprehensive designs for high-performance schools

- Demonstrate that schools using these designs can help all children perform at high levels

- Identify systemic barriers to creating high-performance schools

- Operate new schools at costs comparable to existing schools

- Develop a strategy to implement the designs widely and build the capacity to support the strategy

Several premises, based on research and past experience with school and systems reform, support this mission. First, in order to significantly improve the public education system in this country, the creation of isolated model schools is not enough. Lasting, widespread reform requires that individual schools continually revitalize themselves, and that opportunities to do so are available to large numbers of schools. Second, experience indicates that most schools need help in this ongoing process of improvement, both from administrators within education systems and from specialists in teaching and learning from outside the system. Third, the culture of schools varies widely, depending on leadership, student population, location, history, and other factors. Therefore, it is extremely unlikely that all schools will choose an identical process of growth and change. Fourth, the opportunity for schools to choose among designs for improvement is a valuable impetus for change. Teachers who have the chance to explore different designs and work as a group to select the design most appropriate for their school will often have a heightened investment in the successful implementation of the design and the transformation process as a whole.

This chapter describes the history of the New American Schools' effort and the process through which it has worked to create school-based designs and to test their effectiveness. It outlines the strategy for scaling up the designs to enable the transformation of large numbers of schools to high-performance learning environments. Finally, the chapter discusses the lessons learned to date and how these lessons have shaped the scale-up strategy.

New American Schools: A Brief History

The New American Schools Development Corporation was founded in 1991 by a group of business and foundation leaders interested in investing in innovative designs for school transformation. They pledged to use a venture capital model of investment: At each stage of development, they would critically examine the success of the designs and continue to fund only those that demonstrated real potential for transforming large numbers of schools. At its inception, several unique characteristics set New American Schools apart from other school transformation efforts. First, the effort was founded by private sector leaders, with a promise to neither request nor accept any government funding. Second, the New American Schools initiative has a lifetime of only five years, after which schools and districts will take ownership of the transformation effort. The five-year timeline includes a one-year development phase, a two-year testing and refinement phase, and a two-year scale-up phase.

Along with a small central staff, the New American Schools' team includes a Board of Directors, made up of chief executive officers from some of the nation's largest companies, and an Education Advisory Panel, made up of researchers and educators.

Immediately after the founding of the company, New American Schools issued a Request for Proposals (RFP) for designing high-quality, effective, and exciting schools. The proposals were subject to only three rules: A proposed school had to be open to all students, it had to hold students accountable to high standards, and it had to be designed to operate at a cost comparable to today's schools (following an initial investment period).

The RFP generated an enormous response: Nearly 700 proposals from around the country arrived on Valentine's Day, 1992. Each proposal was submitted by a team representing a broad array of educators, businesses, nonprofit organizations, and other groups. A corps of 500 volunteers—including leaders in education, policy, and business—read the submissions and selected eleven school design proposals to participate in Phase 1, the development phase. These eleven Design Teams received funding for one year to develop their ideas into workable designs for school transformation.

A year later, nine of the Design Teams were chosen to continue with Phase 2. During this phase, the Teams collectively worked with almost 150 schools in 19 states for two years. Working closely with teachers and administrators in these sites, the Teams further developed their designs based on the practical experience of implementation and refined the core components of the designs. All Design Team activities during this period were funded by New American Schools.

During Phase 2, according to the RAND Corporation, schools working with the Design Teams made more rapid progress with initiation and initial implementation of a comprehensive school reform effort than schools included in studies of comparable school change approaches. RAND attributed this success to several factors:

- Each design is a whole-school design that covers virtually all aspects of schooling, rather than a piecemeal, fragmented approach to reform.

- Teachers and principals in New American Schools know where they are headed before they start; the designs unite faculties and school improvement efforts around a common vision for transformation.

- Each Design Team places a high priority on intensive, ongoing professional development for teachers.

- The tight New American Schools timeline forced schools and Design Teams to stick to aggressive schedules and meet demanding deadlines.

The pace and quality of implementation during Phase 2 varied somewhat from school to school and from design to design based on several factors. First, some Design Teams existed before the RFP and had already had opportunities to implement their designs in schools, while others were created specifically in response to New American Schools' RFP and started from scratch in 1993. Second, several of the designs emphasize core elements of schooling (e.g., curriculum and instruction), while others have a more comprehensive scope (e.g., include governance and integration of community services). The former category tended to experience more rapid implementation than the latter.

Phase 2 proved that one of the strengths of the designs is their flexibility. None of the designs is a rigid, cookie-cutter model for school reform. Each offers a distinctive vision and set of components, but permits considerable adaptation by each unique site. The intention is not for the designs to be "replicated" but to offer a focus and a set of broad guiding principles for reform. As a school implements a design, it maintains an ongoing relationship with the

Design Team, driven by the needs of the school. The school, not the Team, has ownership of the change process; the principles and vision of the design serve as a framework for change.

Collectively, the New American Schools Design Teams represent a potent force for change, and they are the effort's most important assets and source of credibility. They represent a vast wealth of education expertise, decades of experience, and innovative ideas. The Design Teams offer different methods, philosophies, and styles, reflecting the different cultures and needs of schools. They are evidence that, at its heart, any significant reform of our nation's schools must be built on the actions of individual schools to transform themselves into highly effective learning environments capable of helping all students perform at high levels, and that the mission of true reformers lies in helping schools achieve this transformation.

Seven of the nine Design Teams that tested their designs during Phase 2 were selected to participate in scaleup, bringing their designs to large numbers of schools across the country. Table 1.1 briefly describes these seven Design Teams.

Bringing Success to Scale

The experiences of the Design Teams indicate that exciting changes are under way in many schools across the country. But innovative, dynamic designs at work in isolated schools—treated as exceptions, operating on the margins, and involving small numbers of students and teachers and families—are not enough. The problems of the public education system today demand solutions that cut through systems and demonstrate real potential to improve educational outcomes for a significant proportion of American students. However, despite decades of education reform efforts, there is not one district, much less a state, of any size or diversity in this country where good schools are the norm. The success of the New American Schools mission rests on changing this fact.

Building a scale-up strategy to accomplish this mission began with a decision to identify a small number of school communities (defined as states, districts, or groups of neighboring districts) and concentrate on transforming a large proportion of the schools in these communities. These communities can then serve as models for other communities around the country.

The New American Schools Development Corporation joined forces with several other organizations to craft a strategy for scaling up school transformation. With the formation of this partnership, the effort officially became known as "New American Schools,"

Table 1.1

The New American Schools Design Teams
Brief Descriptions

➤ *Atlas Communities* (based outside Boston) combines and builds on the work of Ted Sizer, James Comer, Howard Gardner, and the Education Development Center. The design's goal is to create a unified, supportive school community of learners in each K–12 feeder pattern, called a pathway. Teams of teachers from across the pathway work together to design curriculum and assessment strategies based on locally-defined standards and, in collaboration with parents and administrators, to implement sound policies and management structures that support teaching and learning.

➤ *Audrey Cohen College* (New York City) offers a design that organizes each semester's curriculum and instruction around a complex and meaningful Purpose that contributes to the greater good of society. Each Purpose involves core academic skills and focuses learning on student-directed projects involving the larger community; students demonstrate mastery of skills through an interdisciplinary project related to the Purpose.

➤ *Co-NECT Schools* (Cambridge, Mass.) provides a comprehensive, technology-supported framework for learning and communication within schools and districts. Co-NECT's vision for curriculum is project-based, interdisciplinary, and focuses on helping students reach a school's performance standards. Students stay with the same teacher and within small clusters for at least two years. The design was developed by Bolt, Beranek and Newman (BBN), a leading technology company that helped develop the Internet.

➤ *Expeditionary Learning Outward Bound* (Cambridge, Mass.) offers a curriculum centered around teacher-designed learning expeditions that develop intellectual and physical

Table 1.1 (continued)

NAS Design Teams Brief Descriptions

skills and character. The design, based on the principles of the Outward Bound program, helps schools focus instruction on interdisciplinary, challenging projects, structure scheduling to allow for flexibility and in-depth learning, and keep students and teachers together for more than one year.

➤ *Modern Red Schoolhouse* (Indianapolis, Ind.) combines traditional education principles with modern instructional methods and technologies. The design, based at the Hudson Institute, focuses on providing the fundamentals of education in core academic areas through individualized instruction made possible by sophisticated technology. The Design Team has developed its own set of high standards and accompanying assessments to guide improved teaching and learning.

➤ *The National Alliance for Restructuring Education* (Washington, D.C.) places school-level transformation in the context of broader systems change, and the Design Team works with both systems and schools. States, districts, and schools working with the Alliance organize around five tasks: standards, learning environments, community services and supports, public engagement, and high performance management. The hallmark of an Alliance school is the Certificate of Initial Mastery, a high standard of accomplishment for high school graduation.

➤ *Roots & Wings* (Baltimore, Md.) extends the Success for All model developed by Robert Slavin and his colleagues at Johns Hopkins University. The elementary school design focuses on helping all students, regardless of background or challenges, perform at or above grade level. The "roots" of the program are intensive instruction in reading, writing, and language arts along with tutoring and family support. The "wings" elements include a constructivist math program and an integrated social studies/science program.

reflecting a shift in emphasis from development to scaleup. Each of the scale-up partners plays a critical role in the broader effort. All share the same mission—to dramatically improve student achievement—and goals—to build a demand for transformed schools, to meet that demand with high-quality school designs, to ensure that operating environments support transformation, and to measure the results of the effort and tell the story to the public. The primary partners in the school transformation initiative are discussed next.

Ten school communities around the nation will introduce the designs to their schools and support school and system transformation. In late 1994, New American Schools orchestrated a process to select a small group of states and districts to participate in Phase 3. To be considered, a school community was required to indicate the presence of the following criteria: (a) demonstrated commitment to establishing an environment supportive of school improvement; (b) commitment to transforming a critical mass[1] of its schools within five years; (c) commitment to acquire and allocate, or reallocate, significant resources to invest in school restructuring using the New American Schools or other proven designs; (d) the presence of institutions and processes that provide continuity in the face of changes in political and educational leadership; and (e) evidence of wide support for and participation in reform efforts by local educators and business, higher education, community, and political leaders.

Following an intensive process of site visits, interviews, and a review of proposals, the following ten school communities were chosen in March 1995 to participate in the scaleup of the New American Schools designs: Cincinnati, Ohio; Dade County, Florida; Los Angeles, California; Memphis, Tennessee; Philadelphia, Pennsylvania; Pittsburgh, Pennsylvania; San Diego, California; State of Kentucky; State of Maryland; and the Washington Alliance for Better Schools (a group of five districts in the Seattle metropolitan area).

Seven Design Teams are participating in scaleup. Each will work with schools in states and districts around the country to provide technical assistance related to design implementation. In

---

[1] Research indicates that a critical mass of transformed schools is reached when so much change has occurred that it would take more effort to revert to the old than to maintain momentum toward the new. Thus, a critical mass of schools can act as a lever to inspire other schools to transform. New American Schools has defined a critical mass as 30 percent of schools within a state or district.

addition, the Teams will create (or extend existing) design networks to support schools that implement their designs.[2] One Design Team, The National Alliance for Restructuring Education, has a history of working with state and district personnel on systems reform in these sites (Kentucky, Pittsburgh, and San Diego). The National Alliance will continue to work at the systems level and will work with New American Schools to introduce the other Design Teams to schools.

The Education Commission of the States contributes to several parts of the New American Schools' effort. They co-coordinate the communications and public engagement aspects of the effort, define policy barriers to school transformation, disseminate information about the Design Teams nationwide, and enlist the support and involvement of state policymakers.

The RAND Corporation continues its relationship with New American Schools as a third-party evaluator and critical friend. RAND will provide feedback throughout Phase 3 on the performance of the Design Teams and will collect and analyze information that will help publicly document the entire effort in a complete and accurate manner. Their analyses will include student performance data (measured by both traditional and authentic assessments), information about other measures of school improvement including attendance rates and discipline referrals, studies of perceptions of teachers and parents about design-related benefits, and information on school context and its relationship to change in student outcomes.

Transforming Systems to
Support Transforming Schools

High-performance schools exist today, but they tend to be the exception rather than the norm. One reason is that the policy and operating environments in which schools find themselves often present real or perceived barriers to the development of such

---

[2] Most of the Design Teams envisioned building some form of design network in their original proposals and, indeed, several have spent considerable effort doing so during Phases 1 and 2. Experience and research suggest that networks of like-minded educators provide important reinforcement to individuals during the difficult process of change. Networks facilitate meetings among supportive colleagues, are a means of transmitting technical expertise, and provide a forum for collaboration in solving problems.

schools. Limited numbers of revitalized schools, inspired by and using New American Schools designs, can be created without changes in these environments. Fostering the transformation of such schools would constitute an important accomplishment in itself. However, a strategy that creates a limited number of New American Schools across the country likely will produce schools that succeed only because their states and districts treat them as exceptions. In all probability, they will be schools operating on the margins, based on waivers to current regulations and procedures. Only when the number of New American Schools in a state or district becomes a significant fraction of all schools in the state or district will policymakers and administrators recognize the need for major adjustments to the administrative and regulatory practices governing all schools. Thus, to realize the New American Schools vision, policymakers and educational leaders must commit to changing the operating environment to support large numbers of good schools. In short, New American Schools require New American School Systems.

To begin the difficult process of addressing these issues, stakeholders in each partnering school community have agreed to negotiate and sign a Memorandum of Understanding (MOU). The MOU is intended to serve as a catalyst to spark cooperation and consensus among all the stakeholders in education and provide a tangible symbol of their shared commitment to improving the public schools. In every community, the school district and the teachers' association play a major role in the MOU process and promise to be pivotal in supporting school transformation. Other partners often include local business leaders, parent representatives, school board representatives, principals, and political leaders, along with New American Schools and the Education Commission of the States.

New American Schools states and districts commit, through the MOU process, to working toward an operating environment that includes these elements:

- The willingness to give schools wide authority and autonomy to make decisions regarding all aspects of schooling, including staffing, budgeting, curriculum, and scheduling.

- Common, publicly supported standards of achievement for virtually all students, accompanied by institutional mechanisms through which schools or systems of schools can petition for the acceptance of self-developed standards as equivalent to or exceeding the established standards[3] (footnote on p. 19).

- Rich and reliable systems of assessment that help schools demonstrate that they are meeting the standards and help teachers make improvements in their programs.

- Sources of assistance in choosing and developing curricula and instructional strategies that are consistent with the standards and responsive to individual students' needs (for schools using New American Schools designs, assistance may come primarily from a Design Team or organizations the Design Team has trained, while for schools more generally, teacher centers, institutions of higher education, or district-based curriculum centers that understand the needs of transforming schools may be appropriate sources).

- A system for professional development and certification that is responsive to the needs of schools and school professionals, and assures that the instructional staff can help students meet high standards.

- Technology that supports teachers and students in the instructional process, assists in the management of schools, and generally supports the restructuring of schools to provide students with the individual attention and opportunities they need.

- A services and support system that strengthens community and family engagement in the school, reduces health and other nonacademic barriers to learning, and promotes family stability.

- A multifaceted plan to engage the public in the transformation in serious and meaningful ways and to develop a broad and deep public understanding of and support for transformation.

- A capacity and willingness to allocate and reallocate the resources necessary to transform individual schools, at both the system and the school level.

- A management and governance system that ensures that schools have the broad guidance, individual autonomy, and support necessary to achieve their mission.

---

[3] To make this system work, institutions of higher education and employers must agree to recognize these standards and accept performance as measured against them as a basis for school admission hiring.

Along with identifying and removing barriers in the operating environment, each school community has begun linking schools with Design Teams. In order to achieve the goal of involving a critical mass—30 percent—of schools in design-based transformation within five years, each community is embarking on a plan to (a) introduce their schools to the New American Schools designs, and (b) give each school the opportunity to choose to implement one of the designs or another proven school improvement design.

Lessons Learned to Date

The ten school communities, the seven Design Teams, and the other partner organizations prepared and planned vigorously for the launch of scaleup in September 1995. During this preparation, several lessons emerged to guide the progression of scaleup.

First, it is essential that Design Teams and the New American Schools partners communicate carefully and completely with schools, systems, and the public about the nature of the designs, the implications of implementation, the cost of transformation, and the expected outcomes of the process. During preparation for Phase 3, most communities held "fairs" to initially introduce schools to the Design Teams. During these fairs, all of the Design Teams gave short presentations to groups of teachers and principals, who attended presentations by three or four of the Teams. Although these fairs often raised awareness among schools about the New American Schools designs, their effectiveness was limited by the brevity of the presentations, the absence of time for individual discussions between a Design Team and a school, and the participation of only small segments of school faculties. In these and other situations, school and system personnel have not found brief descriptions or broad overview materials to be sufficient to explain what it means to implement a design, the Design Teams' role in implementation, how the designs can be adjusted to fit individual schools, how funds can be reallocated to pay for the designs, and other key concepts. To a large extent, the success of the Design Teams in Phase 3 will depend on their ability to effectively and efficiently market themselves to school-level staff. New American Schools and the Education Commission of the States will provide extensive materials to schools and systems to explain the designs in greater depth to teachers, school administrators, and community members.

Second, the transformation of both a large number of schools and the operating environment requires, at least in the early stages, a high level of attention and active participation on the part of a person or team of people with the time to devote to coordinating activities, building coalitions, and maintaining a focus on the change process. This coordination role is best played by an on-site team, with the assistance and support of an external partner who can marshal outside resources and help mobilize action. New American Schools serves as the outside partner in six sites, the National Alliance for Restructuring Education fills this role in three sites, and the two organizations share the lead in one site. Teachers and administrators have grown accustomed to watching dozens of school reform programs revolve through their systems year after year, and are faced with already alarming workloads. Most do not have the time or, initially, the inclination, to facilitate the process of bringing together stakeholders to change the operating environment and helping schools embark on transformation, both of which require a significant amount of time and energy.

Third, school systems and schools need assistance in developing strategies to dramatically restructure the way they use their resources. The New American Schools designs are intended to operate using about the same level of resources as current school programs on a long-term basis. The designs do require an initial start-up cost, as well as the investment of resources on an ongoing basis for technical assistance, professional development, and technology, but these costs are modest in the context of an entire school system budget. Districts that are willing to create an investment fund to cover these costs best ensure that improvement efforts are successfully maintained. However, school systems are frequently reluctant to change entrenched budgeting and allocation systems, and they are often prevented from doing so by the stringent requirements of different categorical programs. Too often, they view school-based designs as add-on programs, which implies that their costs do not supplant any current expenditures but simply add on to them. This way of supporting schools holds little promise for institutionalizing improvement in education.

New American Schools has expanded the partnership for scaleup to include teams of experts in school finance and budget restructuring. These teams will be available to work with systems and schools to identify how resources are allocated currently, whether that allocation makes sense for high-performance schools, and how to reallocate budgets to best support transformation.

Fourth, as anticipated, the support of parents and communities is crucial to the success of a widespread transformation effort, and school systems are hesitant to move forward without confidence in this support. New American Schools and the Education Commission of the States have teamed with outside partners to provide reviews of public attitudes toward education reform and local and state policies governing education in each participating community. Planning groups in each community will receive the information generated by these reviews to serve as baseline data as they develop effective and appropriate communications and public engagement strategies.

Fifth, in order to support the transformation of a large number of schools, Design Teams and school systems will first need to transform themselves. The Design Teams need to develop the capacity to assist large numbers of schools. This will depend to some extent on their ability to specify the core elements of their designs, separate design development from design implementation, and clearly describe the technical assistance necessary to help schools implement the design. It also will depend on the ability of the Teams and school systems to leverage existing sources of technical assistance and align their work with that of the Design Teams. For example, many districts work closely with universities and teacher preparation programs, whereas others have district-sponsored teacher academies or professional development centers. School systems, in turn, will have to structure themselves to support individual school autonomy and flexibility. School boards, in particular, may need to play a different role than they currently play in many communities if schools are to have the opportunity and the resources to transform themselves into successful high-performance teaching and learning environments.

Sixth, all partners in school transformation, including the school, the Design Team, the district/state, and external partners, must consider themselves accountable for raising student achievement. Designs themselves are not responsible for nor capable of generating results. Rather, design-based assistance with support from districts, states, and external partners can help schools restructure and revitalize teaching, learning, and climate in an effort to raise student achievement.

Moving the Vision Forward

Around the nation, children are learning in exciting and effective school environments. These children are the best evidence that the New American Schools vision is becoming a reality. With a continued focus on changing operating environments and helping schools transform, New American Schools intends to leave three major legacies at the close of its ambitious five-year initiative.

First, the education system will be enriched by the existence of a group of design-based assistance organizations, capable of supporting the transformation of large numbers of schools. Second, the early implementation of the designs will yield compelling evidence that school districts of considerable size and diversity can create and sustain good schools as the norm, not the exception. Third, future transformation efforts will benefit from a well-documented and packaged history of the findings, lessons learned, successes, and failures of this enterprise.

As this book goes to press, the New American Schools Design Teams stand ready to work in partnership with schools and districts around the country, using their school transformation designs to help create revitalized learning environments. In just three years, these designs have grown from good ideas to fully operational, exciting designs for successful and effective schools. They have touched thousands of students, teachers, and parents in hundreds of communities, and they have opened up the possibility of a renewed education system, one that truly prepares today's children for tomorrow's world.

Notes

David T. Kearns is Chairman of the Board and John L. Anderson is President of New American Schools (formerly the New American Schools Development Corporation).

2

Audrey Cohen College System of Education®

Purpose-Centered Education®[1]

Audrey Cohen
Janith Jordan
Audrey Cohen College

What is the goal of education? This fundamental question is almost never seriously addressed by schools today. As a result, a cursory glance at a typical school curriculum would incline one to conclude that education's goal is simply to transmit knowledge, and more specifically, to transmit the knowledge embodied in particular disciplines. Today, such limited goals are causing massive failure in our school system, precisely because of what they ignore. Effective education must direct itself not only to imparting knowledge, but also to accomplishing ends that are far more complex and difficult in their achievement.

Education must develop in students the abilities that contribute to using what they learn for attaining positive ends throughout their lifetimes. It also must enable them to work with others whose traditions and values may differ markedly from their own. And education must give students the ability to assess the consequences of their actions, and to both acquire and utilize knowledge in an informed way that furthers socially beneficial goals for the short and the long term.

Knowledge is a powerful tool for self-transformation and social improvement. Yet in the traditional system of education, the acquisition of knowledge in no way guarantees that this knowledge will be

---

used for personally inspiring and socially meaningful goals. In fact, the dominant subject-oriented approach to learning, and the failure to fuse academic learning with effective action, tend to ensure the contrary. Education, therefore, should direct itself to teaching the higher art of responsible application. Students should learn to think and behave in such a way that they can take information and perspectives from vastly different areas of life, synthesize them, and use them to achieve positive social accomplishments. The larger mission of education, to teach people how to use what they learn for their own and for the common good, is so completely absent from contemporary education approaches as to require a new educational paradigm. The following pages chart the outlines of such a paradigm, one founded on years of research and successfully implemented in numerous environments over the last three decades.

The changing nature of society, as it moves from an industrial organization of nation states to a global society based on service and high technology, makes transforming education all the more imperative. Rapid change, instant communication, and diminishing resources all point to one conclusion. At the same time that life seems to be becoming more competitive, it also is clear that both survival and prosperity depend on positive social interdependence. Such interdependence, in turn, depends on our ability—as individuals, professionals, and citizens—accurately to assess our role and place within a larger whole, and to find vehicles for identifying our personal self-interest and empowerment with the empowerment of others. The required shift in self-perception and orientation is crucial. The capabilities individuals will require are not among those fostered by the industrial era of our recent past. But they are vital for a global economy based on technology and information that operates in a world of limited resources.

The industrial era was founded on an individualistic and consumer-oriented ethos. Because it assumed a world of unlimited resources, individuals could afford to ignore the impact of their own actions on others. The advances of the industrial era also required a division of labor and its accompanying specialization of knowledge. During the last half of the 20th century, however, specialization has moved from being an undisputed asset to creating serious liabilities. During the 19th century, the requirements of specialization were reflected first in the growth of universal education, then in the separation of students by age and the introduction of the time clock to the classroom, then in the separation of study from practice, and finally in the proliferation of subjects studied. Fragmentation within the school both reflected and supported fragmentation in corporations and bureaucracies. Unfortunately, extreme fragmentation of knowledge cripples the capacity for effective and responsible action. Today, the destructive impact of fragmentation is widely recognized. For example, corporate reformer Peter Senge, whose work has contributed to a rethinking of corporate structure and function, comments in the very first paragraph of his acclaimed book *The Fifth Discipline:*

> From a very early age, we are taught to break apart problems, to fragment the world. This apparently makes complex tasks and subjects more manageable, but we pay a hidden, enormous price. We can no longer see the consequences of our actions; we lose our intrinsic sense of connection to a larger whole. . . . [A]fter awhile we give up trying to see the whole altogether (Senge, 1990, p. 3).

The disastrous consequences of the tunnel-vision approach fostered by fragmented thinking are only too evident in the global crises of environmental pollution, overpopulation, devastation of third world areas, war, rampant commercialism, and a universal youth culture of alienation and despair. Because fragmentation is firmly entrenched in the very structure of traditional education, this structure must be transformed if we are to move into the next century successfully.

Traditional education assumes the scope of knowledge is confined to *information,* that this information can be divided into discrete disciplines, that these disciplines can be studied independently, and that their study involves no active engagement but a passive absorption by the learner. Every one of these assumptions must be challenged at its core. First, it should be recognized that knowledge includes more than information: Important additional aspects of knowledge are the ability to apply and evaluate information through practical action, and to generate effective change in oneself and in others. Schools should teach these related competencies as part of knowledge. Second, academic learning no longer can be divided into discrete disciplines that are studied independently of each other. More and more, the real test of learning should be the ability to fuse and relate information from different areas. If learning does not include this transdisciplinary and holistic ability to synthesize and relate information from different disciplines, the cost will be high. Third, passive absorption must be replaced by active engagement and application. The real test of learning is not in what we know but in what we can accomplish with what we know.

In traditional education, the dynamic of learning is unrelated to the purpose of what is being learned. Generally, students study a subject to pass an exam or receive a certain grade, not to meet a challenge and achieve a purpose. Thus, in subject-oriented learning, the intent is to know a particular subject matter for itself, with no regard at the moment for the use to which that subject matter may be put. Application is not addressed and is left to much later examination. Unfortunately, when practical application is ignored in the present, students no longer study with an eye to how they will use what they learn. Their learning takes place in a vacuum, and often results in poor motivation, passivity and lost potential.

The structure of traditional education turns a deaf ear to the obvious fact that a driving and passionate sense of purpose is one of the most profound engines of learning. When we learn most effectively, it is because we want to fulfill a vision or solve a problem: finding the cure for a disease, creating a mode of transportation that will accommodate mass urbanization, helping people deal with loss, fostering artistic creativity, and so on. Business and technological inventions, medical and scientific discoveries, all are developed primarily in response to real challenges, and in dealing with them necessary knowledge is both acquired and acted upon. On the personal and aesthetic levels, the motivation to pursue and refine artistic talents, the particular form those abilities take, and the power of their articulation express the urgency of a personal quest. Purposive learning actually starts at birth and should continue through life. Children learn to sit, stand, walk, and run in the process of marshaling sensory resources toward meeting the challenges and possibilities of the world around them. The same purposive drive that impels the infant's learning and the passionate inquiry of the inventor, the social reformer, the dynamic business entrepreneur or the artist should impel the student's learning at school.

As soon as we begin to consider for what purpose we are learning, we also confront questions of *value*: If I pursue this purpose, who will benefit from it? What values do my objectives express, and how do they relate to other people's values? How do I decide which goals are valuable ones to pursue? For more than a century, questions of value systematically have been removed from educational curricula. Ethical issues are often considered to infringe on the pursuit of objectivity, and are given little or no consideration. The requirements of a global society indicate that this orientation needs to be reconsidered and transformed. A global culture is founded on diversity, and diversity can become a source either of enhanced cooperation or of increased polarization. It will be a source of cooperation if the fundamental value of each individual and of all different cultures is thoroughly absorbed by each child in the process of growth. Teaching children how systematically to understand and respect, negotiate, and work effectively with individuals of different backgrounds and persuasions should be an integral part of a curriculum, not just an addendum. An ethical concern for equality, a respect for others, and a commitment to building a better world also are fundamental to the global society. Unlike the industrial society of the past, the global society incorporates a large emphasis on service and interpersonal relationships, and citizens prosper both professionally and personally to the extent they can offer effective service to others. Effective service is a form of empowerment, and for the service professional, serving or empowering others is serving or empowering oneself. A central goal for education therefore should be to help students identify and work with others toward achieving goals that are genuinely and mutually beneficial.

There are other reasons that ethical concerns should be central to education. Questions of value are part of establishing and responsibly pursuing any purpose. If schools neglect the ethical questions that surround all conscious action, then students fail to learn skills that are essential for productive lives. They may learn to do whatever they do well, without learning to evaluate whether what they are doing is in itself valuable. A simple example will illustrate this point. Studying structural engineering may enable us to build a bridge over a congested highway, but it may leave us unable to decide whether it would be better to build that bridge, to create alternative highways, or to develop mass transportation options. Those kinds of decisions can only be based on a clear understanding of the relative values of the choices involved. Ethical concerns, both large and small, permeate all of our activities on a daily basis. Purging these concerns from the curriculum—except through token recognition in occasional "ethics" courses—has eliminated one of the most powerful and important functions of education: to foster the development of individuals who consciously seek to use knowledge for achieving meaningful and worthwhile social purposes.

A New Paradigm for Learning

Primacy of Purpose

The problems facing education, together with the needs of a successful global society, together dictate a clear educational solution. Fostering this solution has been the mission of Audrey Cohen College since it was founded in 1964, and began developing a new paradigm for education. That paradigm first emerged out of a number of years of research on the educational implications of the changing economy. It reflected the perception that the emergence of a technologically based global society required a fundamentally new approach to learning. The paradigm was invented in 1970 and used with great success initially at the graduate and undergraduate level. Subsequently, the College expanded its work to have its paradigm used at elementary and secondary levels of education. In 1983, Audrey Cohen College was invited to begin working in elementary and secondary public school classrooms in New York City. By 1995, and with significant assistance from New American Schools and the Hasbro Children's Foundation, approximately 20,000 children were attending full public schools that had adopted the College's system of education.

The fundamental principle of the educational system of the College is an emphasis on purpose. The Purpose-Centered System of Education® is based on the premise that students learn best when they use their knowledge and skills to achieve a purpose that makes a positive difference in their lives and in the lives of others. Through this system of education, students acquire the range of knowledge and abilities, and the commitment to ethical action that characterizes productive, socially concerned citizens. By using what they learn in the larger world as well as in the classroom, students learn that life is about finding opportunities to make a difference, and that their creative energy can achieve exciting and valuable purposes.

Purpose-centered learning happens when people learn in response to a practical challenge, and the Purpose-Centered System of Education enables students to use their academic learning to make positive changes in the world. While in the traditional classroom, subjects are studied independently of each other and without relationship to how knowledge from the disciplines can be used (see Fig. 2.1), in Purpose-Centered learning, knowledge from the disciplines—from mathematics and science to English, social studies, geography, and other subjects—is refocused each semester around the process of achieving a specific Purpose (see Fig. 2.2). As part of achieving their Purpose (the term *Purpose*, as the explicit focus of a semester's learning, will be capitalized hereafter), students are required to develop not only substantive knowledge but also other critical skills, including complex thinking, problem solving, synthesizing, communicating, researching, and negotiating.

Each Purpose encompasses a socially important thrust and a major area of knowledge that will be developmentally enriching for the student. Each Purpose also provides the basis for fusing the core

Figure 2.1

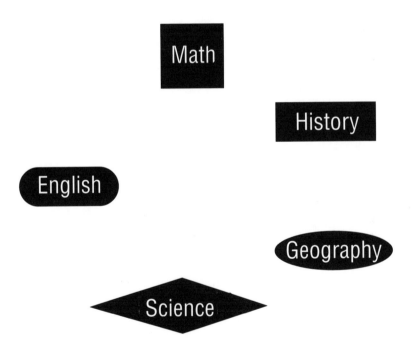

The traditional
subject-oriented curriculum...

Knowledge is isolated in separate compartments.

Figure 2.2

is transformed...

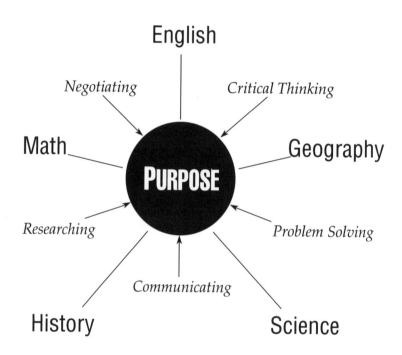

Knowledge and skills are focused on Purpose.

subjects meaningfully, and every educational activity that children perform in school or the community is directed to the achievement of the Purpose in the community or the larger world. Knowledge and action-oriented abilities are thus fused around a Purpose and implemented through taking Constructive Action® in the world.

Purposes appropriate to specific grade levels are provided in Table 2.1. In addition to incorporating the content covered in traditional subject-based learning, Purpose-Centered Education[SM] also encourages students to make ethical and social concerns part of the very framework of their thinking. For example, it is the rare student in a subject-based curriculum who will use what she or he learns about American history to deepen her or his understanding of the complexities of contemporary social institutions. In the traditional school, it is the history that is primary, and not the ability to use that history for dealing with current situations and goals. By contrast, in a Purpose-Centered curriculum, a child might study American history as a resource for comprehending existing institutions within his or her own community.

The paradigm shift represented by Purpose-Centered learning is fundamental. Unlike traditional educational approaches that separate learning from its use, Audrey Cohen College's approach links learning directly to action. Students learn in order to use what they learn, and they use what they learn to reach specific goals. This gives them an appreciation for how deeply they can affect the world around them and builds a lifelong interest in learning.

In many instances today, the classroom and the world remain very separate, and a majority of students receive inadequate exposure to addressing real challenges and learn skills that have little application toward meeting the needs of their social environment. Purpose-Centered education, however, links education and life, bringing the classroom into the community and the community into the classroom. Community involvement becomes a central part of learning and is no longer either ignored or treated as an addendum. Students learn to view both the community—or the larger world accessed through communications—and the classroom as settings for learning and action. From their earliest years, students spend time each week outside the classroom in the community, researching their Purpose, discovering opportunities for improvement, meeting with community members from all types of organizations and businesses who can help bring about those changes, and implementing specific goals to achieve their Purpose outside the classroom. Similarly, students regularly invite civic representatives and professionals into the school to share their expertise and under-

Table 2.1

___

Purposes Appropriate to Specific Grade Levels

Kindergarten
  We Build a Family-School Partnership^SM
  We Care for Living Things^SM

First Grade
  We Work for Safety^SM
  We Use Transportation to Bring the World Closer^SM

Second Grade
  We Make Our Neighborhood a Better Place to Live^SM
  We Use Government to Improve Our Community^SM

Third Grade
  We Help People Through the Arts^SM
  We Share Information with Communities Around the World^SM

Fourth Grade
  We Work for Good Health^SM
  We Use Inventions to Make Life Better^SM

Fifth Grade
  We Improve the Environment^SM
  We Use Technology to Meet Human Needs^SM

Sixth Grade
  We Develop School-Business Partnerships^SM
  We Draw on the Community's Wisdom to Build a Better Future^SM

Seventh Grade
  I Take Charge of My Learning^SM
  I Share My Learning With Others^SM

Eighth Grade
  I Earn Responsibility at My Internship^SM
  We Bring Our Community Together^SM

Ninth Grade
  I Take Charge of My Life and Learning^SM
  I Take Constructive Action in the Global World of Work^SM

Tenth Grade
  I Use Science and Technology to Help Shape a Just and
      Productive Society^SM

Eleventh Grade
  I Gain Wisdom from the Past and Present to Build a More
      Promising Future^SM

Twelfth Grade
  I Apply My Special Knowledge to Make a Better World^SM
  We Reinvent Cultural Relationships for a Stronger World^SM

standing of the larger world. They learn to view such people as resources in their own learning and decision-making process.

Some examples will demonstrate how Purpose can organize a semester's learning. The Purpose of one semester in fourth grade is *We Work for Better Health.* The intent of this Purpose is twofold. First, it enables young students to appreciate how deeply both their own health and the health of the community can be influenced by the choices they themselves make, the knowledge they acquire, the goals for which they use their knowledge, and how they share what they learn with family and community. Second, it gives them the opportunity to empower themselves and their community by taking informed action to influence the health of members of the community as well as of themselves. Children in one school decided that as part of achieving their purpose of working for better health, they would conduct a health fair to increase school board, local agency, and public awareness of health needs of the community that they felt were not being addressed. In the process of preparing for and achieving their Purpose, they researched local health care services, explored the health of family and peers, compared what they learned to the health of other cultures and communities, studied aspects of the history of health care, nutrition and agriculture, and explored a great deal of basic biology.

Early in the semester, the fourth graders studied and mapped out the structure of their own bodies—the skeleton, muscles, organs, and so on—and learned about what foods and exercises affected different parts of the body. They explored the four food groups, learned how to assess the nutritional contents of packaged and canned foods, and discussed their own eating patterns. They gained perspective on their lives by exploring the relation between nutrition, health care, and demographics in different cultures and historical eras. For example, they looked at the era of American westward expansion, finding out how the long months of slow travel, overcrowding in prospecting camps, lack of fresh food, and other problems created health risks on the frontier.

The children learned about medicine, and solicited visits from community health care professionals who introduced them to basic diagnostic procedures, including the use of stethoscopes, testing of nerve reflexes, and others. They also visited local health facilities to research the type and extent of services available to the community. They explored the history of health care, read about Nobel Laureates who had contributed to the development of medicine, and investigated issues in medical ethics. Using what they were learning to collaborate productively with others, they interviewed family members about eating and exercise patterns. In the process, they often discovered they could act as resources to their own relatives.

In preparing for their health fair, the children wrote and assembled two information pamphlets, one with nutritional tips and the other with information about community health care facilities. They wrote poems and songs about health issues for the fair, displayed wall drawings of the body and its organs, organized skits and surveyed visitors on their health. They held mini-workshops for children from the community and from other classes, explaining to them the basics of nutrition, anatomy and physiology, benefits of exercise, dangers of smoking, and so on. They offered free evaluations and recommendations on the dietary habits of visitors. And at the end of the fair, they conducted a survey of the participants to determine what had been learned and how the information would be used.

The semester's Purpose of working for better health enabled the students to take greater charge of their own lives through an exciting exploration of science, to use history and social science to understand their own social institutions, to find out about local, state and national organizations, to develop oral and writing abilities, and to apply basic geometry skills in designing booths for their fair, all in the process of doing something beneficial for the community. Like all the Purposes that form part of the Audrey Cohen College System of Education, this Purpose is appropriate to the cognitive, emotional and physical level of development of the child, and effectively challenges the child's sense of social responsibility.

During a semester whose Purpose was *We Use Inventions to Make Life Better*, fourth graders in one school decided to use their learning to create devices that would improve the lives of people with disabilities. They interviewed paraplegics and others with disabilities, visited local hospitals for the disabled, studied systems of the body, and learned about men and women who had helped the disabled. As part of a general exploration, they looked at inventions made by Native American Indians and early Spanish missionaries. To develop a grasp of simple machinery, they studied levers and were introduced to magnetism and electricity.

Toward the end of the semester, each student built his or her own practical and creative invention. One student made a door opener operated by mouth for persons unable to use their hands. Another created a video game controller with oversized brightly designed handles that disabled persons could easily manipulate. And a third created a color-coded labeling system in Braille for clothing. The children's inventions were evaluated for actual use by a panel of disability experts in the city, and students received several formal letters of commendation for their service.

A fifth-grade class spent one semester on the Purpose *We Improve the Environment.* They read novels with an environmental emphasis, studied the art of Ansel Adams and the history of the country's national parks, and read selections from nature writers John Muir and John Burroughs. They broke into small groups to research specific environmental issues such as acid rain, the ozone layer, and endangered species. Each group presented arguments to the class as a whole for a plan of action focused on their topic.

The class eventually decided to achieve their Purpose by designing and planting a xeroscape garden that would display drought resistant plants that thrived in their arid area, and that would promote local awareness of how to maintain balance in the ecology. They wrote articles for community and school newsletters, researched and mapped water sources for the area, interviewed government officials about how they regulated water consumption, investigated properties of a wide variety of local plants, explored the mineral requirements of plant life, and used measuring skills to design and plant their garden. In the process, knowledge from the core subjects was used to inform their actions.

Reorganizing Learning and Action around Dimensions®

How does one organize a semester's learning around a Purpose when the learning we have to work with is already organized in quite a different way, around independent disciplines? The answer is a radical reorganization of learning that eliminates the framework of the disciplines while maintaining their content. Audrey Cohen College's solution to the fragmentation of learning is a restructuring of the curriculum around five Dimensions® of effective learning and action. These Dimensions represent the entire range of knowledge that should be brought together to achieve any worthwhile Purpose. They include not only materials from all key disciplines, but also areas of knowledge that include the kinds of skills necessary for using knowledge to achieve a Purpose.

The Dimensions structure the achievement of Purpose and replace courses as the organizing framework for each day's learning. During each semester, the same Dimension classes are taught. The specific academic materials addressed within each Dimension, however, change each semester to relate to the developmental stage of the students and to the Purpose to be achieved. Dimensions avoid the fragmentation typical of traditional classrooms and encourage the student to see his or her learning as a tool for constructive change. The result is a rigorous learning experience in which the semester's Purpose is viewed repeatedly from different directions.

The five Dimensions around which learning and action are organized each semester are: Purpose, Values and Ethics, Self and Others, Systems, and Skills. As shown in Fig. 2.3, these Dimensions provide the framework through which students use their learning to understand their Purpose and then take effective action to implement that Purpose in the world. All the Dimensions are rich in traditional content areas. In addition, the Purpose and the Values and Ethics Dimensions represent indispensable areas of learning and action that have been dismissed from most of traditional education. The Dimensions cannot be seen as parallel areas of knowledge in the same way that traditional subjects are. Each Dimension has a very different part to play in the student's understanding and interaction with the world. Together, they address all the areas of understanding that need to be taken into consideration in order to plan and implement effective and socially responsible action. They also provide a world view and analytic frame of reference for understanding human events.

Purpose Dimension.® The Purpose Dimension stands at the center of the curriculum, giving meaning and focus to the other dimensions. In Purpose Dimension classes, students use the knowledge that is explored and researched in the other Dimension classes to pursue their semester's Purpose through a Constructive Action® (see discussion below) that will benefit themselves and their communities. They identify opportunities to improve the world outside the classroom. They develop a plan for achieving their Purpose and monitor and adjust their performance along the way. They marshal knowledge and skill of every appropriate kind, including the core subjects, to make a plan and carry it out successfully. And together with teachers and appropriate community members, they evaluate the results achieved.

*Values and Ethics Dimension.*ˢᴹ An ethos of respect and concern for others and a sense of responsibility for contributing to build a better world are at the very heart of effective citizenship and a successful adult life. Students must learn to appreciate, on both a practical and an intellectual level, the fundamental ethical questions that occur when dealing with other human beings and with organizations. In this Dimension class, students take into account the host of ethical issues involved in planning and achieving their Purpose. Why are we pursuing a particular goal to achieve our

Figure 2.3

Knowledge and skills are organized into action-oriented
Dimensions® focused on Purpose and used to plan and
perform Constructive Actions® to improve the world.

Purpose? Why is it truly valuable? Who will benefit? How do we deal with conflicting values and interests? What are the rules of ethical reasoning? They explore perspectives from history, literature, philosophy and government that help them develop the sense of respect for and responsibility towards others that are the basis for effective citizenship and productive work. The materials they study help them deal with real value conflicts, with making choices and negotiating differences in an ethical manner, and with clarifying how best to achieve their semester's Purpose.

Self and Others Dimension.[SM] The Self and Others Dimension class develops students' awareness of how they function in their relations with others and vice versa. Literature, reading and writing skills, and the creative arts help students improve their understanding of themselves and others, and enhance their ability to communicate effectively and to develop productive relationships with people of all ages and cultures. Students also learn the important part that imagination, intuition and creativity play in helping us understand ourselves and the world. Such explorations of the human condition are vital for success in our global society and for developing the interpersonal and communication skills that are now necessary.

Systems Dimension.[SM] Through the Systems Dimension classes, students develop an awareness that to be effective in reaching their goals without creating unintended negative consequences, they need to understand the systemic organization of nature, life, and society. Each student develops a theoretical and practical understanding of the systems of which he or she is a part, including the family, community and larger social organizations, government, economic systems, and the world of science and technology.

This Dimension is, relatively speaking, underexamined in traditional approaches to education. Yet the more we operate as members of interlocking institutions, the more we need to understand the systems of which we are a part, see how they affect us and we them. In Natural Systems Dimension classes, students examine systems in chemistry, biology, physics, and technology as they relate to achieving their semester's Purpose. In Social Systems Dimension classes, students explore aspects of history, civics, economics and geography that pertain to their Purpose. These classes also assist students in developing their research and complex thinking skills.

Skills Dimension.[SM] Skills Dimension classes are particularly concerned with abilities related to mathematical and computer literacy, technical skills, second language skills, and physical education abilities. In these classes, students develop some of the more complex symbolic abilities they will need to convey information and achieve purposes in their adult life.

Together, the five Dimensions encompass all the components of effective performance, or the range of considerations that must be addressed in order to achieve a meaningful Purpose. They represent five essential viewpoints that enable one to understand and take action in any situation. They also embody a way of organizing a semester's learning holistically around the achievement of a Purpose. This learning includes both content from the disciplines and specific abilities related to purposive and responsible action.

Let us look at a hypothetical example of how academic material might be used in Dimension classes in the process of achieving a semester's Purpose. The fifth grade devotes one semester's learning to achieving the Purpose *We Use Technology to Meet Human Needs.* During the first few weeks in school, the children devote their Purpose class to exploring broad categories of technological advancement—biomedical, agricultural, industrial robotics, aerospace, and so on. They ask themselves whether the community is using the best technology for their specific needs. Subsequently, after considerable research and brainstorming, the students decide to use video technology to serve the community by creating a documentary about the ways technology is used to provide the community with sufficient water, and about the relative benefits and costs of existing methods. They decide to focus on irrigation and how the community uses irrigation technology to turn desert into farmland. They obtain permission to produce a video for the public access channel of the local cable television station. As the semester proceeds, they log their activities moving towards this goal and evaluate results.

In their Values and Ethics Dimension class, the fifth graders explore the advantages and disadvantages of technology. They look at how life has changed as a result of technological advances. They examine how technology affected the quality of family and community life in the past, from agrarian times to today's global, high technology society. They look at some of the difficult ethical issues that need to be addressed in the use of technology and explore the ways in which irrigation can be beneficial or harmful, both in general and in their particular community. They also look at the equity issues which arise in considering who has the best and easiest access to water in the community.

In their Self and Others Dimension class, students look at what life was like on a personal level in cultures with older forms of technology, and what life might be like in the future. They explore a variety of technologies, including traditional and electronic music, audio and digital recording, and film and video technologies. They develop oral and writing skills, and put together chapters in a book on technology for the local library. They read biographies of such technological trail blazers as Telsa and Eastman. They visit museums and art galleries that reveal artists' uses of advanced technology and invite experts in technology to the school to speak to their class. As the semester progresses, the students analyze the components of a documentary, prepare storyboards for their own documentary, and write the script. They rehearse and shoot each segment of the documentary, prepare a mass mailing on the program to community residents, and create press releases, flyers, and posters.

In the Social Systems Dimension class, fifth graders investigate the history of technology in the United States, including agricultural, industrial and high technology development. They learn how the development of the technology of each age influences life in that age and affects the development of the next age. They learn about less technologically developed countries, and about how geography and limited resources influence technological development. They chronicle the history of irrigation technology from ancient times in Egypt and Babylon to great dams today in the United States and Egypt. They study the national and international organizations that make building such dams possible. And they explore which social institutions impact the use of irrigation technology in their own community.

In the Natural Systems Dimension class, students explore how natural resources are used in creating technological products and study where these resources are found on the planet. They visit the community's water department and learn about condensation pyramids. They also explore computer technology and read books on television, video, and computer technology.

In the Skills Dimension class, students explore how mathematics is used in different areas of technology. They use different kinds of graphs—picture, line, circle—to compare facts and numbers that reveal the impact of technology on society during the agricultural, industrial, and present day time periods. They diagram video camera equipment. They prepare a budget for their video. They also study place value in bases other than ten, to better understand the binary system which is used with computers. And they explore the impact of computers and calculators on problem solving today.

In each of the Dimension classes, children both explore written materials within their area of study, invite local experts to speak at the school, and visit community facilities—museums, the water department, and so on—to enhance their understanding. Throughout the process of achieving the Purpose, the world serves students as both resource and laboratory.

The example of a fifth-grade Purpose described above shows how Dimensions focus learning. History, literature, and sciences from the past—for example, the history of ancient Egypt or of the United States, biographies of famous inventors, bygone methods of irrigation, cultural changes that accompany technological change—become not only a source of interest in themselves but also a resource to thinking responsibly and deeply about the present, developing conceptual models of irrigation systems, and planning effectively for the future. In addition to developing oral and written presentation skills, they learn how to brainstorm together, to research resources in the community, to communicate and negotiate effectively with professionals and community members, and to plan, implement and evaluate a course of action. These competencies so vital for mature life emerge and develop spontaneously in the course of planning and achieving a Purpose that the students identify with and whose specific content they determine themselves.

The Constructive Action®

While the College's Purpose-Centered System of Education focuses all learning each semester around achieving the semester's Purpose, the specific way that Purpose is researched, planned, achieved and evaluated is through a Constructive Action.® The Constructive Action identifies all the aspects of the process by which the Purpose is achieved. The goal of the Constructive Action is determined by students, with the assistance of their teachers acting as facilitators. In the example given above, while the Purpose of the semester was to use technology to meet human needs, the goal of the Constructive Action was to create and broadcast an informative video documentary on the costs and benefits of the community irrigation system. From the beginning to the end of the semester, the Constructive Action process guides learning and action. Children brainstorm together to decide what their goal will be for achieving their Purpose, research possible goals, log their progress in implementing their plan, and evaluate the results achieved. The Dimension classes provide depth and focus to their endeavor.

The nature of the Constructive Action depends on students' age and capacities as well as on their Purpose. Constructive Actions must improve the world outside the classroom and must be sufficiently comprehensive to ensure that the knowledge and skills that are being developed in the classroom will be fully utilized. At the primary and elementary levels, entire classes may plan and carry out a Constructive Action to achieve their Purpose, although groups of students and sometimes even individual students also can plan and carry out Constructive Actions with the support of their teacher. Older students spend more time in formal settings outside their schools—such as businesses and nonprofit organizations—that allow them to carry out their own individual Constructive Actions.

Constructive Actions define an entire methodology for thinking and learning about and achieving a valuable purpose. Each Constructive Action includes the process of researching the Purpose, planning and implementing it, using knowledge for achieving the purpose, and negotiating with others and persuading peers and adults alike of the value of what one intends to do. It also includes an ongoing review and critique of one's decisions, strategies, and actions. Moreover, the Constructive Action is the basis for assessing a student's knowledge and ability to achieve the Purpose, using complex skills and knowledge for achieving goals.

Assessment is intimately tied to the College's transdisciplinary approach. Students are assessed not only for their understanding of knowledge acquired in the classroom and community but also for their ability to use knowledge and skills to make a positive difference in the world. Learning only for the sake of learning is not enough. Students must demonstrate that they can use knowledge to meet challenges. This is what adults must do on a daily basis if they are to be successful in their personal and professional lives. In Purpose-Centered learning, children have the opportunity to learn and be assessed in an intertwined manner.

The College has identified approximately 25 abilities that are generic to the achievement of any Purpose. Each semester, these abilities are developed and assessed in relation to the achievement of a different Purpose. With each succeeding semester or learning stage, a student is expected to attain a higher level of competency in these abilities.

The focus on Purpose, the reorganization of knowledge around the Dimensions, and the Constructive Action process that guides the achievement of Purpose and assessment of student performance together define the paradigm for education of Audrey Cohen College. In this paradigm, the content of traditional disciplines (math, English, geography, history, science) are refocused along with crucial thinking skills (negotiating, complex thinking, researching, synthesis, problem solving, communicating) around achieving a Purpose in the world. The five Dimension classes (Purpose, Values and Ethics, Self and Others, Systems and Skills) are used to plan and perform Constructive Actions aimed at improving the world, and the Constructive Action process itself becomes both the process guiding learning and action and the vehicle for student assessment.

Implementing the
Purpose-Centered System of Education

By the fall of 1995, approximately 20,000 children nationwide were learning and achieving in 21 schools that had been authorized to use Audrey Cohen College's Purpose-Centered System of Education. Additional schools are adopting the College's paradigm in 1996. Audrey Cohen College anticipates that, given the support of New American Schools and the very favorable response of school districts to date, the number of students involved in its system of education will grow in an exponential manner.

The first years of the College's involvement in elementary/ secondary education were devoted primarily to having its paradigm used on a limited basis in a few schools. These small scale but crucial pioneering efforts were supported in part by the Edwin Gould Foundation for Children in New York City. In 1989, the College received a grant from the Hasbro Children's Foundation to implement its paradigm in complete elementary schools in strategic locations in the United States. In 1992, New American Schools selected the College as one of 11 from almost 700 applicants, to receive funding on the premise that its educational design had the potential to change education nationwide.

The first entire schools to adopt Purpose-Centered Education faced an enormous task. They became the trail blazers. With extensive assistance from the College, and from required staff development specialists in each one of the schools, teachers had to refocus the materials they used for teaching around Purpose and find additional materials for study that were appropriate to the Purpose of the grade they taught.

Teaching in a Purpose-Centered System of Education requires ongoing and intensive teamwork. Given the isolated nature of traditional teaching roles, most teachers who entered the College's system had very limited experience of teamwork. Simultaneously with meeting the challenge of working with a new paradigm, they also were confronted with the task of transforming professional relationships. To help them do this, the College provided orientation and planning sessions, putting new teachers in grade teams and working with them on examining the College's prototypical materials in relation to the specific needs and interests of their students, also factoring in state and local mandates. Of course, these tasks were approached in the context of getting used to the new language that accompanied the College's paradigm, and becoming comfortable with replacing Math, English, and other classes with Dimension classes. Moreover, teachers had to research and contact community and regional resources—something most of them had never done— and engage community members in participating in the educational experiences of the school. Without other schools that had accomplished the transition to serve as role models, the first schools to implement the Purpose-Centered System of Education faced both a daunting and an exhilarating year. New beginnings are like that.

The principals of these early schools found themselves plunged into public relations campaigns with families. Parents had to be reassured that traditional materials were being adequately covered and had to be educated about the new system of education. Articles about Purpose-Centered education in PTA bulletins, regular tours of the schools, and a continual open door policy to parents were invaluable in smoothing the transition to the new paradigm.

And what about the children's response? Here, too, the transitional period was demanding of those involved. Purpose-Centered learning both requires and cultivates initiative, participation and the potential for strong leadership by students. For example, fairly early in the semester, students in a Purpose class devote themselves to brainstorming about how they will achieve their semester's Purpose, researching different options, and debating them. Rather than leading their students, teachers essentially facilitate this process. During the first semester of working with the College's approach, teachers frequently found it difficult to engage the children in this process. The children simply were not used to taking charge of their learning and being decision makers. Teachers had to work hard to get students not to be passive.

Not only did things become easier after the first year. The strong benefits of a Purpose-Centered approach to education became increasingly evident. Principals reported that after a year with the Audrey Cohen College paradigm, the attitudes of students had changed dramatically. According to one principal, "The children blossomed and became very independent. They are very involved now in the learning process, and everyone sees this."

Children, who are challenged by the College's approach to take charge of their own learning, sometimes adapt more quickly than teachers, who have functioned differently in the past and are now challenged to give up much of their control and become facilitators.

New children coming into the school in turn quickly learn from their peers that they can take the initiative, and the growth in children is reflected in enthusiastic parental support which spreads by word of mouth within the community. Parents are now more engaged than previously in their children's education. Their children bring home from school their own intense interest in achieving their semester's Purpose, and talk with their parents about what they are doing. And parents frequently participate in the curriculum as experts on the semester's Purpose. For example, a parent who is a lawyer, business person, or doctor can share with the children in school how his or her profession serves the community and relates to the semester's Purpose. Other parents have voluntary activities in the community, or deeply held social or community commitments, and they too serve as experts for different Purposes. Increased parental involvement has not been limited to individual schools, but rather is a universal consequence of schools' using Purpose-Centered Education. High levels of family engagement in schools that have adopted the College's design is one of the unquestionable benefits of Purpose-Centered Education.

For teachers, building a relationship with the community started slowly. They had to research what was out there, explore how various community organizations might relate to a semester's Purpose, seek out contacts, and interest community members in participating in the school's educational process. Despite the challenging nature of these changes, school staff development specialists report that teachers' experiences with the community have been almost universally positive. According to one of these specialists:

> Most community organizations are glad to participate, and once a contact is made, these organizations work with the school year after year. By the end of the first year working with the new paradigm, schools have a substantial resource list of experts in the community to call upon. And the end result is extremely healthy. Schools report that after a few years, they are well known in the community, organizations understand and support what they are doing, and frequently volunteer people.

One story from an elementary school in Florida gives a sense of how a relationship can build quickly between a school and the community. Second graders in this school invited a doctor from a local hospital emergency clinic to speak to their class, and afterwards wrote thank you notes to the clinic. As a result, the emergency room decided to provide their expertise to the class. The children, in turn, decided to write stories for other children who ended up in the emergency room. The hospital reciprocated by budgeting for medical professionals on the staff to come to the school on a regular basis.

The transition from traditional education to a Purpose-Centered System of Education becomes easier and easier as more schools within a given area decide to become involved and are then authorized to use the new paradigm. For example, the second school in San Diego to implement the Purpose-Centered approach was able to utilize the first school's list of community resources, capitalize on already established community support, and on the reputation that the system had built among parents in the community. While in the beginning only one school in the San Diego school district had adopted the College's design, by the fall of 1995 six schools in the school district were utilizing it. Teachers in these schools network with one another on regular district-sanctioned staff development days, sharing ideas about curriculum and assessment, about how to implement a semester's Purpose, and critiquing results of their work. They also compare notes on the goals that students have set for achieving their Purposes. The collaboration and networking that initially began between teachers teaching a single grade and then spread to include a network between all the teachers within a school is now operating between schools within a given district and even between districts. By 1995, the College had assisted schools in establishing the basis for a national network for teacher collaboration around its Purpose-Centered System of Education.

For participating schools, the most surprising and unexpected result of using the Audrey Cohen College design has been the growth of a real sense of community among teachers and staff. Although collaboration among teachers initially can be difficult because of lack of experience, it always is healthy and over time transforms the schools. The first teachers to begin using the Purpose-Centered approach did not anticipate how much the change in educational paradigm would turn them into a community. They expected changes for the children, but not for themselves. Consequently, the growth of a real sharing of knowledge, an interest in each other's work, and a common effort towards mutual goals has created an expanded professionalism and a new sense of belonging. The willingness with which schools network with one another is clear proof of the value teachers attribute to the growth of professional interaction.

Each summer, Audrey Cohen College offers orientation and planning sessions for new schools that have been authorized to use its system of education. These training sessions last five days, and thoroughly introduce teachers and staff to planning and functioning within a Purpose-Centered approach to learning. Representatives from the College, staff development specialists, and teachers at existing schools demonstrate the educational paradigm and discuss how it affects the role of teachers. New teachers learn to brainstorm together around a semester's Purpose, and to work in grade-level teams. They hear extensive case studies of actual experiences in different schools, and are guided through planning their first semester. This process includes assessment, curriculum realignment, classroom organization and teaching pedagogy. For example, prospective teachers learn how to relate assignments to the Constructive Action and the achievement of Purpose, and organize testing around the Constructive Action as well. They also discuss grading procedures which focus around evaluating students on the 25 generic abilities that the College has identified.

Throughout the training process, it is important that prospective teachers learn how to learn and work together *in the same way that their students will learn and work together*. Once they have grasped how effectively they can brainstorm, research, and implement a purpose together, they have taken a major step toward believing in empowering their students to do the same thing.

During the school year, all elementary schools initially are required to maintain on staff a resource specialist whose function is to support and facilitate the implementation of the system. These specialists maintain regular contact with the College and assist teachers both in implementation and developing community networks. Typically, their presence is necessary for one to three years duration. At the end of that time, the system is self-maintaining and the resource specialist's functions have been taken over by faculty and other staff. The College has not yet found it necessary to require middle schools and high schools to fund a staff resource specialist, although some high schools are doing so for the first year of implementation. During the time of transition, assistant principals generally can take over the functions performed by these specialists.

Costs for participating in the Audrey Cohen College's design are very moderate, and are of three types. All schools pay for initial orientation training prior to the first semester of using the College's design. Districts also pay a licensing fee and a modest annual participation fee for each school using the system. Finally, schools contribute to payment for College personnel who support the implementation of the system—assessment specialists, elementary and secondary education specialists, liaisons, etc.—For all schools, implementation fees also tend to diminish after the second year of participation in the College's design.

Plans for the Future

All schools participating in the Audrey Cohen College Purpose-Centered System of Education have demonstrated a number of clear and unequivocal benefits deriving from that participation. In addition to the fact that the great majority of students, by completing the Constructive Action process, have begun to develop lifelong tools for learning and action, student performance on standardized achievement and local criterion-referenced tests has consistently met or exceeded school and district expectations. Student attendance data have improved at all participating schools, and discipline problems have decreased. Parents have become increasingly involved in school affairs and in their children's learning, and businesses and non-profit institutions as well as community residents have become involved in all school districts. The College anticipates that student performance will continue to be strong, and become stronger.

Over the next decade, the College anticipates expanding to serve all schools in the New American Schools jurisdictions that want to use its system of education. The College already is reaching out to other districts as well. In addition, Audrey Cohen College will be expanding in the area of teacher education. The College is establishing a School of Education, now under consideration by the New York State Education Department, that would prepare prospective teachers in the College's Purpose-Centered System of Education. The school would help develop the professional staff needed for further expansion of the College's system.

Prospective teachers will be educated for their roles as Purpose teachers by learning in the same way as their future students. In other words, a Purpose relevant to becoming effective teachers will provide the focus for learning and action each semester. For example, in their second semester, prospective teachers will focus on the purpose Developing Effective Relationships with the Key Constituencies in a Community that can contribute to a child's learning. More generally, the curriculum for teacher education will prepare its students to see their role as teachers in the context of a larger role as responsible leaders and major contributors to constructive change within the community. This emphasis on community participation and leadership is so completely lacking from traditional education that reliance on traditional teacher curricula can only retard the process of educational reform. The College believes that deep change, to be effective, can not come simply from focusing on schools. Change must begin and be carried forward by teachers. When they learn, through their own experience, that organizing learning around achieving a meaningful purpose is both personally and socially empowering, they will naturally teach children to learn in the same way.

As Audrey Cohen College looks toward the future, its own pledge to contributing to the transformation of elementary and secondary education is shaped by years of experience and by the wisdom such experience offers. Success and failure are both determined largely by the relative commitment of the community, and by that community's openness to exploration and to change. When key constituencies have supported the efforts to transform education, the College's paradigm has taken root rapidly and flourished. These key constituencies include superintendents, principals, teachers, parents, community organizations, and businesses.

With commitment generally comes a climate of openness to reexamining how things are done, and a willingness to find the means to make changes that support the educational process. A good example of this willingness can be found in one school district that has six elementary schools. Initially, each school had its own separate staff development days. The district superintendent, however, saw the advantage of establishing the same staff development days district-wide. This gave teachers the opportunity to do joint curriculum and assessment planning, and to learn effectively from each other's experience.

Commitment and receptivity are a given where individuals and institutions see themselves as part of a national initiative to heal the educational process. Where the vision is large enough, enthusiasm, patience, and a sense of sacrifice come naturally. Audrey Cohen College asks each school to see itself for what it really is—a participant in the transformation of our educational foundation.

References

Senge, P. (1990). *The fifth discipline.* New York: Doubleday.

ATLAS Communities
Authentic Teaching, Learning, and Assessment for All Students

Cynthia J. Orrell

First a Word from the Principal Investigators

The authentic teaching, learning, and assessment of all students—ATLAS Communities—design is the product of collaborative effort among three school districts and four school reform organizations: the School Development Program, Project Zero, The Coalition of Essential Schools, and Education Development Center, Inc. Each of us brought to the table differing experiences and points of view about schools and learning. Even as our particular histories have varied, all of us found that we agreed on fundamentals. The task was not only to draw the best from each of our enterprises, but to create a coherent design in its own right, more than the sum of these parts.

Our plan is comprehensive, a full pathway from kindergarten through high school. It involves complete communities, not only the schools themselves. It is intensely respectful of the differences among these communities and among individuals.

We rejoice in the diversity among students and adults—in their individual paths of development, in their varying ways of knowing, in their particular familial and cultural surrounds and the convictions that emerge from these, in their readiness and ability to work hard at school—and we wish to accommodate and nurture those differences within a sensitive school pathway design, one that assumes that all children can succeed even if their routes to success necessarily vary.

We know that any design is but the beginning of serious schooling, that the heart of teaching and learning rests with those close to the task. The authority of these people is crucial. The function of a design is to provide sensible scaffolding and a wealth of powerful examples of good practice. What specifically is built on that scaffolding is for those close to the children to shape. Our design should suggest and persuade, not mandate.

We value the authentic—teaching and assessment that is rooted in real intellectual activity (the wise analysis of an actual problem), not tokens of that activity (the solving of brain teasers remote from actual issues). We value an education that builds on the student's natural curiosity; that draws on the best thinking in and across the disciplines; that fosters deep understanding of crucial questions and issues; and that puts student understandings to work in education, the workplace, and other communal settings. Real work has an allure for learners; the challenge for teachers is to place before students authentic ideas and situations that provoke in them further serious thought and eventually the habit of such inquiry.

We recognize that what we intend has not and will not emerge neatly and quickly. ATLAS is a complex project yet in its early years. The experience of the design partners, and those others that join us, will affect the design and provide examples of emerging practice, thereby clarifying, reshaping, and refining our collective work. The description that follows, written for us by Cindy Orrell, shows where we have come in the opening phases of our collective efforts. The work happily continues.

—James Comer
—Howard Gardner
—Theodore Sizer
—Janet Whitla

The Vision

ATLAS Community—a community supporting Authentic Teaching and Learning and Assessment for all Students. The name describes an appealing vision for schooling, a vision that most adults wish for their children, their neighbor's children, and the children who, as adults, will participate in the businesses, religions, governments, civic and charitable organizations, schools, and neighborhoods of the future.

An ATLAS Community envisions schools where all children learn well. Students use their minds in creative, thoughtful ways and express themselves with precision and elegance. They achieve high academic standards as they use their skills and knowledge to wrestle with questions that interest them and that are important to their community and their society. An ATLAS Community recognizes that in order to achieve these goals, students must have long-lasting relationships with adults who care for their intellectual growth, their social and physical development, their success in the society, and their general well-being.

The vision that ATLAS Communities hold out is, in many respects, deeply rooted in traditions of the past. At the same time, it is fashioned to prepare students for the future. In the early part of this century, students routinely demonstrated what they knew through their achievements rather than standardized test scores. Families and schools worked together, and at graduation students were prepared to assume their roles as workers and citizens.

In the future, today's students will be workers and citizens in a world that families and teachers now can barely imagine. Whatever shape this world takes, it is certain that students will face challenging situations to which they must apply their wisdom. They will be called upon to manage information, understand new ideas and technology, express themselves clearly, and create wholly new solutions to problems. As well, they will need the values and habits of well-rounded individuals, comfortable in the global village, a world of different cultures and points of view (Comer, 1980).

Components of the Design

The ATLAS Communities design is a comprehensive plan for reshaping a feeder pattern of schools to focus on authentic teaching and high levels of student achievement. The design is based on a set of guiding principles derived from research and best practice. The principles are accompanied by norms for personal interaction and tools for implementation. By putting into place plans that they have developed themselves, educators in the school communities, those who are closest to the students, shape their policies and practices to align with these principles.

The design grows out of a partnership of four leading organizations in educational reform working with colleagues in three school districts. Each partner contributes its special expertise to the design for comprehensive school reform.

James Comer and the School Development Program at Yale are best known for attention to the interactive social systems and human supports needed for successful school management. Howard Gardner and Project Zero contribute groundbreaking ideas about multiple intelligences and alternative forms of assessment. The work of Theodore Sizer and the Coalition for Essential Schools has helped hundreds of American high schools rethink their pedagogy, curriculum, and supportive school policies. Janet Whitla and Education Development Center, Inc., develop K–12 innovative, hands-on curricula, teacher development programs, and supportive technologies that have influenced the shape of learning throughout the world. The school-based partners—Gorham, Maine; Prince George's County, Maryland; Norfolk, Virginia; and others that join them in the future— ground the design in the practical everyday world of teachers, students, administrators, and families.

The principles and norms underlying the ATLAS Communities design have implications for all strands of the educational system— how school districts are organized and managed, how students and teachers work together, and how the schools and the broader community work together to support students. Implementing the design is a cyclical process in which changes are made in small steps. As any one strand changes to focus on improved student learning, the other strands change as well, because each is part of an organized, whole system.

As an example, when teachers plan to teach more interdisciplinary units, they learn that 45-minute periods don't allow enough time for students to work on a project in depth. Changing the class schedule may cause families to wonder how interdisciplinary work and block scheduling will affect their children's educational progress. In working through these concerns with families, educators learn more about the community's interests. For example, they may learn that families and local businesses want students to have more experiences with computers. At the same time, teachers and students may realize that telecommunications technology can be a real resource in their units of study. Using computers and telecommunications technology then results in further classroom change and teachers' realization that they need different forms of assessment— it is difficult (if at all possible) to assess a student's skill in finding information on the Internet, for example, with a paper-and-pencil test.

Because each community decides how the design principles are best implemented, no two ATLAS Communities look exactly alike. Each ATLAS Community reflects in its own way the principles, norms, and practices of the design while shaping the design to its particular strengths and priorities.

The Pathway

The cornerstone of the design, and the basic organizational unit of an ATLAS Community is the pathway. A *pathway* is a feeder pattern of schools, kindergarten through high school, in which educators plan and work together. Each school in the pathway works to achieve two fundamental goals of the ATLAS Communities design: to enhance student learning and to shape other parts of the system—school policies, professional development, and school management—so that they support good teaching and learning. The idea of a pathway is not new; many people might consider it good sense for educators to hold common goals for students and to coordinate policies across grades. The ATLAS Communities design lets common sense guide practice by specifying that key tasks and responsibilities of schools be approached and carried out at the pathway level. Pathways—

- define academic goals essential for all students, including standards of performance.

- collaborate with families and community members in supporting students and in achieving the educational goals of the schools.

- coordinate the work of individual schools.

- forge new relationships between schools and district administration.

- foster communication and professional collaboration within the pathway and with other ATLAS Communities.

Pathway educators, families, and community members define the specific academic goals they consider essential for all students. They also define standards of performance at each grade. Teams of teachers across the pathway, then, coordinate curriculum and pedagogy so that students have consistent, mutually reinforcing learning experiences from kindergarten through grade twelve. For example, teachers in the pathways of Norfolk, Virginia and Gorham, Maine discovered that the same concepts and topics were being taught in several grades. Their K–12 reviews of curriculum also showed important concepts that were not included at all or were included with less attention than teachers thought appropriate. By eliminating unnecessary overlap, teachers found more time for working in-depth with the most important concepts and skills.

ATLAS Communities also work at the pathway level to involve the extended community in supporting students' development and in achieving the educational goals of the schools. All the adults in the community center their work around the academic success and the social–interactive and psychoemotional development of children. Families in the pathway build relationships with individual teachers and principals, and these relationships are nurtured to last through-out the child's public education. Because the pathway's academic expectations are clear and public, community members more clearly see how their strengths and talents can play a part. In some cases, community members have become mentors for students preparing presentations of their work. In other cases, they have arranged student internships in places of business or worked in classrooms to free teachers' time for professional development. Teachers in a pathway can better accomplish long-range learning goals because providing a supportive environment, planning curriculum, under-standing student achievement, and assessing student work is a shared responsibility.

The concept of pathway influences school management as well. A pathway-wide committee, the ATLAS Communities Team, is re-sponsible for coordinating the work of individual schools. At both the pathway and school level, policies are evaluated by how well they support student development and achievement. Scheduling, stu-dent assignment, or other policies that get in the way of student achievement are changed or eliminated.

The ATLAS Communities Team is also responsible for reshap-ing the relationship between schools and district administration. The two join in a partnership that draws on the best of top-down and bottom-up reform: By negotiating problematic existing policies, the district learns how new policies created by teachers can improve student achievement. These new policies may then be adopted by the entire district. Administrators in the Norfolk pathway, for example, believed that good teachers continually seek ways to improve their teaching. The district evaluation policy, however, reflected the view that only teachers who were failing in their jobs would benefit from an improvement plan. The salaries of those teachers were frozen until their improvement plans were successfully completed. The ATLAS Communities Team raised the issue of teacher evaluation with the district administration, and eventually the entire district revised its policy so that all teachers could work to improve their practice.

Communication and professional collaboration are paramount to the work in a pathway; at the same time, they often present great challenges. Teachers and administrators are busy. While they often need to work face to face, they also need a way to collaborate regardless of the time or the availability of each individual. The ATLAS Communities Exchange (ACE) is an electronic network with e-mail and conferencing systems. ACE allows teachers within schools and in pathways across the country to be in contact with one another and with the ATLAS Communities Central staff.

ATLAS pathways build a collaborative culture, because the notion of pathway underscores the responsibility for all adults to understand one another's practice and examine the effect of their work on student achievement and school climate. Research shows that risk-taking, reflection, and long-lasting change require trust and mutual respect (Comer, 1984; Lord, 1992; Miller, Lord, & Dorney, 1994). Ongoing professional development and collaboration within the pathway are vehicles for building trust and respect.

Authentic Teaching and Learning

The primary goal of teaching and learning in ATLAS Communities is to help students develop valuable skills and habits while building deep understanding of ideas central to the academic disciplines and directly relevant to students' lives. To accomplish that goal, each school in a pathway involves students in authentic work—engaging, purposeful units of study that center around interesting questions and require real intellectual activity.

Recent research has changed the traditional view of human learning as a passive, receptive process to the view that understanding something requires that learners actively construct, apply, and demonstrate their growing knowledge. Authentic work helps students develop understanding. Students see the purpose of authentic work, where they are asked to use their skills and knowledge to analyze complex problems. Motivation is high, skills are learned in appropriate contexts, and students discover that they can use what they know to pursue questions that interest them. As an example, tackling the questions: Does the order in which you add, subtract, multiply, or divide numbers make a difference? If so, when? Why or why not? leads students to understand the algebraic concept of order of operations. At the same time, students invent and carry out problem-solving strategies and practice their computational skills. This is a very different activity than memorizing an algorithm and applying it to a set of problems (Gardner, 1991; Sizer, 1984).

Authentic teaching and learning takes time—time to work with ideas, share insights, relate new ideas to old, and demonstrate knowledge in meaningful ways. Since the school calendar is already overcrowded, each pathway community must make choices about the concepts and understandings that are most important and meaningful. By focusing on essential skills and understandings, teachers and students have more time to work with ideas in depth and to develop understanding.

ATLAS Communities implementation tools support educators in developing understanding in students. A curriculum planning framework helps teachers to select engaging topics for a unit of study and to develop the important questions that will drive students' work. The same framework can be used to pare down or reshape existing curriculum materials. ATLAS Communities also use several innovative curriculum products developed by Education Development Center and other organizations that embody the principles of authentic teaching and learning (Education Development Center, 1994; Zorfass, 1991).

Specific teaching materials alone have not proven sufficient for changing classroom practice in the past, and so the ATLAS Communities design includes school-based Study Groups for teachers. In these on-going forums for professional collaboration, teachers in a school develop a common language and approach to making instructional and curricular change. They share strategies and insights as they try out new strategies, review student work, and give each other constructive feedback. Study Groups use ACE, the electronic network of ATLAS Communities, to share examples of good practice and receive information from colleagues in other schools and pathways.

The ATLAS Communities' focus on authentic teaching and learning shifts classroom activity away from covering facts and learning disconnected skills. Instead it requires students to understand big ideas more fully and to apply their skills and knowledge to new challenges, important requirements for the citizenry of tomorrow. This approach to teaching and learning also requires a broader, more inclusive view of assessment.

A System of Assessment

In an ATLAS Community, assessment is inseparable from teaching and learning. It both measures learning as in traditional schools and informs teaching and learning on a daily basis. Assessment is the system of collecting feedback, formal and informal, that lets students know what they have learned and helps teachers see how best to shape instruction.

ATLAS Communities assess learning primarily through performances, portfolios, and exhibitions, although tests and other traditional measures can play a part. In performances, students demonstrate what they know through writing, discussion, work products such as scale drawings and pieces of music, or other ways that show their understanding of important ideas or skills.

A typical unit or activity begins with a discussion of what the unit is about and what students are expected to learn. As the unit continues, students regularly share their ideas, drafts, and final products to get feedback from peers, teachers, or even outside experts. Based on this daily, embedded assessment, students revise their work and teachers adjust classroom activities and the kinds of instructional support students receive. The unit concludes with individual or group performances in which students demonstrate and reflect on their accomplishments.

Throughout the year, students and teachers select portions of their work for portfolios. By regularly reviewing the portfolios, students, teachers, and families can see how skills and understanding develop over time. The items placed in portfolios, carefully selected and annotated to show different facets and stages of work, provide first-hand examples of what students know and can do.

Exhibitions are a particular type of performance, often required as one condition for promotion or graduation. Exhibitions are done at benchmark grades, typically five, eight, and eleven, and are based on the skills, habits, and understandings the community has defined as essential. In some cases exhibitions are complex, interdisciplinary tasks such as researching and reporting on a question, creating a video, designing and conducting an experiment, or giving a musical performance. In other cases, they are presentations of portfolios or of class projects that students feel best represent their progress. Achievement standards that students are expected to meet are clearly defined and known to both students and the community.

Performances, portfolios, and exhibitions are powerful because of their public nature, their ability to show how learning develops over time, their requirement of deep understanding, and the ways in which they engage students and families (Gardner, 1992; Sizer, 1984). An eleventh-grade student in Gorham, Maine reflected on exhibitions in this way:

> You had to know your stuff, which was good, because in class you can do your work, but you may not understand why it all happens. Like for chemistry, you do labs, but you may not really know the difference between the physical and chemical changes . . . just the whole process. That [the exhibition] was being presented to adults and community members and stuff, it had to be good. The only thing that I was worried about was having them ask some questions that I didn't know the answers to. So you needed to know your topics really well (White, Fanning, & Muncey, 1995a).

ATLAS Communities in Norfolk, Prince George's County, and Gorham have found that implementing a performance-based system of assessment is a powerful catalyst for change across all strands of the educational system. In order for students to be successful in demonstrating what they know, classroom activity must shift toward building understanding through authentic work and interdisciplinary units.

Teachers develop new skills in analyzing student work both to understand how best to fine tune instructional strategies and to assess student achievement. Implementing a system of assessment also involves the extended community in new ways—helping to define goals and standards, understanding students' progress through portfolios, and participating as mentors and evaluators in the exhibition process. For these reasons, ATLAS Communities are urged to develop and fully implement a performance-based system of assessment within five years.

Organization and Management Structures

The organization and management groups in ATLAS Communities are responsible for creating a school climate that promotes authentic teaching and that allows children to feel safe and ready to learn. The groups are charged with creating policies that are responsive to the needs of teachers and students, promoting professional collaboration, monitoring and improving school climate, working with district administration, and developing comprehensive short- and long-range plans of action. Students' academic success and a supportive school climate are the goals of each group; they are also the gauges by which to measure each group's effectiveness. The norms of collaboration, consensus, and no-fault problem solving are proven ways for adults to build trusting relationships; these norms guide the work of all ATLAS Communities management groups (Comer, 1980, 1984).

ATLAS Communities Team. The ATLAS Communities Team leads the pathway by coordinating the work of the individual schools. While its exact membership varies from site to site, the team usually includes two or three representatives from each school and represents a mix of administrators, teachers, parents, and support staff. A school board member, union representative, or other community member may be included. The issues facing the group and its responsibilities, detailed in the section describing the pathway, are to:

- lead the process of defining pathway essential skills, habits, and understandings and structuring the performance-based system of assessment;

- link the pathway to district administration and to other ATLAS pathways;

- represent the K–12 view in individual school's plans and initiatives;

- strengthen links between schools and community.

School Planning and Management Team. School Planning and Management Teams govern the schools and are the primary decision-making bodies in the pathway. Membership includes the principal, teachers, support staff, and community members. In middle and high schools, students may participate. The School Planning and Management Team:

- maintains a schoolwide focus on student achievement and school climate;

- builds community and strong relationships;

- evaluates policies and changes those that present barriers to authentic teaching, learning, and assessment;

- develops a long-range, comprehensive plan that guides the school's work in teaching and learning, professional development, family involvement, school climate, and exhibitions; and

- shares its plans and with other schools in the pathway, the extended community, and as appropriate with other pathways.

Community Health Team. The Community Health Team operates on the belief that schools promote high student achievement when they attend to the physical, psychoemotional, and social-interactive development of students. The Community Health Team is made up of health care and social service providers; its goal is to prevent and address behavior problems and to create a school climate that is safe and supportive. The committee works with teachers to sharpen their observation skills and alter classroom practices to meet all children's needs. It coordinates the plans of social service and health care providers as they work with individual students. It also tracks and analyzes the individual referrals to identify issues of schoolwide concern that the School Planning and Management Team can then address (Comer, 1992).

All organization and management groups work through repeated cycles of planning, action, and reflection. In planning, groups focus on an issue and decide on a course of action, including the kinds of evaluative data they will collect as plans are implemented. Ongoing reflections, informed by data, measure a plan's success in improving student achievement or school climate. These reflections point the way for the next step or the next course of action. Throughout the process, group members agree to collaborate, reach consensus, and find solutions rather than fault.

The following example shows how an ATLAS Community management group uses the norms of no-fault, collaboration, and consensus and fulfills its responsibility through a process of planning, action, and reflection.

Task Force on Time, Prince George's County, Maryland. After the first year of implementing the ATLAS Communities design, elementary teachers identified one major obstacle to what they considered worthwhile goals of collaboration and interdisciplinary curriculum: time. After seven-and-a-half hours of working with as many as 35 students, there was little time or energy to reflect on teaching practice or to plan collaboratively.

The school formed a Task Force on Time, which included several volunteer teachers and the principal. The task force was to create joint planning time so that grade-level teachers could work on interdisciplinary teaching. The first plan, hiring substitutes, was happily put into place, perhaps in part because there was outside funding. Within a year the plan was discarded. Teachers found that preparing for and following up on substitutes' work increased demands on their time, and the task force realized that while grade-level teachers could work together, physical education, ESL, Chapter 1, and other specialists were excluded. Also, the cost of substitutes could no longer be covered by outside funds.

The task force put together a second, more long-lasting plan that created teaching teams from the professional staff of the school, including the specialists. By using the physical education, arts, and media specialists in creative ways, the task force designed a weekly block schedule in which time for joint planning rotated among the teams. Teachers used the time to plan interdisciplinary projects and coordinate teaching, to collaboratively assess student needs and strengths, and to develop common instructional strategies.

The task force's work had its intended results; teachers had time to collaborate and were able to shift their teaching to include more interdisciplinary, project-centered units. Further reflection revealed that teachers developed stronger, more collegial relationships that supported them in trying out new practices as well as giving and taking critical feedback. Grade-level teachers also found increased respect for the physical education and creative arts specialists, whose work they had had opportunities to see and discuss. An unanticipated bonus was that the teaching techniques familiar to ESL and special educators, such as different grouping practices and the uses of ideas about multiple intelligences, were shared with grade-level teachers—to the benefit of all students.

Extended Learning Community. The notion of community is embodied in many ways and at many levels throughout an ATLAS Community. The ATLAS Communities design is based on the belief that those closest to the children, the families and educators in the pathway, hold responsibility for deciding how best to implement the design. Stemming from this belief are such practices as community-defined essential skills and understandings, community-based learning activities, and a pathway-wide emphasis on both informing and responding to community concerns. Within the classroom and school, the norms of no-fault, collaboration, and consensus help to guide the whole pathway toward common academic and interpersonal goals. Among teachers, these same norms help establish collegial relationships and a supportive community of professionals.

A key tool in building a learning community is an assets inventory, a systematic procedure to uncover the special expertise, resources, materials, and talents of individuals or groups. Some pathways, considering themselves part of a global electronic community, have included the resources of ACE and the Internet in their inventory. People have found that the process of mapping and building on assets can cause a shift in attitude toward members of the community. Children and adults come to be seen in light of what they have to offer, rather than their problems or special issues, and talents that otherwise might be undeveloped can be brought forward and celebrated.

Another tool is a school climate survey, a survey of opinions about attitudes and morale intended to surface social issues that might interfere with student achievement. Teachers, students, and parents rate their agreement with statements such as *School is a safe place* and *Teachers help students to do their best.* The concerns raised by the school climate survey can then be addressed through deliberate, thoughtful attention from school and pathway management groups. Information from these and other surveys can serve both as measures of the effectiveness of pathway initiatives and as grist for the creative mills of a school, whether they be for planning classroom activities or squeezing the most from limited resources.

Building an extended learning community also includes student–family conferences and other forums for involving the community in raising levels of student achievement. Regular communication about the activities of the school and about students' work gives families the information they want about their children's learning. As an example, teachers in Gorham, Maine involved families in the assessment of students by sending home tape recordings of students' oral reading at three times during the year. After receiving the second tapes, one parent reflected:

> I do appreciate [receiving] this because I'm not there during the school day, and I can't see what [my daughter] has done or what she has learned through the school year. So to get this [tape] and compare the two is a wonderful experience. I, myself, am very proud of [her], because when she first started in class, she was very reluctant to sound out words because she was embarrassed she might not get them right or someone would laugh at her. I've seen that confidence be built up in her this year in particular (White, Fanning, & Muncey, 1995a).

Professional Growth and Collaboration. The practices and activities of educators in ATLAS Communities come from research and examples of best practice; many of them are part of the repertoire of the best teachers and administrators. Other ATLAS practices, though, may be new and require thoughtful attention, training, trial, and reflection. Research shows that the most successful programs for professional growth include a balance of more formal learning opportunities—workshops, professional readings, or focused training programs—and ongoing opportunities to try new practices and reflect on their effectiveness with colleagues and peers. Formal adult learning opportunities must be informed by and embedded in the real work of schools or families (Lord, 1992; Miller, Lord, & Dorney, 1994; Muncey & McQuillan, 1991; Schifter & Twomey Sosnot, 1993). A teacher in Gorham, commenting on a unique summer institute that combined professional workshops in the morning with an afternoon summer school program of special interdisciplinary projects, commented on her own professional growth in this way:

> I think so frequently when you have staff development and you learn a new idea, you say, "Oh, that's great, I'll try it in the fall," and you never do anything with it. And this [summer institute]

really provided people with a perfect opportunity to be sharing some new things, to be thinking about it, and the vehicle to talk it over with other people. . . . That aspect of bringing the kids in right then and seeing what works, what doesn't work, how you can modify it, is really valuable (White, Fanning, & Muncey, 1995b).

The ATLAS Communities design encourages professional growth in several ways, the most important of which is by promoting a school culture of reflective practice, a culture in which continued learning is valued, expected, recognized, and supported. Regular, formal, learning opportunities on topics that teachers have identified as priorities are detailed in the comprehensive school plan that guides the work of each school. Suggestions for professional readings or structured learning opportunities are also posted on ACE, the ATLAS electronic conferencing system. Study Groups are the vehicle through which new ideas become part of teachers' reflective practice.

Implementing the Design

The ATLAS Communities implementation plan is based on the belief that the ongoing work of school reform should be based in and stem from the needs of the pathway. To that end, ATLAS Communities Central staff support new pathways through leadership institutes and structured Study Group learning materials. A Site Liaison from ATLAS Communities Central staff provides customized technical assistance to each site. The Site Liaison works as both a colleague and consultant to a person in the district, the ATLAS Coach, who is responsible for coordinating ATLAS reforms. While initially the Site Liaison guides the work, over time the leadership and support for change shifts from the Site Liaison to the district-based pathway team. Each of these materials and activities are designed to help educators understand and work with the design such that they can continue their reform work independently after two or three years.

The implementation plan itself mirrors the building blocks of the ATLAS Communities design: cycles of planning, action, and reflection that focus on authentic teaching and learning. Within each phase of implementation, school personnel collect information for use in action plans. Plans are put in place and people reflect on their impact on student achievement and school climate. The cycle begins again for the next phase. Successful implementation of the ATLAS Communities design should result in the following accomplishments within five years:

- The pathway's essential skills, habits, and understandings are clearly defined and publicly understood.

- Curriculum includes project-based units, driven by questions and focused on essential skills, habits, and understandings.

- An assessment system that includes performances, portfolios, exhibitions, and requisite policy changes has been operating for at least one year.

- The pathway and district administration have established new working relationships.

- Pathway and school-based organization and management structures are working to create an extended learning community and coordinate activities of schools across the pathway through five-year plans that address each strand of the design.

Phase I: Exploration and Initial Implementation

The goals of this initial phase, which is expected to last up to a year, is for the pathway community to put in place the key structures and practices.

Initially, stakeholders in the district explore the design with ATLAS Communities Central staff. The stakeholder group varies from site to site, but usually includes members of the board of education, district administration, community and business leaders, parent organizations, and school personnel. The group considers the implications of the ATLAS Communities design, including delegating significant decision-making authority to the pathway and focusing teaching, learning, and assessment on community-defined essential understandings.

Districts that find a match between the ATLAS Communities design and their goals designate a pathway of schools and begin the process. The stakeholder group begins to identify assets within the pathway and community. Teachers and administrators form Study Groups that meet regularly to build a common understanding of authentic teaching and assessment. Organization and management groups are formed. The pathway establishes procedures for communication among schools and installs hardware and software necessary for its electronic connection with other pathways and with other ATLAS Communities. New relationships are formed—among school personnel, with families and community members, and with district administration. The insights gained from the work of this phase actually begin to shape the design to a particular community. For example, the particular activities teachers develop using the curriculum planning framework become an initial reference point for understanding what essential questions are and how they drive learning. The reference point will change over time and with more experience and reflection, but its beginning is here, in the work of the initial implementation phase.

At the end of Phase I, the stakeholder group, schools, and families reaffirm their decision to become an ATLAS Community. The pathway prepares a portfolio that describes its work with authentic teaching and learning, assesses the use of Study Groups as a means of professional development, reviews the range of opportunities for school-community collaboration, and defines the expectations and relationships between the pathway and district. The portfolio informs the community's next steps in working with the ATLAS Communities design.

Phase II: Full Implementation

Phase II is the pathway's first full, year-long cycle of planning, action, and reflection. The organization and management groups work with the information contained in their portfolio to further teachers' work with authentic teaching and to develop comprehensive pathway and school plans. Among the pathway's initial challenges is to begin defining the skills, habits, and understandings it considers essential for all students. To do so, pathway educators must consider state and local requirements, work with families and community members, and define specific academic expectations. Part of this work involves articulating standards of performance and developing plans for a performance-based system of assessment to be implemented within five years. At the end of the school year, the pathway community reflects on its work, ensuring that plans for the coming years address the school and pathway's most important issues and needs.

By the end of Phase II, organizational structures are established and operating. Schools, parents, and community members have a clear understanding of pathway goals and of each school's comprehensive school plan. In classrooms, families and community members can expect to see many changes, including project-based units of interdisciplinary study and frequent performances or demonstrations of student work. Issues of importance to the school, such as school safety, self respect, or working through conflict, are the focus of some classroom work.

Throughout Phases I and II, ATLAS Communities Central staff provide technical assistance tailored to a pathway's needs and priorities. In addition, people from the pathway work closely with ATLAS Central staff, developing the understanding and expertise necessary to continue the work over time.

Phase III: Expanding and Refining

In Phase III, pathways expand and refine their implementation of ATLAS Communities practices and principles in year-long cycles of planning, action, and reflection. The work is guided primarily by the comprehensive school and pathway plans, with technical assistance and support coming from within the pathway and from other ATLAS Communities more than from ATLAS Communities Central staff.

At the time of this writing, four years after engaging with the ATLAS Communities design, the school-based partners in Maine, Maryland, and Virginia are solidly in Phase III of implementation. The ATLAS Communities Team and the School Planning and Management Teams guide school and pathway activity; each site has developed, at least initially, a system for assessment and exhibitions; curriculum is increasingly driven by authentic work and important questions; families and communities are deeply involved in the schools. As anticipated, each site has followed a slightly different course, moving more quickly or cautiously in developing some design components depending on its strengths, opportunities, and interests.

The ATLAS Community in Prince George's County, Maryland gave first priority to establishing its organization and management structures, while maintaining significant but slightly lower levels of effort in the area of authentic teaching, learning, and assessment. This focus came in part from the superintendent's willingness to support principals and the School Planning and Management Teams in the change process. The pathway made significant changes in scheduling, class assignments, multi-age classrooms, and other policies that affect teaching and learning. Reshaping the curriculum was fueled by the enthusiasm of teachers and by success at the middle school with *Make It Happen!*, a program of inquiry-based thematic units culminating in a written research report on topics of student choice. Reading scores at the elementary school increased by up to 30 percent.

Fully implementing a performance-based assessment system has proceeded more slowly. The pathway standards committee has worked carefully through complex issues—mandatory state assessments, college entrance requirements, the understanding of family and community members, and curriculum changes necessary for students to be successful with exhibitions. A timeline for fully implementing the assessment system has been set.

In Gorham, Maine, the pathway is the school district, so there have been fewer issues in coordinating the work of individual schools and district administration. In this community, establishing smoothly-functioning management structures presented particular challenges in the first months. Members of the management teams needed more time than they had anticipated to discuss their school's particular issues and to get organized for action. There was also some attrition in the management teams, which made it difficult to build relationships and sustain momentum. The pathway eventually organized its work through seven design teams, each responsible for different aspects of the ATLAS Communities design.

Prior to engaging with ATLAS Communities, teachers in Gorham had been using student portfolios and other forms of alternative assessment. Their initial ATLAS work built on this strength and on another self-identified strength, student leadership. The Standards and Exhibitions Design Team led the community in establishing a set of compulsory performances (essential skills) for all students kindergarten through grade twelve. Students throughout the pathway also assess themselves orally or in writing in regard to five essential habits: self-directed learner, collaborative worker, complex thinker, quality producer, and community contributor. This pathway's comprehensive system of performance-based assessment helps inform curriculum and daily classroom practice. It has become a model for other districts in the area.

In Norfolk, work initially centered on reshaping curriculum to focus on developing understanding. From this strong beginning, the pathway decided to implement an exhibition system, and that process quickly became a driving force for change. The ATLAS Communities Team worked with district administration to waive expectations for student test scores. In planning for exhibitions, teachers identified several conditions that were necessary for students to succeed. First, families and community members needed to be involved in establishing essential skills, habits, and understandings. As the work continued, teachers realized that students needed additional support in preparing for the exhibitions themselves. Community members and teachers each were assigned as a mentor to each student making an exhibition. Class schedules had to be rearranged to allow students time to plan their exhibitions, do the work, and prepare their presentations. The relationships between students and teachers shifted a bit, with teachers taking on a role more similar to a facilitator than an expert. After all students had made their presentations, teachers discussed the need to develop among themselves a thoughtful process for evaluating achievement fairly and uniformly. The community as a whole identified many tasks that would improve student performance for the next year, including continued work in reshaping curriculum and a review of the standards of performance for all students. After the fourth year of ATLAS implementation, test scores in all disciplines related to exhibition work have increased significantly.

Costs of Implementation

New pathways can expect certain costs as they implement the ATLAS Communities design. The actual demands, whether time or money, depend on the individual circumstances of the district, for example size of the pathway, staff currently available to guide the reform process, resources for staff development, cost of teacher release time, existing technology, and level of readiness for reform.

The work of becoming an ATLAS Community is labor intensive. The pathway should expect to fund a full- or part-time Site Liaison for the pathway. The time required for support from ATLAS Communities varies, but new sites should plan for two years at a minimum. The district should also expect to fund one part-time person from each school to help ATLAS Communities staff guide the reform process and then to continue the work in later years.

There are expenses for travel, professional development, and teacher release time. At the outset of Phase I, staff from each school in the pathway participate in a week-long ATLAS Communities Institute, typically held in the summer, to explore in depth different ATLAS principles and practices. These people then become Study Group leaders for all faculty and staff in their respective schools. During the school year, Study Groups need time to meet and work, typically two to five hours per month. In subsequent years, districts can choose to participate in additional ATLAS Communities Institutes focused on school leadership and curriculum. Other professional development costs, outside of the typical expenditure for each school, depend on the needs identified in management teams or Study Groups.

ATLAS Communities vary widely in their use of and plans for technology. For professional collaboration and communication with ATLAS Central, each school is expected to have access to ACE, a minimum requirement of one computer and modem per school. Depending on the district's hardware configuration, there may also be installation and usage costs for telephone or data lines.

Taking the Next Step

The challenge of changing public education for the better is an exhilarating—and enormous—one. The potential gains for children and for our nation make the choice for today's educators not whether to but how to shape an effective system of schooling that gives students the skills, habits, and understandings they will need for their future success.

References

Comer, J. (1980). *School power: Implications of an intervention project.* New York: Free Press.

Comer, J. (1984). Home-school relationships as they affect the academic success of children. *Education and Urban Society, 16*(3), 323–337.

Comer, J. (1992). *For children's sake: Comer School Development Program discussion leader's guide.* New Haven, CT: Yale Child Study Center.

Education Development Center, Inc. (1994). *Math and more.* Atlanta: IBM Corporation.

Education Development Center, Inc. (1995). *Seeing and thinking mathematically.* Portsmouth, NH: Heinemann.

Gardner, H. (1991). *The unschooled mind: How children think and how schools should teach.* New York: Basic Books.

Gardner, H. (1992). Assessment in context: The alternative to standardized testing. In B. R. Gifford & M. C. O'Connor (Eds.), *Changing assessments: Alternative views of aptitude, achievement, and instruction* (pp. 78–119). Boston: Kluwer.

Insights: An elementary hands-on inquiry science curriculum. (1994). Newton, MA: Education Development Center, Inc.

Lord, B. (1992). *Subject-area teacher networks, teacher professionalism, and staff development* (Res. Rep. 92-2). Newton, MA: Education Development Center, Inc., Reports and Papers in Progress.

Miller, B., Lord, B. & Dorney, J. (1994). *Staff development for teachers: A study of configurations and costs in four districts.* Newton, MA: Education Development Center, Inc., Reports and Papers in Progress.

74

Muncey, D., & McQuillan, P. (Sept. 1991). *The meeting of many worlds: Professional development in a grassroots educational reform movement*. Paper presented at the annual meeting of the Coalition of Essential Schools: Restructuring from an important perspective, Chicago.

Schifter, D., & Twomey Sosnot, C. (1993). *Reconstructing mathematics education: Stories of teachers meeting the challenge of reform*. New York: Teacher's College Press.

Sizer, T. (1984). *Horace's compromise: The dilemma of the American high school*. Boston: Houghton-Mifflin.

White, N., Fanning, K., & Muncey, D. (1995a). *Exhibitions in the Gorham and Norfolk ATLAS Pathways, 1994-1995. Third report of the ATLAS Seminar ethnography project*. Unpublished manuscript.

White, N., Fanning, K. & Muncey, D. (1995b). *Professional development in the ATLAS project. Second report of the ATLAS Seminar ethnography project*. Unpublished manuscript.

Zorfass, J. (1991). *Make it happen: Inquiry and technology in the middle school curriculum*. Newton, MA: Education Development Center.

The Co-NECT Design
for School Change

Bruce Goldberg
John Richards
BBN Corporation

The future, the poet Paul Valery once noted, isn't what it used to be. Not so very long ago, we took the future more or less for granted. We planned its arrival in a state of relaxed, almost lazy anticipation. Our future and that of our children seemed relatively assured. The future had a soothing ring to it, an optimistic chord created out of deliberate forethought and the hard-earned results of past effort.

We knew, more or less, what to expect. There would always be plentiful and meaningful jobs, progressively higher standards of living, shared respect and understandings among communities, and groups grown less diverse over time. If there were one constant to post World War II American life, it was that change, even relentless change, was progressive and continuous.

That was before phrases like *global competition, downsizing,* and the *information age* invaded our collective consciousness and began changing our lives. Today, these and other related events have made the future appear less orderly, its agenda less certain. No longer a comforting and familiar figure, the future has become more like a shadowy trickster in our crowded present, shoving us at times in unfamiliar and uncomfortable directions and forging radical discontinuity with what had gone before.

For the historically privileged populations of the western world, a number of things have changed and changed dramatically. The global economic landscape has begun shifting the balance of the world's wealth and productive capacities from nations like ours rich in natural resources to nations with the foresight, creativity, and skill to utilize and manipulate information in increasingly sophisticated ways. In the wake of this seismic realignment, virtually all public (and private) institutions and organizations are shedding top-heavy bureaucracies, and becoming increasingly more flexible and entrepreneurial in response to shifting customer demand. And as part cause, part result, we are living through one of the most dramatic and relentless technological revolutions in modern history.

All the changes are not global, technological, or institutional, however. Some are sociological and more directly related to the recent and profound shift in our national demographic profile. Simply put, we have become a nation whose individuals are relatively older, less frequently European and White, and more sharply divided economically into camps of the haves and have-nots, than our counterparts of only 50 years ago.

What has this meant for our schools and education system? On the surface, not much. Most schools still see their mission divided into a few time-tested purposes: to teach core academic skills, to prepare students for productive work, to inspire good character and citizenship, and to help students develop their individual talents and interests. But while the mission might still be the same, the best means to achieve it are no longer clear.

It was in the context of the above perspective that New American Schools issued their challenge to create "break-the-mold" schools. The factory model of schooling, designed in the first two decades of the twentieth century, is no longer effective—if it ever was.

Clearly, we can do better. But we will have to do better for all schools—and for all students. We must reassert our fundamental commitment to the belief that all children can learn (Howard, 1992). But we must do more as well. We must see to it that students demand of themselves an unrelenting commitment to achieving excellence in a world of ever-changing contours.

This is not an argument for a few well-wired "schools of the future." Such schools have become an irrelevancy. After all, what is the alternative, "schools of the past"? Schools rich with technology and built with lifelong learning in mind can no longer be marginalized and slotted for specialized market niches, appealing only to those who have a self-proclaimed interest in "computers." Either all schools will become "schools of the future," or the future will be bleak.

The Orientation of Co-NECT

For their first project cycle this year, middle-school students at the A.L.L. School in Worcester, Massachusetts asked the following critical question: How does smoking affect the quality of life in the United States? The teacher, Tim O'Brien, gathered resources and, before the project began, made contact with organizations such as the Lung Association and political action committees with home pages on the net. Additional resources were collected throughout the project. This type of advance preparation is necessary for project work. Relying on students to identify, request, and establish all project sources, information, and interchanges, could seriously hamper a project's needed capability to have resources available in a timely manner.

Tim provided a menu of standards that correlated well with the project (see Fig. 4.1). Each student had to choose at least three, but not more than five, standards with which to work. He coached them along in the decision-making process, encouraging them to select and incorporate standards they had not addressed in the past, or standards for which they had earned the designation "developing" in past projects.

Tim set many deadlines (first draft, poster plan/layout, etc.) as part of the project work plan. He held individual conferences on an as-needed basis (low performance, encouragement, and compliments) and facilitated whole class conversations on issues such as work habits, and project progress. Status reports were given by groups and individuals nearly every day. These were sometimes held at the end of the class to gauge overall progress. At other times these reports took place at the beginning of the class to set goals for the session and then later at the end to see if they met the goals.

The main question led the students to research various topics—from laws that deal with minors purchasing tobacco, to diseases caused by smoking. The students involved the community in their project in many ways. For example, they consulted with a neurosurgeon to better understand the biology of smoking and the effects of nicotine on the brain.

They learned that the Food and Drug Administration (FDA) considers smoking a pediatric disease because the majority of smokers start before age 18. The students observed how surprisingly easy it was for minors in their own community to purchase tobacco products because only a few stores bothered to check the age of their customers. They concluded that there is no incentive for proprietors to obey the tobacco laws because they are not enforced.

Figure 4.1   Brainstorming Chart Linking Project Activities to Standards

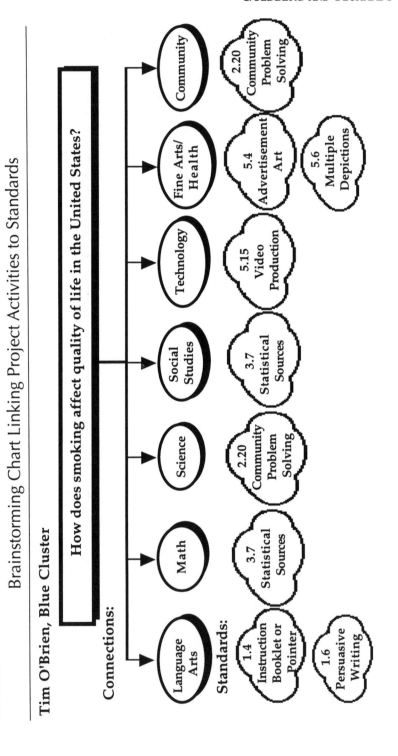

Figure 4.1 (continued)

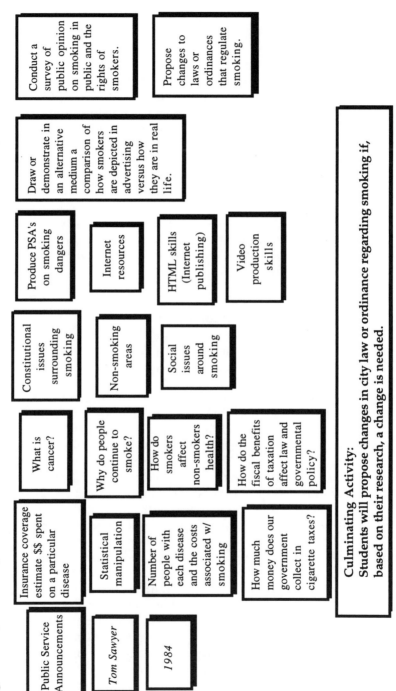

Conduct a survey of public opinion on smoking in public and the rights of smokers.

Propose changes to laws or ordinances that regulate smoking.

Draw or demonstrate in an alternative medium a comparison of how smokers are depicted in advertising versus how they are in real life.

Produce PSA's on smoking dangers

Internet resources

HTML skills (Internet publishing)

Video production skills

Constitutional issues surrounding smoking

Non-smoking areas

Social issues around smoking

What is cancer?

Why do people continue to smoke?

How do smokers affect non-smokers' health?

How do the fiscal benefits of taxation affect law and governmental policy?

Insurance coverage estimate $$ spent on a particular disease

Statistical manipulation

Number of people with each disease and the costs associated w/ smoking

How much money does our government collect in cigarette taxes?

Public Service Announcements

Tom Sawyer

1984

Culminating Activity:
Students will propose changes in city law or ordinance regarding smoking if, based on their research, a change is needed.

Based on their findings, the students proposed changes in the laws governing smoking to the City Solicitor, Michael O'Mara. Those changes are now incorporated into a draft of a new ordinance. The students are on the agenda to present their findings and voice their support for the new ordinance to the City Council. O'Mara is enthusiastic about the students' involvement. Their physical presence at the City Council meeting will be a powerful statement of their concern. And their recommendation for stricter tobacco laws for minors, he believes, ultimately will have more influence in passing the new ordinance than would the typical bureaucrat's presentation.

The students were also interested in smoking practices outside their own community. To pursue this, they created a survey on the World Wide Web (WWW), posing several questions to the general Internet community. The survey encouraged anonymous e-mail responses be sent to the students. Responses came from several other states and countries. Their survey and findings may be found at the following URL:

http://nis.accel.worc.k12.ma.us/WWW/Projects/formtest.html

Co-NECT—The Learning Organization

The political, social, and economic environment in which formal education now occurs is clearly different from that of Horace Mann's time. The relative equilibrium of the past is gone, and anxiety exists concerning the ability of traditional institutions to face up to more demanding circumstances. In this new environment, all organizations and institutions must be capable of responding to and learning from the rapid and discontinuous changes that are occurring in society. In our view, there are four critically related tasks education must address. First, we must redefine the nature of school curriculum so that students are producing academic results in terms of world class quality products and performances. Second, we must provide students and teachers with a technological infrastructure that allows them to participate as knowledge workers in an information society. Third, we must create the conditions by which individual and social diversity enhance the nature of lifelong learning, rather than detract from it. Finally, we must develop strategies capable not only of initiating these changes, but of sustaining them.

Finding a solution to the aforementioned four tasks requires a whole school design and a coherent framework for change—one that combines simultaneous changes in integrating curriculum, assessment, instruction and governance with a strategy for maximizing the likelihood that the effort will be an ongoing one. Co-NECT was our response (cf. Fig. 4.2). This dynamic combination of design and change is what makes Co-NECT, in Peter Senge's (1990) words, a "learning organization."

> "[L]earning organizations," [are] organizations where people continually expand their capacity to create the results they truly desire, where new and expansive patterns of thinking are nurtured, where collective aspiration is set free, and where people are continually learning how to learn together (p. 3).

It would be foolish for us (or, we think, for any reform effort) to claim our approach is unique. Sharing successes after all is part of what a learning organization is all about. So it is that the Co-NECT approach shares some core beliefs with other reform initiatives. For example, like many other designs for reform, we believe that each of our schools needs the autonomy to create self-managed and flexible social structures (clusters) to perform the work they undertake. We also believe that curriculum should be oriented around the accomplishment of real-world projects—whose solutions are related to the concerns and lives of the communities in which they originate.

But there are differences as well. Unlike some reform efforts, we do not place our trust in any one indicator, test, or new assessment instrument to gauge the success and quality of student work. Instead, we believe in a balanced and comprehensive assessment system—one that includes exhibitions, portfolios, performance assessments but traditional tests as well.

We also differ from many other reforms in our enthusiastic embrace of technology as both a learning tool and catalyst for change. The Co-NECT project-centered curriculum, therefore, is likely to include collaborative Internet-based projects among far-flung geographical sites that incorporate new found colleagues, students, mentors, and experts. And by incorporating advanced communications technologies, we can expand the boundaries of the school's professional community to include others who share a similar commitment to change. In fact, we believe that sustaining reform is almost unimaginable without widespread use of the newer just-in-time communications technologies. Every Co-NECT school, therefore, must eventually have a technological infrastructure permitting each member of its community access to information and participation within the larger knowledge-producing community.

These differences illustrate a pronounced re-norming of the culture of the school. It is up to the individual school, however, within the context of its own culture and vision, to work towards actualizing widespread technology use. Each site must evolve its own sustainable technology culture in which the integration of communication, simulation, modeling, systems thinking, and other tools within project work, becomes transparent and commonplace.

Of course, in many (if not most) instances, realizing a basic technology infrastructure will be heavily dependent on a district's understanding, capacity, and commitment. A district technology plan is necessary, of course, but not always sufficient. Additionally, a district will often require assistance in assuring that the technology plan is phased in over time so that it satisfies critical educational, technological, and financial considerations. We not only provide this assistance, but encourage districts to include within their oversight of Co-NECT schools an equally firm commitment to creating the eventual infrastructure for all their schools.

Co-NECT—The "Unlearning" Organization

These differences also entail an unorthodox approach to the task of implementing change. The challenge of breaking the mold and creating a school as a learning organization is a radical departure from current schooling. We do not believe that it is possible to make this shift by a series of small incremental changes. Co-NECT schools are premised upon a notion of discontinuous change, of change that is often so radical and unpredictable that it requires shared commitment and skill to *unlearn* what has gone before.

In this sense, educational institutions are no more immunized against a changing environment than any other institution in our society. All of them, private or public, business or governmental, face a future as unfamiliar as it is shared. For all of us, change is now not only imperative, but qualitatively distinct from the kind to which we have become accustomed (cf. Nadler, Shaw, Walton, & Associates, 1995). Most important, it is no longer possible to think of (and plan for) change as simply incremental.

> Incremental changes are made within the context or frame of the current organization. The fundamental definition of the organization—its identity, values, and mission—does not change. These form the boundaries and borders of change. Incremental change happens within these borders, as indeed it should. Changing the frame is difficult and even dangerous, because it involves fighting against the forces of balance, fit, and congruence. So we think of these incremental changes as changes within the frame. Discontinuous change is qualitatively different, since here the goal is to change the organizational frame itself (Nadler, et al., 1995, p. 29).

The orientation of Co-NECT is one that takes account of what we perceive as a very different organizational frame or context for education. In perhaps an odd but very real sense, therefore, the orientation of Co-NECT is slanted as much toward becoming an unlearning organization as it is to becoming a learning one. In addition to mastering and integrating the five disciplines (personal mastery, team learning, systems thinking, shared vision, and mental models) that Peter Senge outlined as critical to the learning organization, we believe that we must also learn how to unlearn what has gone before—how to continuously recognize, manage, and structure organizational responses to the tumultuous era of discontinuous change (Senge, 1990).

What is meant by an *unlearning* organization? Most broadly, we have found that there are a number of organizational, attitudinal, and behavioral shifts that schools and districts must make in order to be responsive to the changes demanded by a learning organization:

- *Subtraction is more important than addition.* Too often schools (and districts) are predisposed to add to their reform agendas rather than subtract from what they have traditionally done. In order to become an effective learning organization, it is necessary to ask what programs and practices can (and perhaps ought) to be eliminated, and then follow through and subtract them.

- *Organizational fluidity and constancy are not opposed.* Organizations that break themselves down into small focused teams or units can encourage constancy of purpose and intimacy—but sometimes at the cost of innovation and wider communication. Creating processes, forums, and technologies in which new social relationships can be readily formed and reformed without overloading students and teachers is a fundamental requirement of the new learning organization.

- *The role of the teacher / school district is not to "teach, test, and hope for the best."* Establishing a culture that not only pays serious attention to results, but also to the importance of learning from experience (successful and less successful), is the hallmark of a learning organization characterized by reflective practice. In schools, as with all organizations in a state of discontinuous change, every opportunity to seize learning from what is being experienced should be exploited. In this sense, schools must think of themselves as organizations performing in a jazz idiom. To the experienced jazz group, once the standard melody has been introduced, no subsequent note is a "wrong" one. Rather, every note is an invitation to incorporate something unexpectedly rich and new into the familiar (cf. Senge, 1990, p. 298).

In our judgment, schools and districts need assistance in changing and sustaining new organizational frames. So in addition to the Co-NECT design framework, we have also developed a framework for implementing the design within a context of discontinuous change. This framework combines a phased implementation strategy with an overall change process that recognizes the need for schools to periodically revisit their design over time. Or, to put it yet another way, in Co-NECT schools, design and change are indissociable.

The Co-NECT Design Framework

Our school is a Co-NECT school. The difference is that in Co-NECT you are challenged more and you get to work with more hands-on stuff and you get to work with people that are at different levels in grade wise and experience wise (Webmasters, 1995).

In the Co-NECT design, a school is not a building; it is a community. That community can be composed of the students and teachers who share a common physical space, or it can be virtual—a community involving schools, museums, workplaces, homes, and libraries spread geographically across the globe and engaged in a common pursuit. In either case, if the design is to succeed, the school districts of which Co-NECT schools are a part must also be committed to a radically new kind of community-building through systemic reform.

Co-NECT is a K–12 design that provides the framework for a school to transform traditional rules, roles, and relationships into that of a learning organization. Our focus is simple—helping to create a school's local capacity to sustain the changes it is making over time. Technology plays an integral role in this transformation, both in the infrastructure and by transforming the nature of what and how students and teachers are learning. We believe that in the context of systemic reform of a district, with three to five years of professional development and on-line assistance, each Co-NECT site can become self-sustaining.

Co-NECT schools combine an emphasis on academic excellence with a commitment to making learning challenging, engaging, and productive for every student. We share a belief in the benefits of learning by doing, assessments that measure actual student and school performance, grouping practices that give every student a chance to succeed, and continuous professional development for teachers and staff. We also place strong emphasis on the role that modern technology plays in changing the way people work and learn together.

The Co-NECT design is based on five key interrelated elements: project-based learning; cluster-based governance; comprehensive and multi-faceted assessment; access to the best available technology; and a strong professional community. These design elements combine to create productive, exciting new ways of organizing teaching and learning (see Fig. 4.2).

Project-Based Learning

Co-NECT projects unfold within a community no longer identified by geographical contiguity. A community can be constituted by a neighborhood or by a community of interest shared across the globe via the WWW and other communication technologies. The curriculum is inseparable from this community, and it comes alive in the community's engagement with multi-disciplinary projects. Small teams of students, teachers, and, on occasion, community members collaborate on investigations of compelling interest and value to themselves and those around them. It is this focus on project-based learning that stimulates the growth of an inquiry culture and transforms traditional student-teacher relationships. Skills and knowledge are acquired in the process and context of producing authentic work, work that has meaning and relevance out of school as well as in school.

Projects also result in tangible products—in things and activities like exhibits, books, research reports, planning documents, and community services. To be genuinely authentic, these products must demonstrate an in-depth understanding of issues and problems that routinely occur within the various fields of knowledge they explore (see Brown, Collins, & Duquid, 1989). The products exemplify high standards and become part of the students' growing portfolios.

> What we are basically doing is learning physics and the motions of physics. The most important thing is learning about roller coaster rides, amusement parks, and what projects we can

accomplish. Most of our projects that we are doing are made up by us, the students at Scott School. We are going to have a carnival to raise money for the trip to Great America and Indiana Beach. We are having games, prizes, candy sales, and raffle tickets.

Mostly what our project is about is exploring the basic laws of physics and how these laws are applied to the designs of amusement park rides. We have constructed an actual working model of a roller coaster. We also have built a double Ferris wheel, merry-go-round, and swings (Webmasters, 1995).

A complex and dynamic interaction exists between project work and the standards that are internalized through them. It is necessary to establish criteria to identify the characteristics of a particular product or performance that the school community values by citing examples of what good projects should look like. Short-term goals are set in individual meetings between teacher, student, and parents. The student and teacher then work towards demonstrating competence in these standards within the context of project work.

Of course, all this takes time. Richard Carstensen, a naturalist in Juneau, Alaska, begins his foreword to Dzantik'i Heeni Middle School's trail guide, *Take A Hike . . . The Outer Point Trail*, by writing:

"Oh no! Another Draft?" This was the typical refrain from the young authors of *Take a Hike . . .* as press time approached. Creativity outweighs patience among middle school students. But as professional writers and artists learn, the occasional sparks of genius must often be fanned for hours and days before a product is worthy of the public eye . . . Quality takes time, as any of the collaborators on this guide can tell you. These are our careful portraits of Outer Point, one of Juneau's great places, in prose, poetry and drawings, supported (not hastened) by computer technology (Aparezuk, et al., 1995, p. iii).

For the students, teachers, graphic artists, naturalists and others working on Juneau's trail guide project, the experience of project work has made an indelible impact on what it means to demonstrate real-world competence and skill. It has also shown them how curriculum and performance standards developed by the state can enhance, not detract from, genuine learning.

Not all knowledge or skills, however, derive from project work. In addition to projects, seminars and workshops focus on specific topics or skills that need to be addressed in order for project work to

Figure 4.2

The Co-NECT Design Elements

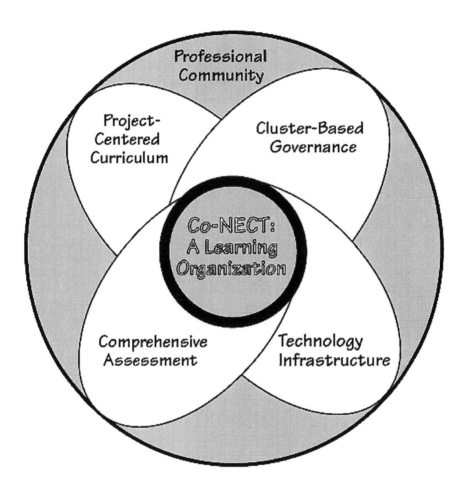

be successful. These may arise within a particular project, (e.g., a seminar on acids and bases for a project on acid rain), or a more general need that finds expression across a range of possible projects (e.g., representing data on bar graphs).

Cluster-Based Governance

Co-NECT is committed to students and teachers organizing themselves into small and manageable clusters or "houses," (if possible, of anywhere from 80–150 students and 4–7 teachers depending, of course, on local student–teacher ratios). Students stay within this community for several years. Because children learn in different ways and at different rates, this arrangement provides both a mix of ages in the cluster, as well as a longer term relationship between students, parents, and teachers. Absent is the stultifying anonymity prevalent in many of today's large urban schools. New social relationships, therefore, are critical to Co-NECT, not only because they are nurturing and supportive, but because they are integral to creating a community of inquiry.

Certain implications follow. For example, it is preferable to have the clusters in close proximity to one another in order to avoid traffic problems within the school building. It is also important that the cluster teaching teams, now armed with additional responsibilities and authority, find effective ways to communicate with other cluster teams. In part, this is also the responsibility of the principal, whose new role also requires the organizational skills necessary to create, support, and sustain cross-disciplinary teams of teachers.

Comprehensive Assessment

Successful schools embrace high standards of performance for all students. Stated in concrete forms that everyone understands, challenging standards give administrators, teachers, students, and parents a strong sense of purpose and provide an authentic means of demonstrating and measuring progress, from kindergarten through high school. The Co-NECT team assists schools in incorporating performance standards that are based on existing national, state, and district standards. A school also needs to set its own benchmarks for its performance as an institution of learning, monitoring its ability to provide all students with the opportunity to achieve high standards, and periodically reporting results to the community.

The key reason for engaging in these activities is to enhance the quality of student work, such as the work accomplished in *Take A Hike . . . The Outer Point Trail* cited above. What counts as quality work, however, is transformed over time as new information becomes available, as circumstances and challenges change, and as we learn better to reflect and act upon what we do. The Co-NECT design requires the ongoing examination and creation of products and performances that constitute high quality. It is results-oriented. But results and quality of what?

A steady stream of research over the past decade has pointed out how different school knowledge is from the knowledge eventually brought to bear in out-of-school contexts (Resnick, 1987). The failure to recognize this radical divergence has resulted in deleterious educational consequences. Many students tend to be less motivated to learn, not seeing any direct relationship between what they learn in the classroom and what they need in the world outside.

There are other problems as well. Because the work of traditional schools is mostly formal, abstract, and decontextualized, it is difficult to find measures that accurately account for what students actually know and can do. Traditional measures alone won't suffice. The results gathered from existing standardized, norm-referenced, multiple-choice tests, for example, reveal only a kind of abstract and disembodied understanding. These results are usually cloaked in the statistical garb of percentiles and stanines. Although helpful for certain purposes, they can not reflect *in toto* the work of a project-centered curriculum whose clear and compelling standards are meant to highlight real-world situations and performance.

The Co-NECT design understands the meaning of *quality* and *results* differently. We begin by recasting the chief work of school as the successful completion of projects. These originate from real-world situations, issues, and problems. Most often, they involve many disciplines. They extend over time, often many weeks, and are designed so that they tap into students' pre-existing interests and knowledge. Embedded in their design are periodic and ongoing assessments and portfolios requiring high performance and content standards agreed to by local, state, and national communities.

Best Available Technology

In a Co-NECT school, students and teachers function in a technology-rich environment.[1] This is defined more by accessibility—having what you need, when you need it, where you need it—than by computer-student ratio. The technology is distributed around the school. Learners can access the local area network (LAN) from any area within the school. Having the technology everywhere—ubiquitous computing—is best defined by access to this network. The technology is an integral part of the design. Putting lots of technology into a school will certainly make some difference in the school, but it will not be transformational unless it is part of a larger educational design.

---

[1] For a more extensive discussion of technology in a Co-NECT school, see Goldberg and Richards (1995).

The Co-NECT design is oriented to participatory, active, learning. Learners are producers, not just consumers, of information—that is, students and teachers are responsible for contributing to the overall information structure. Technology heightens the opportunity for participation. Exhibitions of students' work, whether published on the school internal web, WWW, or school television studio, are products that are meant to communicate to other people.

Having students become technology literate means much more than being able to keyboard, use word processors, databases, and spreadsheets. As we move into the 21st century, there are many new and different kinds of literacy that will be required of our citizenry. Video and audio literacy entail knowing how to view or listen, and how to create, edit, and present visual and audio concepts. Information literacy entails knowing how to find what you need, how to represent it in different ways, and how to share it with others. This prompts us to recommend a real mix of machines and technologies: portable computers for teachers, powerful multimedia workstations, intelligent keyboards that can only do word processing, Ethernet network drops in every room, video cameras, and digitizing photo cameras, synthesizers, and a television studio for production and broadcasting.

In order to use technology to support fundamental change in the organization, it needs to be integrated into all parts of the organization—from school governance, to assessment, to instruction. The kinds of learning (or habits of mind) that we hope to see as the product of a Co-NECT school include skills in sense-making, self-motivated research, collaboration, and the ability to learn how to learn. The development of these skills requires new kinds of conversations among students and teachers and new kinds of work arrangements among both students and teachers.

Communications Infrastructure. The specific Co-NECT technology and communications design grows out of more general research considerations. At BBN Corporation we have conducted a variety of research studies on the design and effectiveness of communications technology in the schools. In particular, Newman, Bernstein, and Reese (1992) reported that, as of 1992, wide area network (WAN) connectivity was constrained to a single computer with a modem. Even where there were local area networks (LANs), they were usually used for computer-based instruction, and were not connected to the WAN. This structure resulted in islands of connectivity, in which most computers were not connected to the outside. Schools typically gained connectivity from a local college or university. In a college or university there is an individual, or group, that can manage the UNIX interface needed to control the network resources. Depending on a sophisticated college or university network meant that schools were usually constrained to terminal emulation access to a host computer. The interface was unfamiliar and very difficult to use. The schools were "guests" on someone else's computer. As guests, they were restricted in the number of accounts possible, and to a very limited form of access (with many of the standard Internet services not being available).

In order for schools to have genuine Internet connectivity to the desktop, they need to have a LAN infrastructure throughout the school connected to the source of continuous connectivity to the Internet. The schools then need a way to manage their own resources. As a result of the Newman, et al. (1992) study, BBN decided to develop a low-cost Internet server for the K–12 audience, designed to be managed by a teacher, student, or secretary. The BBN Internet Server provides the basic Internet services—e-mail, news, ftp, gopher, and web—which can all be managed from a point and click interface on a Mac or Windows machine. As important as the LAN flexibility is the continuous connection to the Internet. We recommend a minimum of a 56K leased line directly connecting to an Internet point of presence. With an Internet Server, schools can control their own resources—teachers, and students with appropriate permissions, can add or delete users, create mail lists, and create their own Gopher or Web pages. Students and teachers have an opportunity to publish their own work (see for example: http://Hammond.k12.in.us). Current estimates are that only nine percent of schools have "Internet to the desktop," that is, a LAN with leased line connectivity to the Internet.

In addition to the underlying technology, it is critical to have an understanding of what students and teachers are going to be doing with the technology. Hunter (1993, 1995) points to a variety of instances where Internet-based projects are being used as instruments of change in schools. And in the National Science Foundation-funded School Network Testbed, BBN is working with more than 100 organizations that are exploring different models for Internet working projects that link schools with their communities. This critical mass of projects and resources allows us to build curriculum structures on the assumption of Internet-to-the-desktop technology.

Management Infrastructure. Unlike more directed learning environments, Co-NECT communities require an extraordinary amount of flexibility in order to respond adequately to the many twists and turns that project-based learning inevitably takes. Unfortunately, there are few flexible management (including school-based budgeting) and assessment tools at present to fill this small but rapidly growing market niche. There are, however, an evolving set of tools designed to support collaborative work in business learning organizations, and we are exploring ways to adapt some of these ideas to the realities of the K–12 environment.

We need to create scheduling tools that permit the constant organization and reorganization of students into the distinct learning communities of project groups, workshops, and seminars. One or two scheduling programs (MacSchool, for example) go some of the distance in providing greater flexibility, but none of these tools begins with the pedagogical assumption that students are workers, as opposed to administrative units assembled for the purpose of bureaucratic convenience.

The situation with project-based curriculum tools seems more promising. Here, tools that permit both communication and provide the scaffolding necessary to initiate in-depth inquiry are becoming more plentiful. In project-based science, for example, tools developed (Collaboratory Notebook) or incorporated (Cornell's CUSeeMe) by Northwestern University's CoVis Project allow multimedia documentation and collaboration to occur among a geographically dispersed set of students and scientists.

Similarly, the University of Michigan has developed a Project Integration Visualization Tool (PIViT) that enables project-based planning around key or driving questions connected with assessment activities and instructional examples. And Chancery Software is developing a Curriculum Orchestrator that ties subject specific standards, textbook resources and teacher-initiated lesson objectives in a dynamic and evolving fashion. Finally, agents or *knowbots* that navigate the maze of Internet resources in search of project-appropriate materials are beginning to make their way out of engineering departments into the educational and commercial marketplace. At BBN, we are developing tools for students and teachers to mine the kinds and quantity of information each wishes to parse from the daily mountain available over the net. We are also constructing electronic tools to support distributed learning communities to create and collaborate in various modeling environments.

Much the same evolving story exists regarding new assessment tools. Scholastic's *Learning Profile* and *Electronic Portfolio* are steps taken in the direction of placing greater overall management control in the hands of students and teachers. And we have been working with Boston College's Center for the Study of Testing, Evaluation and

Educational Policy (CSTEEP) to develop accountability tools that permit an efficient yet rich approach to testing in which open-ended, performance and writing samples share the stage with multiple choice questions. Yet, much remains to be done before the inclusion of such tools and programs can be said to constitute a seamless fit with radically restructured learning communities such as those envisioned by Co-NECT.

Professional Community

School change is demanding and requires serious commitment. But in exchange for all the hard work, there exists the promise of tremendous intellectual growth and personal fulfillment. Much of this growth occurs through the school's commitment to reflective practice and continuous and ongoing professional development. By *professional development*, however, we mean much more than *training*. We also mean *consulting, facilitating, and planning*—activities that in tandem, transform the isolated and fragmentary occurrences of in-service sessions into the reflective life of a professional community.

Respecting teachers as continuous learners is as necessary to professional development as any specialized two-hour training session in the use of the latest software application or piece of equipment. Simply put, without a wider professional development context, there is no culture of continuous learning, and without a culture of continuous learning, there is no hope for sustained and lasting impact.

Developing such a culture is no easy matter—especially when it requires the sophisticated use of various technologies by everyone. First, there are constraints imposed by the absence of the usual twin suspects in implementing reform, namely time and money. The ever-present demand for time is one reason why Co-NECT schools are organized into smaller self-managing units or clusters. That way, teams of teachers can create flexible schedules that permit varied professional development activities within the context of the school day. Incorporating professional development within the school day also helps to ameliorate (but, of course, not solve) the shortage of funding for professional development time (release days, substitute teachers, etc.).

Other means can be found to create learning opportunities. We have found it particularly effective to provide all teachers with portable computers two months prior to summer workshops. Teachers appreciate the professional respect, and respond by spending their time at home gaining familiarity. Second, a series of minisabbaticals (one to five days) allows individual teachers or teams of teachers the time to integrate their learning of some new technology within a project path undertaken by their cluster. In some districts, a whole category of super subs was created. These are teachers, all exceptional and all wishing to retain some connection to teaching, who have been extended a modified form of early retirement in exchange for their agreement to substitute regularly for teachers in need of time to work on technology integration. (Ultimately, of course, a financial commitment to ongoing investment in professional development must be made at the school and district level. We agree with the rising chorus of technology reformers advocating that at least 30% of the dollars allocated for technology purchases be used for professional development.)

Of course, not every teacher will be enthusiastic about technology, nor will all teachers find themselves at the same level of sophistication in integrating it fully in their day-to-day work with students. We have found that attention to market segmentation is useful here (see, for example, Scrogan, 1993). People bring with them different levels of technology sophistication, and won't fit in "one size fits all" sessions. When technology doesn't fit, people are soon bored or overwhelmed. Our experience has led us to avoid pairing the most avid technology users with the most resistant. In many cases, there will be a third class of learners—those "in between" that are just beginning to gain competence and enthusiasm. Often, it is better to pair these with the novices and the resisters.

Our teachers benefited from working with one another in the course of project work. After-school sessions worked best when they were suited to the real needs of the participants. We really felt the difference when, by doing our homework, we were able to connect with what teachers and students were doing, and making sure that what is being learned has immediate and productive impact. That way, the technology being learned is integral to enriching actual student project work. As much as possible, we tried to use the technology to demonstrate its effectiveness. We have established two programs to begin the scale-up process: The Co-NECT Exchange and the Co-NECT Critical Friends Program.

The Co-NECT Exchange. Short-term training, whether one day or two weeks, cannot bring about a change in culture. We are experimenting with ways to provide ongoing support for teachers. The Co-NECT Exchange is a WWW-based communications exchange for members of the Co-NECT community. It contains the standard WWW archival structures—archived versions of information about key Co-NECT programs, pointers to pages maintained by partners and school sites, *Who's Who* directories, and an on-line version of the Co-NECT Design Guide. In addition, we introduced some tools for collaboration that are organized around the metaphor of "desks," analogous to the newspaper "city desk." The idea is that students and teachers with similar interests will communicate through these desks. Sample desks include Assessment and Projects— where teachers and students at different schools, working on similar projects, are able to share information.

We are working on ways to increase teacher participation in the Exchange. We have found that distance communication is enhanced by person-to-person communication (high-tech needs high-touch).

Co-NECT Critical Friends Program. In order to facilitate building a broader professional community, we have instituted the Co-NECT Critical Friends Program. This program periodically brings together school staffs from different sites (electronically as well as in face-to-face meetings) in order to help catalyze these ongoing professional communities. Representative teachers from each site make two visits to observe, learn, and critique Co-NECT schools in other districts. In turn, sites are visited once by teachers in these other schools. The Critical Friends Program is designed to include electronic communication as an integral part of ongoing support.

Critical to building a professional community, however, is producing a whole staff committed to assisting and learning from one another. This does not mean that a specialist in network management or curriculum integration is superfluous. Far from it. But it does mean that although specialized technology positions might be necessary to get things going and to keep them moving, such positions are not sufficient. Professional development requires a learning *community* where responsibility is assumed and shared.

But how likely is it that this can actually happen? What will motivate not one or two dedicated and involved teachers, but the great majority of teachers to become part of this learning community, to integrate technology as an essential ingredient in teaching and learning? Technologies, once utilized, can, in fact, leverage change. But that is the point: They must first be used.

In each instance of change, the question of incentives and disincentives must be raised. What are the rewards and penalties communicated by various institutional practices within the school district and are these aligned with what is valued by those engaged in creating a professional community? After all, why would anyone want to put themselves through the inevitable discomfort that accompanies change if there is no match between personal goals and system recognition?

Every school system has existing incentives and disincentives for change. These can be purely economic; they can revolve around consequential allocations of time and money, or they can be more personal and social. To make a lasting and sustainable difference, professional development structures must take into account the existing system of rewards and disincentives and, if necessary, scrap them for new ones.

The Co-NECT Framework for Change

Phase One: Preparation and Building Local Capacity
Most schools and districts are not prepared to begin immediate and full implementation of the Co-NECT design. At the district level, for example, we found that most school districts do not yet enjoy a robust technology infrastructure in which schoolwide LANS are the rule, much less connected to one another and open to the outside world through wide area networking from the desktop. Similarly, most school districts have not yet coupled their Management Information Systems with their district's strategic goals for learning and teaching so that school staff can transform the inert status of the information they are so often asked to collect into data upon which preventative action and continuous improvement in student achievement can transpire.

It has also been our experience that school districts are not organized well for the purposes of implementing school-based reform. Often, their internal organizational departments and associated functions are balkanized and working either independently or even at cross purposes. Those who work in building facilities might not be aware of how telecommunications or instructional technology personnel are thinking about the issues of network design and implementation. *Unlearning* existing rules, roles, and relationships is a prerequisite to establishing a genuine learning community. That takes time. Change requires a commitment both at the district and school level. That is, there must be a supportive operating environment within the district as well as support at the school level, i.e. both top down and bottom up, or what Nadler, et al. (1995) called *lateral development* (see Fig. 4.3). We require an affirmative vote of the faculty as a precondition for moving out of the prep stage. In addition, we require a minimum of three schools in a district, in order to leverage resources and assure that transforming schools are not isolated.

Figure 4.3

Bottom-Down/Top-Up Change

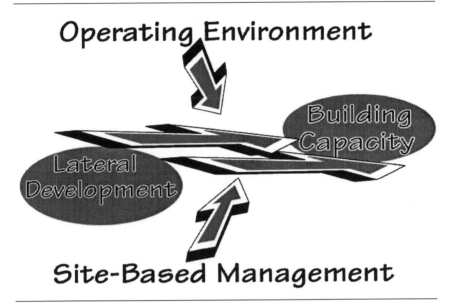

At the school level, there often exists a similar need to prepare more thoroughly for implementation. Although teachers and principals may have some experience with flexible scheduling, teaming, interdisciplinary projects and alternative assessments, the nature of that experience will often have been episodic, isolated, and disjointed. Teachers, for example, might not have shared many of their experiences as team members, and the school might not yet have come to grips with the difficult task of putting together disparate reforms so the whole becomes greater than the separate parts. Large schools may not yet have reorganized themselves into smaller units in which such complicated and hand-wringing issues as flexible multigraded student scheduling are more easily addressed. Similarly, in many of our schools, teachers' familiarity with various technologies varies widely, and they may require specific customized training before the communication infrastructure of the school can come to life.

Because of these factors, we recommend that schools (and districts) set aside a certain period of time during which they lay the groundwork for implementation of the design and for the process of discontinuous change. This "prep period" might extend from a few months to an entire school year. A school design team is formed as well as a district design team. The Co-NECT design team and field representatives then work with schools and districts to assure widespread understanding and ownership of the design, as well as the organizational and technological infrastructure to implement it successfully. Unless local capacity is carefully built, implementation will be exceedingly difficult.

For the preparation and each subsequent phase of the process, we have established a set of design-related results, evidence that schools have achieved these results and an accompanying match of products and services to assist them in doing so.

Phase Two: Implementation

Implementation can take from two to five years. This does not mean that schools will have realized the design at the end of this time but rather that they will have developed the capacity to continuously develop, sustain, and refine it. Like learning itself, schools (and clusters within schools) develop in different ways and at different rates. This means that professional development must be flexible enough to meet their expressed needs.

Summer institutes and regular visits to schools during the school year can and are scheduled in advance, but the exact substance of the training will vary according to school needs and the rate of progress they have made against the benchmarks set.

Generally, however, one can think of the content framework for implementation to more narrowly focus on two activities: Enhancing the quality of student work and building a sense of professional community. These objectives involve at least three major related areas of the design:

- Projects/standards/assessments/rubrics

- Organizational structures/processes related to discussion and improvement of the quality of student work

- Technology

Development (and planning) in each of these areas is more spiral-like than scope- and sequence-oriented—meaning that each area is continuously revisited, and what is learned about a topic, procedure, or tool at one time is taken as a baseline upon which to build a richer and more integrated understanding of the other two.

It should be reemphasized that the exact nature of the school design adopted and implemented depends to a great extent on the co-creation of the design with Co-NECT staff. Use of this participatory design process means that some variability will naturally occur. Thus, for example, Co-NECT schools often differ in the ways in which they interpret the design component of cluster-based management and flexible grouping. Some schools have created K–2 teamed learning environments, others have separated out kindergarten. Some schools are experimenting with "looping," a way of having the same students follow the same teacher(s) through a number of sequenced grades (three through five, for example). What is common to each implementation interpretation, however, is a shared belief in the proposition that children learn in different ways and at different rates, and therefore grouping should occur with the maximum amount of flexibility necessary to accommodate a range of learning situations.

Sharing and discussing different implementation scenarios is a fundamental aspect of building local capacity, and so, is inseparable from the creation of professional communities. Implementation, therefore, includes activities that are directly related to this task: The Co-NECT Critical Friends program builds a sense of professionalism in the visiting teachers, as well as a broader sense of community between Co-NECT schools; the choosing of relevant sample assessment items from established assessment banks, their implementation, scoring, and interpretation schoolwide is another vehicle for creating a collegial environment (as well as a valuable means to discuss the relation of indicators to improving student achievement); and the cross-site collaboration in technology-mediated project-based work both embodies and stretches the professional role of teachers as continuous learners.

Phase Three: Sustaining Local Capacity

At some point during years two or three, focused attention needs to be devoted towards institutionalizing the changes occurring within the schools so that they can be sustained and integrated into the district's overall reform plans. This does not mean that implementation has been "completed" at the school site. Far from it. Implementation involves continuous improvement and so is never truly "completed." But it does mean appropriate venues for tying together school site changes take center stage. In some instances this might mean a "trainer-of-trainers" effort, the creation of a professional development school, or the establishment of a teaching and learning academy that is responsive to principles of "just-in-time" learning. Establishing the internal capacity to absorb and continue the changes will most likely require personnel, budget, and infrastructure realignment. A simple, but effective, barometer of success is the degree to which the school has created a market for itself within its district and real and virtual communities. Do other schools, locally and globally, turn towards it for examples of best practice? Does the school's community rely on it to provide needed services? More generally, is the school seen as a producer of value and not simply as a consumer of value?

The Change Process

Extending through each of the above three phases is a process that encompasses planning, doing, and reflecting. Although the notion is commonsensical, we have learned that it is far easier for reformers to discuss change endlessly than it is to actually engage in it. That is one reason why we believe it imperative, even in the very first phase of building local capacity, that teachers and students begin to experience and reflect upon the kinds of activities that mark the Co-NECT design.

Similarly, throughout each of the phases, a number of instruments are used to chart and gauge the direction of change. Needs assessments, gap analyses, and benchmarking are all directed towards assuring that the results desired from each of the phases are proceeding in accordance with the mutual understanding of teachers, administrators, parents and policymakers. Finally, in order to promote ownership over the changes, the Co-NECT Design and Cluster teams are encouraged to develop their own change "dashboard," an instrument designed to provide timely feedback on elements of the desired changes believed critical to success.

Costs: Products and Services

The costs of implementing the Co-NECT design depends upon three related factors. First, the status of the technology infrastructure (including support services); second, the degree of professional development necessary to implement (including release time and substitute costs); and third, the needed level of associated district consulting services relevant to integrating school-based infrastructure with overall district planning and implementation.

Without question the first two categories (infrastructure and professional development) are the most expensive variables. Although there will always be a need for continual reinvestment in these two categories, the initial up-front investment is likely to constitute the single most costly expenditure. We have estimated, for example, that if one were to begin with only a roof, ceiling, and four walls, the initial technology costs for completely outfitting an average elementary school of 500 students could be as much as $500,000 (including LAN and WAN installation). Add to this the ongoing costs of Internet service, network management, and the approximately 10 percent to 15 percent of the hardware/software budget necessary for annual maintenance and upgrades, and it is easy to sympathize with the painful financial dilemmas facing school boards.

At least two recent developments should prove helpful here. First, the very pace of innovation, accelerating as it has at an unrelenting rate, is resulting in decreased costs while, at the same time, enhancing technology prowess and versatility. The accrued savings can be leveraged even further by economies of scale realized in centralized acquisition schemes. Second, alternative financing strategies (including leasing arrangements) are now providing increased choices tailored to individual district and school needs. There is also a third hopeful sign. As the technology improves and becomes less platform dependent, many traditional and costly practices can be acutely reduced (or totally eliminated), thereby allowing for even greater cost savings. Replace textbooks with on-line resources, for example, and a substantial savings in administrative overhead (cataloguing, warehousing, etc.) can follow.

The second general cost area is that of professional development services—those undergone both at the site and remotely. The average yearly costs for these services have been around $55,000 to $60,000 per school and includes summer institutes (usually one week on site) regular on-site sessions with Co-NECT representatives, electronically mediated remote support, and cross-site visits with other Co-NECT schools. The exact mix of after-school sessions, in-class consultations and release time opportunities requiring substitutes varies according to the available professional development plans and budget of the schools and districts. However, an attempt is made to agree upon the kinds of results envisioned by implementation, the evidence or criteria acceptable in discussing these results, and the amount and kind of professional development assistance, time, and materials estimated to achieve them.

The last area of costs is that associated with district consulting needs. We have found great variability in the capacity of districts to design, manage, and implement complex network systems. Whether BBN or some other consulting service (or vendor) is employed, we believe it critical that communications, instructional, and management systems be designed as flexible, scalable, and compatible.

The Co-NECT Story

The Co-NECT design team resides in the Educational Technologies department at BBN, a company that is a world leader in communications, systems integration, curriculum development, and educational research. Since the early 1960s, educational researchers at BBN have been exploring ways to use the company's computer and networking technologies to improve teaching and learning. We led the development of the Logo computer language. BBN also pioneered the development of the ARPANET—precursor to the Internet. And in the 1970s we were very involved in the evolution of the field of cognitive science. Working in collaboration with practicing classroom teachers, we conduct basic research in human learning and cognition and develop software tools that extend and enrich the traditional curriculum, especially in science and mathematics. We integrate this research within the context of real school and organizational change. As a communications company, we are especially interested in helping schools find ways to make the best use of networking facilities, connecting teachers and students with each other and with national and global resources. Co-NECT partners include Boston College's Center for Study of Testing, Evaluation, and Education Policy (CSTEEP), Earthwatch, and the University of Michigan.

Unlike other designs, our implementation, we decided, would begin minimally, working initially with only two schools. Choosing two locations not far from our Cambridge offices (Worcester and Boston) provided us with the ready geographical access we believed would be necessary to help realize a very ambitious school design. It seemed that both school districts supported our efforts and that the staff and faculties at both schools were ready and willing to engage in the changes called for by the Co-NECT design.

Although the Worcester school remains an important Co-NECT demonstration site, we decided during the second year to discontinue our efforts in Boston. The contrast between these first two efforts has informed the project in many ways. In Worcester, we faced many apparently overwhelming system-level challenges:

• An extremely supportive superintendent and assistant superintendent announced their retirement towards the end of our design year.

• The design called for a K–12 school, but the facility in Worcester was already overcrowded and using portable structures.

- The city of Worcester was going through tremendous demographic changes. In 15 years the city changed from 98 percent White, to a diverse city of 60 percent White, 20 percent Hispanic, 10 percent Black, and 10 percent Cambodian. The city was under court order requiring all schools to reflect the city's racial and ethnic diversity.

Fortunately, these challenges were successfully resolved. A committed and skilled principal and staff persevered through a year of political uncertainty. As the year progressed, it became even more apparent than ever just how critical the continued active support of the central administration and school board is to success. The new superintendent and assistant superintendent have not only supported but contributed substantively to the expansion of Co-NECT in the district. The city creatively resolved the building issue by temporarily leasing and renovating a vacated nursing home facility, and has committed to constructing a new K–12 facility. Finally, the school has made a shining exemplar of its multicultural community by defining itself as a global studies school.

The reasons for discontinuing the Boston school were complex, but essentially reducible to two general lessons: First, we believed that the support extended the school by the district leadership at the time (the district structure was changed midway during the first year and changes in leadership soon followed) was more passive than active. Simply put, there were too many other things going on at the time. Insofar as this was true, the effects of our work and that of the school were marginalized. The school never got the attention it needed if the changes it was attempting were to be sustained and leveraged over time by the school system. The second reason for discontinuing was related. The school itself was struggling to combine a recently launched and major focus (the creation of a comprehensive two-way bilingual school) with yet another even newer and more complex undertaking (the creation of a technology-infused and multigraded, project-based curriculum). Had even the most generous district support been available, it might not have been enough to carry out simultaneously these two heroic restructuring efforts.

The following year we added two additional sites to complement our efforts in Worcester—one in Hammond, Indiana and the other in Juneau, Alaska. The selection process was arduous. It became clear early on that, because we were bringing with us a substantial contribution of technology, it was difficult to discover whether potential sites were more interested in the hardware than the design. We also realized that unless substantial and overwhelming support existed, the design would be difficult to implement in extremely small districts. Small districts have no "release valve," that is, no place for teachers or students to escape to if they really do not like the design.

In Juneau we began work with the Dzantik'i Heeni Middle School and a small but comprehensive new high school named The Phoenix Program. Both undertakings have been extremely successful. Student projects that serve the community and state, while at the same time embedding within them Alaska's new curriculum standards, have made believers of parents and policymakers alike. In Hammond, Scott Middle School continues to attract active parent support as it moves towards incorporating the design in each of its clusters.

Beginning with the 1995 school year, we have paid a great deal more attention to the implementation of a district strategy. In order to aid in building the district's local capacity through leveraging the collective contributions of Co-NECT, we have adopted a policy requiring a minimum of three schools in a district. As a result, we added schools in other locations including four in Dade County, Florida; six in Memphis, Tennessee; and four in Cincinnati, Ohio. In the summer of 1995, we conducted summer institutes in each of the districts.

We anticipate some 20 to 30 schools to be affiliated with Co-NECT during 1995–1996, and perhaps another 20 to 30 the following year. It is only then that we will be more fully prepared to undertake the gargantuan task of scaling up Co-NECT to hundreds, perhaps thousands, of sites.

The lessons we learned early on have been reinforced over time: In order to succeed at implementing and sustaining major change, an ongoing and mutually beneficial partnership is necessary between schools and the systems of which they are part. Because districts do not always (in fact, rarely) have the resources necessary to nurture fledgling attempts at whole school change, we have learned how to better assist schools in brokering alliances with other organizations for needed intellectual, social, and financial capital. We are partnering with the University of Michigan, Boston College, and others in seeking ways in which the resources required by rapid and sometimes unpredictable change can be marshaled to coordinate efforts mutually aimed at improving the quality of student work.

Past Achievements, the Future, and a Summary

Early Achievements

How do we know we are on the right track? Obviously, it is still very early in the process, but we are encouraged by the following:

CSTEEP has been working with Co-NECT to track student performance in reading, writing, science and math. The test battery includes items from the National Assessment of Educational Progress (NAEP) and the Urban District Assessment Consortium (UDAC).

- At the A.L.L. School in Worcester, which has been working with Co-NECT the longest, at intermediate grade levels (3–5) in all areas, significant increases in scores on the group performance items were made based on the CSTEEP Battery administered in 1993, 1994, and 1995. On the NAEP reading items, scores rose from 32 percent correct (fall 1993) to 45 percent correct (spring 1994) to 47 percent correct (spring 1995).

- The A.L.L. School in Worcester was designated one of six exemplary middle schools in New England by the New England League of Middle Schools in 1994–1995.

- Teachers at the Scott Middle School in Hammond, Indiana achieved their goal of improving students' abilities to work cooperatively. On a majority of math and science performance items, the percentage of students who successfully completed the task rose by at least 10 points from the baseline assessment administered in fall 1994 and spring 1995.

- Student scores on open-ended reading items rose at Scott Middle School. Whereas only 31 percent of the students that participated in the baseline assessment were able to construct meaning based on a passage they had read, during the follow-up assessment, 41 percent of participating students performed adequately on these items. On items that asked students to extend meaning, performance rose from 32 percent on the baseline assessment to 46 percent on the follow-up assessment.

- At the Dzantik'i Heeni Middle School in Juneau, Alaska, performance showed noticeable improvement, particularly in the areas of mathematical problem solving and abstract thinking skills, despite already strong baseline performance.

Future Developments

Looking to the future, we anticipate three areas of ongoing development. First, we will continue to expand our internal and external technological capabilities. We will continue on this path so that we can provide ready and reliable interactive communication across geographical boundaries; assure the kind of "just-in-time" and continuous professional development requisite for facilitating lasting change; and enable us to scale up Co-NECT sites from relatively few communities of inquiry and learning into a critical mass of many such communities.

In order to accomplish this, we are in the process of incorporating and developing applications and tools that fit into the kinds of social environments (both real and virtual) in which we work. So, for example, we will be introducing more distance learning technologies such as IRC (Internet Relay Chat), desktop video conferencing, collaborative groupware, project-based software and intelligent search agents into Co-NECT sites during the 1995–1996 school year.

Second, we will be seeking to articulate and promote the Co-NECT Design's contributions to informing youth apprenticeship and school-to-work transition programs. The need is both striking and urgent. Approximately 75 percent of high school students never obtain a degree from a four-year institution. Many of these students have not had the opportunity or motivation to develop the kinds of work force skills required to compete in today's economy. The Co-NECT design's emphasis on project-based work, its incorporation of the kinds of competencies and skills called for in the SCANS report, and its utilization of the most advanced technology available to inform teaching and learning, mean that we are well-positioned to help restructure the conditions and content of learning both at the workplace and in the schools. Over the coming year, we will be developing the organizational and technological bridges that can permit many forgotten students to successfully navigate across both worlds.

Third, we will continue to explore how the newly evolving dynamic between interactive technologies and student achievement can best be conceptualized, documented, and more effectively communicated. To accomplish this, a new evaluative paradigm is necessary. Up to now, an overly simplistic causal model has dominated the discussion of how technology benefits learning. The model is often a simplistic behaviorist one that attempts to negotiate meaning between the stimuli of instructional delivery on the one hand and the results of standardized norm-referenced multiple-choice tests on the other.

At least two problems with the evaluation of technology's effect on learning need to be addressed. First, the technologies (including application tools and software) that embody a delivery model of education bear little resemblance to the kinds of authentic real-world learning opportunities that students must be prepared to tackle. And second, reliance on any single assessment or system, especially one whose chief function is to classify and separate students for accountability and administrative purposes, rather than help improve their performance, is of limited value. More and qualitatively different evaluative models are necessary. We intend to explore how more complex tasks, especially those carried out with the aid of technology, can influence changes in performance, as well as the various ways these changes can be measured reliably and with validity.

Conclusion

We began with a quotation from the poet Paul Valery ("The future isn't what it used to be"). We would like to end with a quotation from another visionary of a sort, who, though perhaps not a poet, was nonetheless a man of unintentional but pointed wisdom—either the Hollywood mogul, Sam Goldwyn, or former Yankee catcher Yogi Berra. "Making predictions is hard to do, especially about the future."

The era of discontinuous change we are now living through makes planning for the future an almost heroic effort. In Co-NECT, we are responding to this challenge by recognizing that no design, ours included, is ever complete, and that creating organizations with the predisposition and capacity to respond to changing circumstances is the unexceptional price of admission to an uncertain future.

We also recognize that in this era, schools and communities need different kinds of assistance and support than traditionally, if they are to succeed as learning organizations. They need support that is timely and improvisational, yet reliable and responsive.

Why are we doing this? Because we are committed to realizing a future in which all children can succeed. We believe that meeting this unprecedented challenge of the future will be impossible unless schools are assisted in developing and managing the dynamics of rapid technological, organizational, and cultural change. We are doing this, because not to do so would be to give up, and giving up is an unacceptable moral and educational alternative. Co-NECT is our response to the present; but it is an invitation to collaborate with us in designing the future.

References

Brown, J. S., Collins. A., & Duquid, P. (1989). Situated cognition and the culture of learning. *Educational Researcher, 18* (1), 32–42.

Goldberg, B., & Richards J. (1995, September). Leveraging technology for reform: Changing schools and communities into learning organizations. *Educational Technology,* 5–16.

Howard, J. (1992). The third movement: Developing black children for the 21st century. In B. J. Tidwell (Ed.), *The state of black America.* New York: The National Urban League.

Hunter, B. (1993, September). NSF's networked testbeds inform innovation in science education. *T.H.E. Journal,* 96–99.

Hunter, B. (1995). Learning and teaching on the Internet: Contributing to educational reform. In B. Kahin & J. Keller (Eds.), *Public access to the Internet* (pp. 85–114). Cambridge, MA: The MIT Press.

Nadler D., Shaw R., Walton A., & Associates (1995). *Discontinuous change: Leading organizational transformation.* San Francisco: Jossey-Bass.

Newman, D., Bernstein, S., & Reese, P. A. (1992). *Local infrastructures for school networks: Current models and prospects.* (Report No. 7726). Cambridge, MA: BBN Corp.

Resnick, L. B. (1987). Learning in school and out. *Educational Researcher, 16*(9), 13–20.

Scrogan, L. (1993). *Tools for change: Restructuring technology in our schools.* Boulder, CO: Institute for Effective Educational Practice.

Senge, P. (1990). *The fifth discipline: The art and practice of the learning organization.* New York: Doubleday.

The Expeditionary Learning Outward Bound Design

Meg Campbell, Harvard University
Emily Cousins
Greg Farrell, Outward Bound USA
Mieko Kamii, Expeditionary Learning Outward Bound
Diana Lam, San Antonio Independent School District
Leah Rugen, Expeditionary Learning Outward Bound
Denis Udall, Expeditionary Learning Outward Bound

To start a school is to proclaim what it means to be human. Depending on the time and the place, it can be obvious and comfortable or startling and radically unsettling. If we are to be true to ourselves and true to learning today, we must prepare for the latter.

Our design, Expeditionary Learning Outward Bound, encompasses the broad range of intelligence and relationships necessary to generate, undertake and complete challenging intellectual and physical expeditions. It responds to the failure in public education today to engage students in their own quest for learning and to achieve their personal best. Our design motivates and accelerates their acquisition of the skills and knowledge required for productive and meaningful lives.

Expeditionary Learning is a framework for school improvement and a comprehensive school design for grades K–12. It is based on ten design principles that grow in large part out of the experience of Outward Bound. Outward Bound, founded in 1941 by Kurt Hahn in England and brought to this country by Joshua Miner and Charles Froelicher in 1962, has been built on a long-standing relationship with formal education. The program grew out of Gordonstoun, a secondary school Hahn founded in Scotland after his exile from Nazi Germany, where he had started his first school, Salem, in Bavaria.

In Expeditionary Learning schools, students spend most of each school day on purposeful, rigorous "learning expeditions" that have intellectual, service, and physical dimensions. Learning expeditions are in-depth studies of a single theme or topic, generally lasting six to nine weeks, and are the core of the curriculum. Each expedition contains several projects and performances. Field work, central to learning expeditions, draws students out of the school building and engages them in real-world investigations, such as interviewing community members concerning neighborhood development or collecting samples of local water to assess its quality. As one middle school student wrote, *"Now instead of reading everything from a text book we go out and do stuff on field trips or like on our pond expeditions,* we didn't just read about the microorganisms. We actually went out to different ponds and got specimens."

Expeditionary Learning places equal emphasis on intellectual and character development. Our schools hold high expectations for student achievement and the quality of student work and require rigorous demonstrations of student competencies. Our design calls for the complete reorganization of time, space, and relationships among persons, across disciplines, between persons and learning technology, and between the school and community. For instance, tracking is eliminated, the schedule accommodates extended blocks of time, and students stay with the same teacher for at least two years.

We focus on whole schools rather than on individual teachers or exceptional principals and our work with faculties is centered on teaching and learning, rather than on governance issues. We have started in close, with classrooms as our base.

Expeditionary Learning schools have been created by converting existing schools all at once, (Dubuque, Iowa) or incrementally, (Boston, Massachusetts and Portland, Maine) or by establishing entirely new schools (New York City and Denver, Colorado). This chapter reflects the work in these "demonstrations" sites, as well as in nine "spirit" schools in Baltimore, Maryland, San Antonio, Texas, Decatur, Georgia, Dubuque, and Portland that have implemented selected aspects of the design since the fall of 1993.

Mission Articulated as Ten Principles

Ten design principles—the foundation for fundamental changes in school culture—provide schools with a framework for their vision and direction. Pursuing these principles requires building a greater continuity of relationships between students and teachers, drawing on the power of small groups, creating a more in-depth and focused curriculum, and building stronger links between school and community.

One of the outgrowths of the school reform movement is the recognition of the value of an articulated vision or philosophy for motivating others to join the change process. Our design draws vision and strength from our ten principles. We incorporate them in everything we do, whether creating learning expeditions, school schedules, or faculty institutes. We design a range of learning opportunities that will give all members of a school community the chance to experience the design principles and to reflect upon their connection to their own values and beliefs.

A vision is one thing; investment by others in that vision is another. We recognize that for our principles to be more than nice words on paper, people must make a deep personal connection to them. The design principles have to mean enough to inspire people to be stewards of them each day in their classrooms and schools. This is an ambitious and continuous undertaking. It is also one of the most distinctive features of our design.

Expeditionary Learning Design Principles

Learning is an expedition into the unknown. Expeditions draw together personal experience and intellectual growth to promote self-discovery and the construction of knowledge. An expedition is a journey with a purpose. We believe that adults should guide students along these journeys with care, compassion, and respect for their different learning styles, backgrounds, and needs.

Given fundamental levels of health, safety, and love, all people can and want to learn more than they do. Expeditionary Learning harnesses the natural passion to learn. It is a powerful method for developing the curiosity, skills, knowledge, and courage needed to imagine a better world and to work toward realizing it.

1. The Primacy of Self-Discovery. Learning happens best with emotion, challenge, and the requisite support. People discover their abilities, values, grand passions, and responsibilities in situations that offer adventure and the unexpected. They must have tasks that require perseverance, fitness, craftsmanship, imagination, self-discipline, and significant achievement. A primary job of the educator is to help students overcome fear and discover they have more in them than they think.

2. The Having of Wonderful Ideas. Teach so as to build on children's curiosity about the world by creating learning situations that provide matter to think about, time to experiment, and time to make sense of what is observed. Foster a community where students' and adults' ideas are respected.

3. The Responsibility for Learning. Learning is both a personal, individually specific process of discovery and a social activity. Each of us learns within and for ourselves and as a part of a group. Every aspect of a school must encourage children, young people, and adults to become increasingly responsible for directing their own personal and collective learning.

4. Intimacy and Caring. Learning is fostered best in small groups where there is trust, sustained caring, and mutual respect among all members of the learning community. Keep schools and learning groups small. Be sure there is a caring adult looking after the progress of each child. Arrange for the older students to mentor the younger ones.

5. Success and Failure. All students must be assured a fair measure of success in learning in order to nurture the confidence and capacity to take risks and rise to increasingly difficult challenges. But it is also important to experience failure, to overcome negative inclinations, to prevail against adversity, and to learn to turn disabilities into opportunities.

6. Collaboration and Competition. Teach so as to join individual and group development so that the value of friendship, trust, and group endeavor is made manifest. Encourage students to compete, not against each other, but with their own personal best and with rigorous standards of excellence.

7. Diversity and Inclusivity. Diversity and inclusivity in all groups dramatically increases richness of ideas, creative power, problem-solving ability, and acceptance of others. Encourage students to investigate, value, and draw upon their own different histories, talents, and resources together with those of other communities and cultures. Keep the schools and learning groups heterogeneous.

8. The Natural World. A direct and respectful relationship with the natural world refreshes the human spirit and reveals the important lessons of recurring cycles and cause and effect. Students learn to become stewards of the earth and of the generations to come.

9. Solitude and Reflection. Solitude, reflection, and silence replenish our energies and open our minds. Be sure students have time alone to explore their own thoughts, make their own connections, and create their own ideas. Then give them opportunity to exchange their reflections with each other and with adults.

10. Service and Compassion. We are crew, not passengers, and are strengthened by acts of consequential service to others. One of a school's primary functions is to prepare its students with the attitudes and skills to learn from and be of service to others.

It is not possible within our limited space to illustrate each design principle at length. Two sketches, however, may provide a sense of how the principles shape and pervade school culture.

> *Solitude and Reflection*
> I like it when they make us reflect on what we did. It makes you look back and say, "Oh, I can do this better next time." You can reflect on anything after you do it, and it makes you feel like you studied all night for a final exam and you really feel good about it. You feel more experienced when you look back on things and figure out how to make them better.
>
> —*Rory Murray, Sixth Grader*
> *Rafael Hernandez School, Boston*

Reflecting on one's experiences is a major road to building a person's own values. If students are to tap into their own creativity, personal renewal, and thoughtfulness, schools must structure time for meaningful reflection is valued. At Salem, the school Outward Bound founder Kurt Hahn opened in Germany, students took a daily 30-minute "quiet walk" alone to replenish their minds, bodies, and spirits.

"I don't retreat from the world to escape," Robert Frost said, "but to return stronger." Solitude is cocoon time. It helps develop powers of concentration. It requires silence, commitment, and an imaginative use of existing space. It does not cost any money; it can happen every day. People of all ages reap its benefits. Scientists and artists alike attest to the "click," the unanticipated connections they make when constructively immersed in solitude—an experience virtually unknown today in public schools.

Essential for character development, solitude and reflection also enhance academic learning. David Kolb suggests that learning requires explicit time set aside for reflecting on experience (Kolb, 1984). His work describes a learning cycle that has four key elements: concrete experience and observation, considered reflection, synthesis and abstract conceptualization, and testing of concepts in new situations. Each phase leads to the next. If learners are not encouraged to reflect they will not be as likely to derive lessons that redirect and build on their understandings. Kolb's model is especially pertinent to the experience-based field work that makes up much of each learning expedition. Structured reflection, whether through journal writing, discussion or other forms, is one of the tools that Expeditionary Learning teachers use to capture field experiences so they can be explored and deepened back in the classroom.

Teachers regularly integrate structured reflection into each day at all grade levels. Shari Flatt, a first-grade teacher at Table Mound Elementary School in Dubuque, Iowa, said, "At first I thought my children would be too young for reflection. The silence seemed to last an eternity." Slowly her students became accustomed to the silence and enjoyed longer and longer periods of reflection. Flatt has seen the impact it has had on their academic development: "I see it as a way of teaching them to think on their own. Some of my children need to focus on what it actually means to think about something. I try to model different types of reflection, so they realize that *reflection means more than simply thinking about your feelings*." Some of her strategies include reading excerpts from her own journal and starting reflection time with a question such as what their goals are for that day. One of the teachers in her team, Tammy Duehr, remarks: "Now they're so accustomed to reflecting that as soon as I say 'circle up,' they sit down and close their eyes."

> *Service and Compassion*
> You can preach at [students]; that is the hook without the worm. You can order them to volunteer; that is dishonest. You can say to them, "you are needed," and that appeal hardly ever fails.
> —*Kurt Hahn* (1957)

A rich body of research and theory has demonstrated that service, when properly structured, can have a powerful impact on young people's intellectual development. A number of researchers, including Minnesota educator and researcher Diane Hedin, have demonstrated the dislocation between learning that occurs in out-of-school settings, or practical intelligence, and that which goes on in school, or school-related intelligence. This growing body of research confirms what thoughtful teachers have known all along: the most powerful kinds of learning experiences happen when knowing and doing are bound together; that is, when abstract concepts are taught in the context of situations where their meaning and real-world applications are apparent.

Service helps young people see the connection between academic content and problems people encounter in the real world. Moreover, it can provide an opportunity to test and apply knowledge they have gained beyond the settings in which the learning occurred (Hedin, 1989). A number of researchers found that problem-solving abilities increased for students who were involved in community service groups more than for comparable children who were not.

Many of the students at Jack Elementary school, an Expeditionary Learning school in Portland, Maine, live in the Kennedy Park housing project in the Munjoy Hill section of that city. As part of a fourth- and fifth-grade learning expedition on Munjoy Hill, a representative from the Portland Housing Authority came and asked the students what they would like to see in their neighborhood. One student responded, "I think we should have a bike shop. Kids need a cheap place to get their bikes fixed." Most of the children in the community ride bikes, but few of them have the money for repairs. Broken bikes pile up in disuse instead of getting fixed, the student said. All of the students agreed, and the idea for the Kids' Quick Fix Bike Shop was born.

The students began their project by applying for and receiving a $50 grant from the Portland Partnership of businesses and schools. The Portland Housing Authority agreed to let the students use the basement of their Kennedy Park offices for the bike shop. Making the bike shop a success took more than simply finding a space and some money, however. The students had to learn how to repair the bikes and how to manage a business. They called Portland bike shops to set up lessons with repair people. They invited people to come talk about bike safety, and the man who created the Portland Bike Trail spoke to the students and donated bike maps. While the students were learning the repair skills, they were practicing them two afternoons a week in the shop.

Their teacher, Karen White, felt strongly about incorporating the service project into a whole expedition. Because the students were so excited by the bike shop, they were eager to learn the skills they needed to make it run well. They quickly learned words like *lubricant* and *disengage* for their spelling tests. They prepared for phone calls to bike shops by carefully writing out scripts. They consulted with a local banker on opening a checking account. Not only was White impressed with the progress of the student work, she was also pleased with the way the students have grown through their service. "This has been their project through and through," she said. "There has been a great difference in their self-esteem, and the way they feel about themselves. *They know they have done something. I really feel like they believe there is nothing they can't do.*"

Bridging the gap between in and out of school learning is key. But equally important are the social development outcomes of service for students. Service has been shown to improve young people's social and personal responsibility, and attitudes toward adults and others. Moreover, it has a positive effect on growth in moral and ego development (Conrad & Hedin, 1983; Hamilton & Fenzel, 1988; Newmann & Rutter, 1983). But as Diane Hedin has written, "If the objective is real change in the way that young people view their obligation to the community, it cannot be assumed that the young person is the primary beneficiary of the service. Youth service is powerful because it benefits the community as much as it does the student" (Hedin, 1989).

Curriculum and Instruction

I felt like a real scientist looking into a microscope and when I found the specimen I felt awesome. When you are done with the expedition, you go home and tell your mom and dad what you learned and they practically don't even know what you are talking about. It's like you wrote a new chapter in the encyclopedia. Six weeks ago I would never have known about pond life.
—*Journal entry, Fifth-grade Student*
Dubuque, Iowa

We have found that an intensive focus on teaching and learning through the development of learning expeditions has been a lever for whole school change. The design of a learning expedition touches every part of a school (see Fig. 5.1). In order to support extended, multi-disciplinary expeditions, schools have to change the way they organize their schedules, the way teachers work together, and the way professional development is fit into the daily life of the school. For instance, coordinating an expedition's field work outside of the classroom requires flexible scheduling, time for teachers to plan, and extended blocks of time for students to be in the field.

The organizing center of the learning expedition is the theme or topic. A good theme is intriguing and open-ended. It defines the territory of the expedition but also generates questions. It naturally cuts across disciplines, though some themes lend themselves more to one discipline than another. Guiding questions shape an expedition and give it further definition. They are the basic tools of intellectual exploration and give a learning expedition a structure of inquiry. At the School for the Physical City middle school, for example, the question "How can we tell when a community is thriving?" gave structure to the theme Our City, Ourselves. Across all sites, as learning expeditions unfold, teachers weigh which themes and questions work and which seem too broad or narrow. They consider the role of the student in developing guiding questions and in shaping the expedition plan. At Dubuque's Central Alternative School, for instance, teachers include students in planning meetings, offering them academic credit for effective participation.

Figure 5.1

King Middle School Plans an Expedition

Finding a way to sift through learning goals and priorities is one of the toughest challenges of planning a learning expedition. Teachers at King Middle School in Portland, Maine, convened to plan a learning expedition that would allow them to meet major objectives for each discipline. The social studies teacher wanted to cover world culture. The science teacher needed to focus on biology. The language arts teacher's focus this year was writing a major research paper and persuasive essays.

After a lively discussion of possible topics that would allow the teachers to address each of these needs, they settled on the theme "endangered species." Through this theme, the social studies work would examine the complex interactions between humans and the environment of endangered species in selected non-American cultures. The science work would focus on ecological issues, and math would include the collection, analysis, and presentation of data on endangered species.

The teachers then brainstormed ways to integrate the social studies and science content with the writing goals of the language arts teacher. The endangered species projects included a debate, a brochure to inform the school and community about the issue, and an in-depth research paper. Although the teachers had taught writing research papers many times before, they decided the interdisciplinary approach would give the paper added power.

Individual and Group Project Work

A learning expedition is shapeless until ideas for projects are developed. Working on projects comprises much of the intellectual journey and destination of a learning expedition. Projects within a learning expedition unify and ignite student learning by calling for concrete products or actions that address authentic problems and situations. They are in fact "performance tasks" and provide multiple avenues for students' thought and expression.

One of the tensions in the development of major projects is finding the balance between group and individual assignments. Group work fosters community, encourages students to learn to work cooperatively, and draws on complementary strengths. Individual work, on the other hand, helps teachers ensure student engagement, obtain information on the strengths and weaknesses of each student, and provide a body of work from each student for assessment purposes. Individual projects do not mean that students need to work in isolation. Students can help each other through sharing skills and resources and critiquing each other's work.

One can also plan a group project comprised of components that are clearly the responsibility of each individual student. A good example of this approach is the Pond Life expedition in which fifth-grade students at the Table Mound Elementary School in Dubuque completed a field guide to a local pond. Each of the three classes involved produced one field guide, but each student was responsible for one page. As students become accustomed to project work and develop strong work habits and high internal standards for their work, group projects will become stronger.

The Use of Field Work

The conscious use of field work is perhaps the most visible dimension of learning expeditions. It quickly reinforces the changed school culture as student clipboards for field notes and journal entries become essential school equipment. Teachers are discovering the multiple purposes of field work—immersion into a theme or topic, deeper investigation and research, team-building and adventure—as they negotiate the traditional barriers to incorporating out-of-school learning into the curriculum. They are doing away with traditional field trips in which students reluctantly follow a guide through a museum or business. Instead, teachers are guiding students outside to interview community members, sketch buildings, measure shadows, and make detailed observation about how things are and how they work. Students are going outside to answer questions and follow leads that cannot be looked up or found easily in textbooks, enriching their project work with real evidence and experience.

Like other aspects of learning expeditions, purposeful field work is challenging to plan and carry out. It requires flexible scheduling and considerable thought about grouping students and the roles of adults in the school. Field experiences need not be elaborate or long distance undertakings. Much can be learned from a walk in the neighborhood surrounding a school, by interviewing the school janitor, or through developing an ongoing relationship with a local nursing home. Visitors from the community—experts, parents, and neighbors—bring the outside world into the classroom.

The best learning expeditions are based on natural inquiry. Where did this come from? How did it get to be this way? Steven Levy, a fourth-grade teacher in Lexington, Massachusetts, wrote that even "familiar objects that the children take for granted are filled with intrigue and meaning when we explore their origins. It amazes me that one can start with almost anything, and through a process of questioning, reflecting and imagining, see through that object, as if it were a window, into the depth and breadth of the world" (Levy, 1995).

In the first two years of implementation, the process of developing learning expeditions prompts teachers to examine their practice and students' learning. For many teachers in our demonstration schools, it was the first time they had taught with projects and inquiry at the core of their curriculum. The experience of teaching in this new way and engaging in reflection and dialogue with colleagues has sparked exciting, challenging questions. How can we plan learning expeditions so that students deepen their understanding of content and develop their abilities? How can we improve the ways in which student learning is assessed, and make sure standards and assessment are embedded in the curriculum? Perhaps the most useful discovery we have made is that Expeditionary Learning is an unfolding process, rather than a set of fixed solutions.

Standards and Assessment

In all of the school systems with which we work, students are required to take standardized tests. We expect students in Expeditionary Learning schools to do as well as or better on them than students from other schools. Indeed, as recent test scores from our demonstration sites reveal, this has already begun to happen. But, standardized tests have their limits; they shed little light on the practices of teaching and learning. We believe that the first purpose of assessment is not to rank and sort students, but to help them learn better. Assessment that is closely linked to instruction, such as portfolios, exhibitions, and performances of student work, and critique sessions, actually fuels and supports the learning process. Fortunately, learning expeditions and the portfolio of student work were made for one another.

Learning Expeditions and Standards

Learning expeditions are planned and implemented by teachers who have thought about standards—what graduates of the learning community should know and be able to do. Embedded in every learning expedition are projects that require the following:

- Writing, reading, speaking, and listening;

- Inquiring and problem-solving, carrying out investigations, doing research;

- Thinking critically, analytically, logically. Using quantitative reasoning;

- Being inventive, imaginative, creative, and willing to take intellectual risks;

- Working hard, persevering, doing one's best;

- Developing friendship, trust, citizenship, service, and working in a group;

- Getting and keeping fit, being reflective and compassionate, and standing up for oneself;

- Taking the perspectives of others in considering their viewpoints.

Before launching into major projects, teachers discuss the standards with their students and solicit their participation in developing criteria for assessing the quality of their work. Student work is held in classroom "working folders" so that students can revisit the criteria and standards and revise their work. As a project unfolds, teachers and students discover areas in which the criteria and standards need to be modified or revised.

Portfolios and Standards

Periodically, students go through their working folders to choose pieces for their portfolios. Portfolios serve as evidence of the content, quality, and range of a student's learning. They contain the student's explanation of why certain pieces are included and what they are intended to show. What goes into a portfolio depends on for whom the student is assembling it (audience), and what qualities, competencies, or skills she is being asked to document (purpose). Coupled with teacher observations, notes from student and parent conferences, and quiz or test results, this body of work stands as evidence of how well students have met standards. Because portfolios contain drafts along with their final works, and final works produced over time, they are tools for students' personal reflection on their learning.

Shifting to the use of portfolios is a process that requires ongoing discussion and experimentation. Close to the end of the 1994–1995 school year, the teachers at the Rafael Hernandez School in Boston asked students to put together a portfolio to introduce themselves to the next year's teachers and to share with their parents. The teachers decided that the students should choose one piece that represented their best work, one that needed revision, and one that demonstrated improvements through revision. When the time came for students to make their selections, they were overwhelmed by all the material. At the parent conferences, many students found it hard to discuss their work with their parents because they were not used to conversing about work. It became clear that students should select work for their portfolios throughout the year with a clear understanding of the standards that guide their decisions. Students also needed experience in speaking about their work, and so the teachers organized role plays, peer conferences, and modeling to prepare students for those discussions.

In order to judge the quality of a portfolio or a performance and let students know what they must do to improve their work, teachers and researchers have developed rubrics—scoring guides that specify the qualities which distinguish one level of performance from another. Once a group of teachers has been immersed in using a much discussed, well-understood rubric, they are able to score the portfolios of students they have never taught, never met, reasonably well. Ideally, rubrics allow educators to assess the quality of work done by students who have not necessarily completed the same assignments, read the same books, or had the same field experiences. They allow students' portfolios to be evaluated along common dimensions.

In a similar process, the entire faculty of the Rocky Mountain School of Expeditionary Learning (RMSEL) in Denver developed a set of content standards across grades and subject matter in the summer of 1994. Where they were available, the faculty drew from national standards such as the National Council of Teachers of Mathematics. Next, they turned their energies toward developing rubrics for scoring math and writing portfolios, drawing upon the California Learning Assessment System, Vermont Writing Assessment, and the New Standards Project.

The RMSEL faculty also did some groundbreaking work in assessing character development. They began by outlining five essential manifestations of healthy character: integrity, courage, empathy, responsibility, and discipline; then they discussed the ways in which these values could be seen in a student's actions. For instance, on an adventure into the wilderness, students who clean up after themselves and others demonstrate responsibility and self-discipline. The faculty asked adults who see students demonstrating these qualities to write letters describing the students' actions. In order to graduate from RMSEL, students must compile a collection of these letters in their portfolios.

In addition to creating schoolwide standards, schools are also reviewing their respective district or state standards and curriculum frameworks for the purposes of shaping the development of learning expeditions. From this experience we are now able to make recommendations to new sites about best routes to follow. Meeting existing district standards has not been a problem according to recent surveys of Expeditionary Learning teachers. Teachers say learning expeditions not only meet but routinely exceed these standards.

Standards and assessment must be considered as learning expeditions are developed. A thoughtful review and discussion of prevailing standards and how they inform curriculum and teaching ensures that student work will be held up against standards and that standards will be met.

Classroom Assessment

In addition to the use of portfolios, our model includes incidental, ongoing, culminating, and external forms of assessment. Incidental assessment is the teacher's recording of observations as he or she circulates among the students and sees who understands or is having difficulty with a lesson or task.

Ongoing assessment engages students in thinking critically and analytically about their own and others' work, and in revising their own work in practices like student-teacher and peer conferences, small and large group critique sessions, and opportunities for reflection on the feedback students have received. These practices help develop a classroom "portfolio culture" in which students are accustomed to the idea that students exert effort, work hard, critique their own and each other's work, and are satisfied only when they have done their best work.

Culminating assessments centering on students' portfolios can take a number of forms: a year-end portfolio to introduce oneself to next year's teacher; a showcase portfolio of best works; a portfolio submitted as part of a statewide assessment system; a presentation or performance that is judged. Performances, presentations, and exhibitions also invite assessment from sources external to the class: parents, community members, professionals in fields related to student work, and teachers and students from other classes.

Professional Development

The success of Expeditionary Learning depends on lasting changes in classroom practice. Traditionally, staff development in schools has focused on isolated techniques or programs without addressing the fundamental need for personal and professional transformation. Such transformation accelerates visible changes in every aspect of school design. Michael Fullan, a University of Toronto professor whose work focuses on school change, wrote, *"Continuous development of all teachers is the cornerstone for meaning, improvement and reform.* Professional development and school development are inextricably linked" (Fullan, 1991).

Professional Development Design

During the early stages of implementation, orientation experiences which foster understanding of Expeditionary Learning usually include the following:

- one-day community explorations—teachers and administrators conduct investigations of the surrounding community as a learning resource;

- service retreats—small groups design and conduct service projects for local schools;

- Outward Bound educators' courses—school teams learn they can do things they've never done before, build trust, and get firsthand experience with expeditionary learning principles in wilderness and urban Outward Bound expeditions.

- local institutes—introductions and experience in designing and implementing learning expeditions.

Following the orientation phase, our design calls for three years of approximately 20 days a year for professional development experiences for each school's entire faculty and administrators, planned by Expeditionary Learning's school designers and an instructional leader from the school, and tailored to meet its needs and local environment.

Following are the four elements of our professional development program:

Summer Institutes and Minisabbaticals

The act of designing a learning expedition to teach is in itself a powerful mechanism for professional and personal renewal. Designing a learning expedition immediately immerses a teacher in an intellectual and personal challenge that has real-world consequences. In the summer institutes and minisabbaticals, all teachers develop learning expeditions that they are committed to carrying out during the school year. Five-day summer institutes and shorter minisabbaticals that take place during the school year provide structured formats within which teachers design multidisciplinary, thematic projects consistent with district outcomes and Expeditionary Learning standards and design principles. Once they know how their students will be learning, they know what kind of schedule, planning, sequencing, and development is needed to support it.

In a minisabbatical, an Expeditionary Learning school designer meets with teacher teams for three- to five-day periods during the school year. Teams are freed from other responsibilities for the purpose of reflecting on the progress of current expeditions and planning new ones. Creating the time for teachers to collaborate as they learn, plan, and reflect is critical to successful implementation of the design. The minisabbatical format presupposes experience and familiarity with the design principles through an orientation experience such as a community exploration. It is best suited to teachers who have already guided their first learning expeditions.

Common Planning Time For Teachers

Perhaps the most important facet of collaborative professional development is ongoing daily and weekly time for planning and assessment, and administrative support in establishing the schedule and school culture to reinforce it. Certain ingredients of the planning process seem to make it go smoothly and effectively. For instance, sharing sessions work best when they involve an in-depth examination of a single aspect of an expedition which teachers can discuss in depth and detail. Commonly agreed upon ground rules for expedition critiquing sessions are also helpful, for they safeguard teachers' sense of trust and mutual respect.

Sufficient time and an emotional climate that allows for messy, recursive debates and discussion is hard to find amid the clamor and hectic pace of schools. Even in the face of these challenges, many Expeditionary Learning schools have found innovative ways to open the school schedule. At Jack Elementary School in Portland, Maine, school lets out at 12:30 every Wednesday afternoon so teachers have half a day to plan learning expeditions. The students actually gain 15 extra minutes in instruction time through this arrangement, since the school day starts at 8:45 a.m.—15 minutes earlier than in previous years—and lunch lasts 45 minutes on most days and 30 minutes on Wednesday instead of an hour.

Jack used money allocated for lunch aides to pay for Wednesday afternoon enrichment programs for a student body not otherwise able to afford such activities as dance, pottery, theater, or hockey. Other schools have also reallocated funds or taken advantage of district money for specialists to allow teachers to meet in teams. District discretionary funds have also been used for substitutes so teachers can attend full-day development opportunities.

Conferences and School Visits

Teachers tell us they gain a deeper appreciation of their own strengths and areas for growth as a result of school visits. The private sector calls this *benchmarking*, finding out and learning from others' best practices. Expeditionary Learning's teachers' conferences allow teachers from diverse sites to spend Fridays visiting Expeditionary Learning schools and Saturdays investigating an important topic and sharing their progress in implementing expeditions in their classes and expeditionary learning throughout the school. Workshops and presentations by fellow practitioners and outside experts provide an infusion of new ideas. Working groups allow teachers to discuss the content of workshops with colleagues and exchange ideas and experiences.

Cross-site school visits by teachers afford the host school an interested audience for and set of commentators on student work, which prompts reflection by the host faculty and students. What is our best work? What have we really learned? Where are we struggling? Since visits also are structured in small groups, visiting teachers observe learning expeditions in progress and talk teacher-to-teacher.

Summits: Learning Expeditions for Educators

Summits immerse teachers in week-long learning expeditions focused on a particular subject, during which they observe and work with a master teacher. Summits model the kinds of active, adventurous learning that Expeditionary Learning teachers and schools are striving to engage in with their students. Throughout, teachers are confronted with complex problems and practices that invite searching questions and deep connection-making. The content is sophisticated, and the tasks are compelling and seemingly impossible, but actually within reach. Summit topics to date have included fitness and human anatomy, architecture, Native American history, and the Holocaust and its connection to contemporary history.

Teachers often return from summits with immediate applications for their classroom. A recent summit that looked at geology through the exploration of caves, streams, and minerals modeled strategies, ideas, and techniques for teaching scientific concepts such as observation, fact versus inference, hypotheses building, and problem solving. Connie Russell-Rodríguez, an English-as-a-second-language and reading teacher from the Rafael Hernandez School in Boston, attended the geology summit and wrote:

> As a result of that adventure, several colleagues and I planned a 10-week interdisciplinary unit on geology, which was a pinnacle experience for me in terms of seeing immediate results. Both my students and I were excited to come to school for that entire 10 weeks, and the work they produced met all my expectations and more.

Technology

> I am 18 years old. I am attending school at PRVTC (Portland Regional Vocational Technical Center) in the early childhood occupations. I am doing an expedition on multiage classrooms. Anything you could give me would be helpful. Please send mail back (*Electronic Mail News*, 1994).

> Hi! . . . I'm currently a fifth-grade teacher in Boston. I've taught multiage/grade classes several times (most recently last year) . . . I think it's great for several reasons. First, there is always about half the class who can help the new kids feel comfortable. Also, just working with the same students for more than one year helps a teacher establish solid relationships with families and really get to know a child well. I also think it helps create

a "family" feel to classrooms, which has a positive impact on cooperative learning skills and support from classmates. Have you had an opportunity to work in a multiage setting yourself? What sparked your interest in this subject? Good luck with your project! (*Electronic Mail News*, 1994)

Expeditionary Learning's approach to integrating technology into education falls into four parts: First, we have established a continuously-expanding electronic network of Expeditionary Learning teachers, administrators, staff and advisors; second, we are using technology to disseminate our work by posting our monthly newsletter *The Web* and other publications on the Internet; third, we are investigating ways of bringing technology into the classroom; and fourth, we are exploring how to join the information superhighway from the schools. In addition, electronic inquiries about Expeditionary Learning can be made over the Internet to info@elob.ci.net.

Schools and the Information Superhighway

Although reform efforts often speak eloquently about bringing advanced technological capabilities into schools, we have discovered that it can be a challenge simply to hook up a telephone in a classroom. Before they speed onto the information highway, many schools first have to install the most basic tools.

Much of our recent work on technology has been to help schools lay down the infrastructure that will support access to the Internet. One Internet gateway per school is simply not enough. For the most part, the teachers and students who take advantage of our e-mail network of educators have computers and telephone lines in their own rooms. Only when more teachers and students have this opportunity will the Internet be used to its full potential in schools.

And indeed, the potential is great. While many people think of telecommunicating as a means to receive information, it is better understood as a way to share information and ideas with other people—a two-way street. Already, the electronic network of Expeditionary Learning partners includes over 200 people who are able to exchange advice and experience instantaneously.

Tom Lafavore, a teacher at Portland Regional Vocational Technical Center in Maine, described the benefits of the network by saying, "There is a fantastic amount of information that can be passed back and forth. Organizationally and in terms of curriculum, e-mail has tremendous potential for designing and creating expeditions and touching base with [all the Expeditionary Learning people] in the country."

Technology in the Classroom

Expeditionary Learning's commitment to students' technological literacy focuses on increasing teachers' and students' level of comfort with technological tools (computer software and hardware). We have found that when students see technology as a tool to understanding a learning expedition topic, they are more motivated to use it. Students turn to technology when they have to create products for expeditions. For instance, students use spreadsheets to prepare a graph of findings from a water quality survey or desktop publish their anthology of oral histories. Having computers available in the classroom as well as in the computer laboratory encourages teachers and students to view them as integral elements of every classroom and learning expedition. We would like students and teachers to be able to turn to the computer in the same way as we now turn to a book, a calculator, paper and pencil, or a dictionary.

Our focus has been on fostering general, professional uses of technology instead of on disseminating educational software. We would like our students to become well versed in a range of word processing, data management and desktop publishing programs. Through this process, all students will acquire highly marketable skills as well as the skills that will help them master other computer applications.

A prerequisite to having students become familiar with technology is for their teachers to be comfortable using computers with a range of applications. We are working, therefore, on integrating into our staff development the opportunity for teachers to become technologically literate.

School Governance and Organization

Expeditionary Learning has developed and tapped structures for school governance and organization that will support a new definition of teaching and learning. The layers of changes involving time, space, and professional relationships are innumerable and lay the groundwork for deeper changes in classroom practice. Expeditionary Learning schools address the elimination of tracking, the redesign of schedules to obtain flexible blocks of time, the creation of small clusters, school site decision making, the need for shared teacher planning time, for teachers working collaboratively in teams and for preparation of teachers to continue teaching the same groups of students for at least two years.

None of these changes are easy, but because they are synergistic, their simultaneous introduction actually facilitates implementation of each of them. For example, attention to school culture through the establishment of community circles, small advisory groups of 10 to 15 students and an adult, reinforces the development of new approaches to academic curricula. Although reform efforts have made attempts to implement changes like these in isolation, or one at a time, the incremental approach has proven more difficult.

School Site Decision Making

> What has changed in my perception is where I might have said, "I don't think this is a good idea," I now sit back and say, "OK, this is the way I feel about it, but if you guys feel very strongly about going in another direction, that's fine."
> —*Principal Margarita Muñiz*
> *Rafael Hernandez School, Boston*

Power illuminates when it is shared and linked to competence and good ideas. For schools to become high-performance organizations well grounded in the experience and knowledge of those who work there, the power must be shared, not only empowering faculty to act, but also creating the kind of supportive organization in which they will be enabled to seek life-giving experiences for themselves. The key to school improvement is not to be found in systems, technical knowledge, or the authority of experts. All these things can be helpful, but they can also be misleading if the foundation of the learning community is left to disintegrate. Students, teachers, administrators, parents, and community leaders are human beings. To "break the mold," people need something rarely mentioned in discussions of educational reform. They need to be impelled into the experience of working together to develop a shared vision of how teaching and learning can make their communities better places to live.

Expeditionary Learning seeks to place the locus of control for decision making and action as close to the work of teaching and learning as possible. However, site-based decision making is a complex matter, involving new leadership roles for teachers, parents, and other members of the school community, as well as strong leadership and direction from the principal. As school-based management has taken hold throughout the country, there has been a powerful tension between granting authority to teachers and requiring strong leadership and initiative from principals. For it to work effectively, a balance of authority must be achieved in which teachers' initiatives are supported by the principal and vice versa. Such new structures and relationships at the school level must be supported by comparable changes at the district level.

Detracking

One of the striking differences in Expeditionary Learning schools is the inclusion of different kinds of students in the same classroom. Expeditionary Learning holds that all students can and want to learn more than they do, and Expeditionary Learning schools reflect our principle of inclusivity by bringing together students of different strengths and abilities. In most cases, rather than pulling out students for separate classes, special education and Title I teachers enter into classrooms to support the work of the primary teacher. Teachers have found that learning expeditions facilitate this process, because they provide all students with an opportunity to be academically successful. Academically advanced students get to tackle more challenging material at the same time students with academic difficulties get to shine by reaching the high standards of a project or demonstrating leadership.

Expeditionary Learning schools have also begun to tap into the varieties of ways cross-age mixing of students can add value to learning through tutoring, advisory and extracurricular groups, and in some schools through learning expeditions that stretch across several age groups. Detracking requires much more than simply bringing together students of different ages and degrees of academic preparation. It requires a great deal of focused attention on the teaching strategies that will provide academic "scaffolding" for individual students and the support for teachers as they work with heterogeneous groups.

Multiyear Teaching

> We trained hard . . . but it seemed that every time we were beginning to form up into teams, we would be reorganized. I was to learn later in life that we tend to meet any new situation by reorganizing; and a wonderful method it can be for creating the illusion of progress while producing confusion, inefficiency, and demoralization.
>
> —*Petronius Arbiter, 210 B.C.*

Schools may be the only institutions that require their workers (teachers and students) to completely reorganize their working relationships every year. Keeping teachers and students together over multiyear cycles is a key structural feature of Expeditionary

Learning. Although it has not yet become widespread in this country, or researched in depth, multiyear teaching has been used successfully in a number of schools across the United States, including the Waldorf Schools, where students stay with the same teacher for eight years.

Expeditionary Learning teachers observe that multiyear teaching allows teachers and students to get more deeply involved in learning projects. Paul Thompson of the Blackstone Elementary School in Boston explained, "You know how in January students start taking off academically? In the second year, my January happens in October. After a few weeks of getting reacquainted, we get right down to work." Projects reach deeper levels, because all the students share base knowledge and experience from the previous year.

Teachers also become more familiar with students' learning styles, adding to their ability to assess student work. Multiyear cycles also appeal to parents, one of whom noted that she would not want to change her children's pediatrician each year, and to students, who welcome stronger relationships with teachers who know them well. No parent in any Expeditionary Learning school to date has requested a transfer to another class to avoid having the same teacher for another year.

Another potential appeal of multiyear teaching is that it should not result in additional cost to districts or schools. It is only custom, not any state or local regulations, that prevents this organizational change. It is not excluded by teacher contracts. It is an example of an administrative, school-based decision that could happen overnight. Successful multiyear teaching, however, does require a significant change of identity on the part of teachers who are no longer "second-grade teachers" or "tenth-grade biology teachers." The multiyear structure itself is a vehicle for professional development and renewal, as teachers can never teach the same core curriculum for many years at a stretch.

Schedules

Expeditionary Learning holds that time has to be used differently than it has been in conventional, bell-oriented schedules. "If you were to try to find a way to destroy the opportunity to learn, you would use the present schedule of most public high schools," observed Harvard Professor Harold Howe II, former United States Commissioner of Education and member of our Council of Senior Advisors (Cousins & Rodgers, 1995). Expeditionary Learning schools depart completely from conventional scheduling structures. The design eliminates bells. The clock does not drive the curriculum. Instead, the schedule adapts to meet the needs of teachers and students. Learning expeditions provide teachers with creative ways to share and divide time. Extended blocks of uninterrupted time allow students to explore topics in great depth.

As our schools design new schedules, common themes and lessons emerge. Most obvious is the fact that scheduling is a very difficult process. There are no fixed answers, because each schedule must be tailored to the specific needs of individual schools, teaching teams and students. Because students spend a lot of time in the field, the schedule must remain flexible and not tightly bound to a particular space. There should also be constants in the schedule that will punctuate the week and the year with regularity and give the schedule a backbone. Daily morning community meetings for a whole school, advisory groups or community circles, and regular blocks of time for sustained work in core discipline areas provide coherence in Expeditionary Learning schools. Students also need flexible ways to receive intensive academic support and challenge such as tutorials, specialized courses, and Socratic seminars.

Restructuring the School Day

Perhaps the most vexing question is how the schedule can support student learning. For the Wheels of Change middle school expedition, which examined immigration, the industrial revolution, and water wheels, teachers at the Rafael Hernandez School in Boston restructured the schedule and the teaching teams to strengthen their work. The Spanish and English teachers produced a play; the mathematics and science teachers led an investigation of water wheels; and the social studies team examined the industrial revolution. At the end of the first three-week cycle, the students rotated to another team for the next three weeks of the nine-week expedition.

This structure allowed every team to implement a cycle three times, albeit with different grade levels. It also gave teachers an opportunity to ensure greater intellectual rigor in the subject matter than they could in the multigrade, fully interdisciplinary context. During this final phase of the expedition, the students could take the knowledge they acquired during the nine previous weeks and shape it into an interdisciplinary final project. They worked on the project with the guidance of an interdisciplinary teaching team they chose.

Similar innovations have emerged at other Expeditionary Learning schools. Many schools have discovered, for instance, that moving all specialists (art, music, physical education) to the beginning or the end of the day frees up the extended blocks of time necessary for learning expeditions. At the King Middle School in Portland, Maine, which is divided into vertical houses, all scheduling outside of specialists is left to the discretion of each house. Teachers within a house can choose when they want to meet within discipline groupings and when they want to meet all together for project work.

Parent and Community Engagement

Learning expeditions have proven to be an excellent vehicle for engaging parents and community members. Because expeditions have such a defined focus and send students out into the world to conduct field work, parents and community members can easily find a natural way to contribute based on their own expertise. We view an architect, a biologist, a long-distance truck driver, and an immigrant grandmother as potential "experts" for learning expeditions. Parents and community members are also invited to attend and evaluate students' culminating presentations. For students and community members alike, these presentations strengthen the link between participating in school life and being a member of the community.

Some parents may feel less than comfortable in schools because of negative associations with their own school experiences. These parents may have a great deal to offer the school communities, but they may not always find a way to enter. Expeditionary Learning schools recognize that family needs must be addressed in conjunction with the needs of the students. The Jack Elementary School in Portland, Maine, for example, created the on-site Parent Center with Chapter 1 funds. By offering General Equivalency Diplomas (GED), computer programming, and parenting skills classes, the Parent Center welcomes parents who previously might not have felt comfortable within a school community. The classes provide parents with a link to the school. Once in the school environment, parents have begun collaborating with teachers and contributing to the school decision-making process.

Redesign of Space

It has been widely noted that American public schools were founded on a factory model of education, so it should not be surprising that for the better part of this century, they were built to look like factories, too. School buildings and school yards are not generally places one seeks out or wants to be in, and in this sense, they share a certain aura with penal institutions. Educators have not traditionally focused attention on understanding the influence of physical school design on teaching and learning. We have ceded those thoughts to the "experts."

In addition to the reality of school buildings, the notion of "school" as a nondescript, square building with self-contained rooms all the same size divided by a corridor is part of our cultural history. What counts in our minds as "school"? When school boards broke from that idea in the 1970s to impose a different standard of "open classrooms" on teachers and students, the design fell the way of many other well-intentioned projects. There was creative resistance by those living with the changes imposed upon them. The walls went back up and the architects retreated to traditional design layouts. Two of the key sources of the resistance were the open classroom design challenged teachers and students' notions of what school was without involving them in a process to expand their vision, and the design had flaws because it was not grounded in practitioners' experience and needs.

The best work in physical school design, in our view, is underway in Reggio Emilia, Italy. In Reggio Emilia, social space, individual space, and seemingly marginal space is deliberately and thoughtfully constructed to foster communication among children and adults. Rather than being a last priority, aesthetics and creativity of the design of space is central. Parents and teachers invent and build new furnishings, pay careful attention to colors and light, and join in the ongoing care of the space. Our design for use of space within and around schools is most directly informed as well as inspired by these public schools. Loris Malaguzzi, founder of Reggio Emilia schools, has noted, "To be sure our schools are the most visible object of our work. . . . There has never been, on our part, any desire to make them all alike" (Gandini, 1993).

Our design calls for infusing evidence of the ten design principles into how space is used in and around the school. Just as flexibility is required in the approach to use of time, space also must be viewed with a flexible lens. The natural world is evident in the classroom, whether it is a water fountain crafted by kindergarten parents at the Rocky Mountain School of Expeditionary Learning in Denver as part of students' Rain Forest learning expedition, the planarian in the Pond Life expedition at the Bryant Elementary School in Dubuque and the Rafael Hernandez School in inner-city Boston, or the nature walk and pond created on Clairemont Elementary School property in Decatur, Georgia. Such conscious attention to physical space—from tiny details to huge renovations—provides Expeditionary Learning schools with another powerful avenue for creating a culture to support teaching and learning.

Implementation Process for
New Schools and Districts

Expeditionary Learning can be implemented in most existing or new schools, preferably with enrollments of no more than 500 students. The design can also be implemented in several separate schools that share one physical site. Schools can be any configuration of grades K–12. Current sites include elementary schools, K–8 schools, middle schools, high schools (including a vocational school), and one K–12 school, in large and small cities covering a wide range of income levels. These schools serve all students, including those who are bilingual and those who have special needs. A fundamental assumption is that Expeditionary Learning works best in smaller schools where teachers have close relationships with students and decision making authority. A teacher–student ratio of 1:25 or less is assumed.

Expeditionary Learning is a comprehensive school design rather than a program within a school. Because the changes involved in implementing Expeditionary Learning are so radical, it is useful to have strong district support. Having a number of implementing schools (4–8 schools) in one district is one way to ensure that district commitment. It also helps establish Expeditionary Learning as a norm which can't easily be abolished.

Activities Sequence to Implement Design

Exploratory Phase. After districts and schools have expressed initial strong interest in the design, Expeditionary Learning staff will conduct a series of orientation experiences over a two-month period. More schools may begin the exploratory phase than will ultimately be selected as—or decide to become—Expeditionary Learning sites. An initial one-day community exploration will provide faculties with an immediate experience of the design and a good sense of local community resources for learning expeditions. Following that, a series of focus groups will offer teachers, administrators, parents, and students opportunities to grapple with the design principles and build consensus for becoming Expeditionary Learning schools. School teams should then visit existing Expeditionary Learning schools to see what they look like in action and to talk with teachers and administrators who are implementing the design.

One of the standards that Expeditionary Learning uses to assess compatibility is a demonstrated evidence of commitment to whole school implementation on the part of the great majority of the faculty and staff of the school. This evidence may take the form of a written commitment, signed by faculty and key members of the school community, or other clear signs of widespread and informed agreement. Another clear standard is the willingness and ability of the school and the district to invest the necessary time and resources in professional development not only for the transition years but for continuous improvement. During a summer planning institute, the key leadership teams from each district (including school-level personnel) and new school designers will deepen their understanding of Expeditionary Learning and map out the change process.

Implementation Year 1. The initial phase of professional development requires 15 to 20 days of professional development time for each member of the school faculty during the summer and school year. According to plans designed for each school, days will be clustered so that teams and whole faculties can begin to acquire the skills, strategies, knowledge, and beliefs necessary for full implementation of Expeditionary Learning. In addition, several regional conferences will provide opportunities for cross-site exchange and teacher dialogue.

Schools will also begin a relationship with a school designer, the primary link between the central Expeditionary Learning design team in Cambridge and the schools. Each School Designer works with approximately four schools, and is in each school about one day a week to support the implementation of Expeditionary Learning. School designers conduct professional development activities, problem-solve with teachers, foster school-level discussions about standards and assessment in an Expeditionary Learning context, and help administrators set professional development goals.

During the summer, all teachers will participate in a planning institute (5 days) and many will do a summit (5 days). The institutes will focus on designing learning expeditions and doing assessment of student work, and the summits will provide an immersion for teachers into a rigorous, intellectual learning expedition organized around one theme or topic.

If one school has or is building a ropes course in its gymnasium, or plans to use such courses already available in its community, at least some of the faculty should take ropes course training.

To get a vivid and personal experience of Expeditionary Learning Outward Bound educational principles, all faculty should have the opportunity to participate in traditional Outward Bound courses in the wilderness and in the city tailored to support implementation of the design. (See the above discussion of professional development for descriptions of these experiences.)

Implementing schools will also be connected to other Expeditionary Learning schools through an electronic mail server.

Implementation Years 2 and 3. As implementation continues in years two and three, districts will need to provide 20 days a year of professional development for each faculty member. By the second year, we expect all teachers to be doing expeditions.

Maintenance Years 4+. The maintenance years continue to foster the ongoing relationship between the Expeditionary Learning staff and the schools. This phase includes continued professional staff development of at least 10 days that supports the redefined role of Expeditionary Learning administrators and teachers (invitational expeditions; summer institutes; minisabbaticals; summits; conferences; Outward Bound wilderness courses). Teacher and administrator participation in these professional development activities is reduced, but faculty involvement in Expeditionary Learning exchanges with other schools is expected. Established electronic networks and *The Web* will support an ongoing dialogue with other Expeditionary Learning schools.

References

Conrad, D. E. & Hedin, D. P. (1983). The impact of experiential education on adolescent development. In D. E. Conrad & D. P. Hedin (Eds.), *Youth participation and experiential learning* (pp. 65–67). New York: Haworth Press.

Cousins, E. & Rodgers, M. (1995). Slaying the time giant: A discussion with Harold Howe II. In E. Cousins & M. Rodgers (Eds.), *Fieldwork: An Expeditionary Learning Outward Bound reader* (pp. 145-147). Dubuque, Iowa: Kendall/Hunt.

Cousins, E. & Rodgers, M. (1995). *Fieldwork: An Expeditionary Learning Outward Bound reader.* Dubuque, Iowa: Kendall/Hunt.

Fullan, M. G. (1991). *The new meaning of educational change.* New York: Teachers College Press.

Gandini, L. (1993). Educational and caring spaces. In C. Edwards, L. Gandini, & G. Forman (Eds.), *The hundred languages of children* (pp. 135–150). Norwood, NJ: Ablex.

Hahn, K. (1957). Origins of the Outward Bound Trust. In D. James (Ed.), *Outward Bound.* London: Routledge and Kegan Paul Ltd.

Hamilton, S. F. & Fenzel, L. M. (1988). The impact of volunteer experience on adolescent social development: Evidence of program effects. *Journal of Adolescent Research, 3,* 71–73.

Hedin, D. (1989). The power of community service, in caring for America's children. In F. Macciarera & A. Gartner (Eds.), *The Academy of Political Science, 37*(2).

Kolb, D. A. (1984). *Experiential learning: Experience as the source of learning and development.* Englewood Cliffs, NJ: Prentice-Hall.

Levy, S. (1995). *Something from nothing, a fourth grade expedition into economy, community, and history.* Cambridge, MA: Expeditionary Learning Outward Bound Monograph Series.

Newmann, F. M. & Rutter, R. A. (1983). *The effects of high school community service programs on students' social development.* Madison: University of Wisconsin, Wisconsin Center for Education Research.

6

The Modern Red Schoolhouse

Ron Heady
Sally Kilgore
Hudson Institute

The changes in economic and political life in the last half century require commensurate changes in what students are expected to know and be able to do regardless of where these students live geographically or the environment in which they mature (Finn, 1991; Marshall & Tucker, 1992). The skills needed both to participate in civic life and to compete in the marketplace of today and the next century are grounded in technology: The scientific advances that have affected and, in many ways, improved the quality of economic and political life have also created challenges and decisions about our lives together in this society that only a highly informed citizenry can effectively confront and solve.

Visit a modern, successful automobile plant and the knowledge and thinking skills needed by today's students become evident. Workers need to understand and apply statistical evidence, principles of energy, scale and structure, and systems theory. They must participate in making decisions and evaluations that allow them to respond effectively to the demands of the market. Managers and employees must have well-developed communication skills because diagnosing and solving problems are collaborative ventures. These kinds of knowledge and these levels of skill were not needed at an automotive plant 40 years ago. In fact, a great deal depends on the training of the average worker. Marshall and Tucker (1992) reported on the comparison between ordinary American and Japanese workers made by Motorola's director of education and training at a 1987 Congressional hearing:

> Well, almost every Japanese worker would be reading at the twelfth-grade level coming in. He could read that book [on quality control] and pass it on. Number two, they would be quite skilled in math. They would have been used to working in teams [in school] so it's not a change in style for them. And they have been given problems to solve throughout their secondary school education (p. 98).

Just as the marketplace requires much more of its participants than it did previously, so also does democracy require much more of its citizens. Numbers, percentages, and rates—the backbone of most current political debate—require that people be able to distinguish the relevant from the irrelevant, the reality from the propaganda. Environmental debates, arguments about changes in the economy, and the effects of educational programs are just a few of the areas where citizens face statistical and scientific data in assessing the consequences of where politicians would have us go as a nation. Citizens also need an appreciation of historical and scientific evidence to evaluate the performance of elected officials and the complex options faced in securing the public good. Finn (1991) reports on Tom Brokaw's interview of a U.S. Marine in the Arabian desert. "What had he known about Saudi Arabia before getting there, the anchorman asked. 'I never knew it existed,' the young serviceman replied with a grin" (p. 1). As Americans are thrust increasingly into international leadership roles, such ignorance will not serve us well.

As the demands of political and economic life changed in the last half century, educational institutions also changed, but they changed in ways that did not anticipate the needs of the 21st century. Throughout this century, as schools sought to accommodate increasing numbers of students with increasing differences in skill and preparation, policymakers reduced academic expectations for high school graduates. More and more non-academic courses were offered—some vocational, some personal relations, and yet others consumer-oriented training.

By the 1980s, most states required not more than one year of science and mathematics for high school graduation. (National Commission on Excellence in Education, 1983.) Almost 50 percent of course work was elective (Adelman, 1983). In the 1970s the fastest growing track of students was the "preparing for nothing" track, that is, the general track. As noted by many researchers (Adelman, 1983;

Cusnick, 1983; Oakes, 1985; Powell, Farrar, & Cohen, 1985),
general track students in the 1970s and 1980s in public schools
filled their high school days with consumer mathematics, personal
improvement courses, and with any luck, band or chorus.

These changes in public school curricula were driven by noble
purposes. We wanted more young people to stay in school beyond the
eighth grade; yet many of these youngsters' knowledge and skills did
not seem to promise great performance in academics. We wanted to
integrate a multitude of racial and ethnic minorities that often did
not have the same preparation for academic work as other students.
When students were not performing well, we lowered our expectations to make certain that everyone was on board. (Fortunately, this
long-term trend began to change in the 1980s.)

The Modern Red Schoolhouse seeks to keep everyone "on
board," but the strategy this design has adopted is different. Modern
Red Schoolhouse schools raise the academic expectations for all
students and change the way students are taught and the structure
of time available to learn—two elements of schooling that have
changed very little in the past two centuries.

In this chapter we discuss, first, the theory and vision that
serve as the foundation for the project. In the next section, we
describe the structure and processes associated with implementing
the design, using the reactions and experiences of our initial sites to
suggest the peaks and valleys that teachers and administrators
experience during the transition. In the third section (Initial Evaluation) we provide more systematic data on implementation and
student outcomes, and in the concluding section offer some reflections upon our experience and some projections about the future.

Theory and Vision

The Modern Red Schoolhouse is designed to take the virtues and
principles of the little red schoolhouse and make them work in
today's diverse, complex society. It is first, and foremost, a design
that shares across all schools a common set of academic standards
with a common set of assessments. It builds upon the traditions of
its namesake through its efforts to draw all adults in the community
into the life of the school. It also constructs a common culture among
adults and students who participate in that school—finding universal values in their different backgrounds.

The modern component of the design is found in the reconfiguration of time and the diversification of pedagogy, both enabling all
students to reach high academic standards. It is similarly modern in

its use of technology; in fact, advanced technology is an essential requisite to full implementation of the model, not only for instruction but for management of the school and management of instruction as well. Technology provides access to databases, such as stock markets and weather reports, for student analysis; it allows teachers across sites to communicate about instructional strategies, administrators to complete attendance records, and both teachers and administrators to evaluate the relative effectiveness of various instructional strategies.

The Modern Red Schoolhouse design encourages the elimination of age-limited grades where students, by virtue of the mere passage of time, march from grade to grade, year after year (Finn, 1991). Instead, Modern Red Schoolhouses focus on three divisions— *primary*, *intermediate*, and *upper*. The primary division covers the material in the traditional kindergarten through grade four; the intermediate division covers traditional grades five through eight; and the upper division spans the traditional grades nine through twelve. Students will progress toward mastery of the standards in each division at their own pace and in manners appropriate to their individual strengths and talents. The time it takes one student to pass through one division and into the next may be shorter or longer than the time for another student. Unlike some programs which emphasize individually-paced instruction, however, the Modern Red Schoolhouse focuses on all students' achieving rigorous academic standards and provides a system of formal assessments to both monitor and validate students' progress toward high achievement.

Six Tenets Form Basis of Design

The design for the Modern Red Schoolhouse rests upon six basic tenets which imply substantial changes in the practices and the application of resources within schools. Incorporating these tenets into the everyday practices of school requires shifts in the uses of time; modified expectations for students, teachers, administrators, and the community; clear parental or adult mentor responsibilities; and a continual and primary focus on high academic achievement for all students. The Modern Red Schoolhouse design strives to help educators and parents make these shifts occur. We discuss each of these six tenets below.

All Students Can Learn

All students can learn and attain high standards in core academic subjects. Children simply vary in the time they need to learn and the ways they learn best. The primary emphasis in every Modern Red Schoolhouse is on high levels of academic achievement for all students. If given the proper tools, appropriate learning experiences, high expectations, adequate time and encouragement, *all children,* with rare exceptions, can meet high academic goals. In the Modern Red Schoolhouse, mastery of subject matter is the only acceptable goal, regardless of a student's background, learning style, or pace. Different models of learning exist in various research traditions, and the Modern Red Schoolhouse tries to make use of these in appropriate elements of the design. As is evident by this basic tenet, we are changing three basic parameters in education: expectations, time, and pedagogy.

Expectations. Beginning as early as the work of Carroll (1963), researchers emphasized that the amount a student learns is partly a function of what is taught (coverage) and the effort a student expends to master the knowledge. In the 1980s, researchers focusing on the opportunity to learn found critical differences in learning outcomes to be a function of what was taught (Bryk, Lee, & Holland, 1993; Coleman, Hoffer, & Kilgore, 1982; Gamoran, 1992, 1987; Ogbu, 1974; Rosenbaum, 1976). Quite simply stated, not much was being taught to students in the 1970s primarily because students were not enrolling in academic courses. Opportunity to learn, then, begins with what one expects students to learn.

During the design phase of this effort, curriculum experts, national education leaders, and prominent researchers and practitioners collaborated with administrators and teachers from participating school districts to establish academic expectations for students at a Modern Red Schoolhouse. Using the College Board's Advanced Placement exams as initial benchmarks and borrowing heavily from other sets of standards developed in the recent national effort to reform America's schools, the participants developed content standards in English and language arts, history, geography, mathematics, and science for what are currently fourth grade, eighth grade, and twelfth grade—the major transition points for students in a Modern Red Schoolhouse. Subsequently, the design team added standards in foreign languages, health and physical education, and the arts (visual arts, music, and drama).

Four to five performance statements in each discipline establish the broad themes addressed at primary, intermediate, and upper divisions. For each statement, five or so standards specify what a student should know and be able to do. (These standards do not address the level of adequacy of performance; rather, that task has been addressed in developing the assessment system.) The following examples illustrate the form and the content of specific standards at the upper division.

- Mathematics—Each student understands and applies the concepts of instantaneous and average rates of change.

- Science—Each student understands and can apply knowledge of the following concepts in the physical sciences: matter, energy, physical and chemical change, motion and force, waves and light, and electricity and magnetism.

- English—Each student can draw on a broad base of knowledge about the great themes of literature—themes of initiation, love and duty, heroism, illusion and reality, salvation, death and rebirth, for example—and explain how these themes are developed in specific works.

- History—Each student can identify significant features of government and political process in the United States and can summarize the historical development of these features, including federalism, the rise of the party system, the presidency, and the electoral, legislative, and judicial processes.

- Geography—Each student understands the general dynamic of geographic movement and can predict the changes resulting from a major population relocation, an epidemic, a natural disaster, a media broadcast, or the transportation of raw materials and finished goods.

Although districts or individual schools may wish to increase requirements in any of the core subject areas, one of the most important commitments schools must make as they consider adopting the Modern Red Schoolhouse design is to accept the rigorous academic standards for all students. Both an immediate and a long-term implication of that commitment is determining a point or a time at which achieving mastery of the standards is a *sine qua non* for students' progressing from one division of the Modern Red Schoolhouse to another, from primary to intermediate, intermediate to upper, or for graduating from the upper division to the workplace or some form of higher education.

Time. For decades, time, classroom time in particular, has limited the amount that children could learn (Dreeben & Gamoran,

1986; Heyns, 1978). Students have been expected to learn material simultaneously with 30 to 100 other students. At the end of the designated time, instruction proceeded, even though learning may not have kept pace. Instruction in the Modern Red Schoolhouse is organized so that learning time can be tailored to the needs of individual students. Teachers, parents, and students work together to set the appropriate pace of instruction. Some students need and take more time to master certain standards than do others. Others need and take less. But in the Modern Red Schoolhouse, learning is the constant, and time is the variable. Concrete measurements of achievement and mastery will verify students' progress toward the standards. It may become necessary for some students and their parents or mentors to choose to depart from the Modern Red Schoolhouse without having attained mastery of the standards. Even these students, however, would take with them a report that documents the level of their proficiency and accomplishment in terms of the Modern Red Schoolhouse standards.

This component of the Modern Red Schoolhouse design recognizes that some students can learn more if they have, or if they take, more time to learn the material. Most important, there is a substitution effect: Many low-achieving students can match the achievement of more advantaged students if they expend more time and effort (Kilgore, 1993; Sørensen, 1987; Sørensen & Hallinan, 1977). The practices of tracking and ability groups acknowledge that students have different starting points; but seldom, if ever, do schools construct systems that require more time of students with low achievement levels. In fact, the general track structure led to requiring less, not more, time of low-achieving students (Oakes, 1985; Rosenbaum, 1976). The inevitable consequence is less and less learning for low-achieving students (Gamoran & Berends, 1987). The Modern Red Schoolhouse design works to change this common and frustrating dilemma.

The Modern Red Schoolhouse design requires schools to institute practices that allow some students to have more time and some students to proceed at a faster pace than others—a model of continuous progress. Building a system of continuous progress drives the reorganization of the school day, school year, and the development of curriculum. For monitoring the continuous progress of each student, the Modern Red Schoolhouse has developed an Individual Educational Compact (IEC), which also facilitates both responsibility (for the school, the teachers, and the students) and accountability. The IEC is an agreement negotiated by the student, the parents, and an advising teacher; it is an educational road map for the student over a specified period of time. IECs have three major functions: establishing measurable goals for the student; identifying the responsibilities of the parents and teachers in helping the student reach the Modern Red Schoolhouse standards; and identifying special assistance or services the student will need from school, parents, or community to achieve his or her goals. Initially the IEC, particularly in the primary division or elementary school, identifies short-term goals and is negotiated frequently. As both students and the Modern Red Schoolhouse sites mature, however, the IEC becomes more complex and covers longer periods of time. The IEC can be entered into a computerized system and a student's progress continually updated. At any time, students, parents, and teachers have access to a report of the status of the student's current work, achievement levels, progress toward the standards, and performance on both learning activities and assessment activities.

Even the amount of time spent in school may vary by student. Participating schools may be open for more hours than is common today; some students may come to school earlier than others or stay later. Class periods may vary in length, and individual teachers' schedules may vary from day to day. Similarly, the length of the school year may be greater for some students than for others.

Pedagogy. The third parameter we seek to change is pedagogy. Neuroscience research points to different learning styles of children (Damasio, 1994; West, 1991); research in cognitive psychology points to the need for a schema to which to attach new information or concepts (Resnick, 1987). The Modern Red Schoolhouse design calls for teachers to develop curriculum in discrete units, referred to as foundation units, that will over time provide multiple paths to the standards. Some units may rely more on visual applications to learn mathematics, for example, than current practices do. These emerging options provide teachers and students access to more variation in pedagogy than is currently available.

Educators have been limited often by a lack of technology and materials in the strategies they could use to help students master certain concepts. As developing Modern Red Schoolhouse sites increase their use of technological resources both for management and instructional purposes, many of them begin to rethink the methods, the materials, and even the locations they incorporate in their instructional strategies. Working from the premise that all students can master difficult concepts, but also recognizing that *how* they learn these concepts varies, teachers in Modern Red

Schoolhouses will make some substantial departures from their traditional practices. Geometry, for instance, even at the lower divisions of school, has generally been taught as a set of abstract rules. But a learning activity that focuses on simple machines can introduce some of the intricacies of geometry in the context of observable, easily manipulated materials and processes. An intermediate-level unit can examine these concepts at a more sophisticated level in traditional quilt patterns. And a unit at the upper level, ostensibly a fine arts unit, can focus on geometric principles in a study of Picasso and other cubists. Expecting mastery from all students requires a number of new ways of teaching, the direct participation and involvement of teachers in collaboration, and multiple paths to a stated destination.

Transmitting Culture

Schools should help transmit a common culture that draws on the traditions and histories of our pluralistic society and the principles of democratic government that unite us all. At the same time, children should understand the histories and culture of other nations and peoples.

When students graduate from high school, they should, of course, be able to read and write proficiently and know mathematics, science, English, history, and geography. But they should also have the discipline of mind and character to be contributing members of a democratic society. They should be able to advance an argument, foresee its implications, and understand counter-arguments. They must be willing to challenge their own and others' assumptions and be prepared for a lifetime of continual learning. American society offers great opportunity, but only to people willing and able to make difficult choices, accept individual responsibility, commit to a moral road map, and, on occasion, take intellectual and economic risks.

The curriculum of the Modern Red Schoolhouse, which includes a sequenced progression of mathematics, science, English and language arts, history, and geography, enables students to have a broad appreciation of the roots of American culture and cultures of other nations. In addition to the five core academic disciplines, the Modern Red Schoolhouse curriculum—across all ages—requires study of a foreign language, the arts, physical fitness, and health. The range and breadth of the curriculum ensures that a student will be able to put the required knowledge in the larger context of "life."

While individual schools develop specific themes, units, and lesson plans, they retain the consistency evident in the shared standards. Sites are encouraged to offer other subjects based on local preferences and the specific needs of their students. A Modern Red Schoolhouse site, for example, may develop and infuse into the curriculum a more extensive cultural focus that reflects its primarily Hispanic, African American, Native American, or other ethnic population. The overriding goal, however, is for all graduates of a Modern Red Schoolhouse to have the knowledge and skills they need to succeed in adult life. They should understand the essential elements of statistical evidence and the energy involved in chemical reactions. They will have read classical Western literature as well as literature from non-Western traditions. They will know how to evaluate historical evidence and determine the effects of technology on migration.

Grant (1988) and Glenn (in press) argued that effective schools have a history and moral purpose that give form and substance to the life of the school. The Modern Red Schoolhouse design calls for a conscious effort to encourage virtuous behavior in students. Although some people argue that schools should do nothing that promotes values, such an attitude is both impossible to practice and dangerous to advocate (Jackson, Boorstrom, & Hansen, 1993). Most schools encourage children to "take turns," a habit that is integral to making a school safe for children and one that reflects a value common to all Americans. Encouraging such behavior is, in fact, teaching about fairness; and other practices adopted by good schools teach something about the importance of learning, of self-discipline, of honesty. Ignoring such values is teaching something else: that dishonesty is acceptable, that learning doesn't matter, and that self-discipline is irrelevant. The question is really not *whether* values will be evident in school, but rather *which* values will live there.

In the Modern Red Schoolhouse, parents, teachers, and where appropriate, students are encouraged to identify those values that are most important to their community and, therefore, should be nourished by all those who are a part of school life. In so doing, schools develop (or elaborate upon) a history and tradition that calls all participants to a higher purpose.

A common culture, then, is built on two levels. First, across all schools, Modern Red Schoolhouse standards and curriculum give students access to the shared culture of Americans with all the diversity and complexity this implies. Second, the curriculum is built to reflect local priorities and values, many shared by most Americans, some unique to the history and traditions of that locale.

Organizing Instruction, Deploying Resources

Principals and teachers should have considerable freedom in organizing instruction and deploying resources to meet the needs of their students.

Teachers can inspire students, but they cannot be inspirational when they are constrained by mandates about classroom structure and teaching strategies. The Modern Red Schoolhouse implements a common-sense proposition: Principals and teachers know best how to educate students in their schools. While the Modern Red Schoolhouse design requires a curriculum with strong emphasis on the core academic subjects, teachers should be free to use instructional strategies that work for the children in their classrooms. School districts in which the Modern Red Schoolhouse design is being implemented have agreed to increased autonomy for project sites, particularly in the areas of decision making, personnel, and budgets.

Autonomy is important, we think, for all schools. Schools for instance, should be free to choose the services provided by districts and state offices. (Districts and states should, however, retain their rights to establish expectations for student outcomes.) Only when schools have the opportunity to choose other services will these larger institutions become responsive to school needs.

Like all NAS designs, the Modern Red Schoolhouse is committed to maintaining costs that are equivalent to current per pupil costs after the start-up period. To reach that goal, schools need to have greater discretion over their budgets. While district and state officers work with good intentions, the propensity to mandate some expenditures ignores the multiple paths to a stated objective. A school that houses, for instance, a social service agency with numerous social workers to serve students and their families may not need to hire another social worker with school or district funds. Yet state and district mandates can require just that. The Modern Red Schoolhouse design usually requires that schools hire a technology support person. That cost will either be added to the overall per pupil costs or absorbed by reallocating staff funds. A similar scenario can be constructed for funding of textbooks and altering school calendars or class schedules.

At the outset, the degree of autonomy that given schools have will vary, depending on their previous experiences with managing budgets and the districts' processes for providing autonomy. At the end of three years, however, most schools should have control over the essential elements of autonomy—staffing, curriculum, schedules and calendars, budgets, and acquisitions.

Staffing. Autonomy over staffing implies that a school will have control over recruiting and hiring new staff, evaluating and terminating staff, and assigning staff. Exactly how a school proceeds in building this autonomy will depend in large measure on where it is beginning. Changes in this area will require cooperation of both the teachers' professional association and the superintendent.

Curriculum. Both state and district offices have a number of requirements regarding curriculum that can be unnecessarily restrictive. The Modern Red Schoolhouse encourages districts and states to provide schools with expectations regarding what students should know and be able to do rather than with expectations regarding how many hours or Carnegie units a student should accrue in civics or mathematics. Teachers should be free to find ways to meet those expectations in the ways best suited to their students and should be held accountable for achieving those outcomes.

Schedules and calendars. Given the high academic standards expected of all students, Modern Red Schoolhouse sites need considerable flexibility in preparing their calendars and daily schedules. Before- and after-school programs, longer class periods, and increased preparation times are the most common needs that schools encounter as they begin implementation of the Modern Red Schoolhouse design. Lengthening the school year for teachers in order to allow for more professional development days is extremely valuable in the implementation period; it allows for teachers to work on new curriculum and minimizes the disruption of student learning. In the longer term, Modern Red Schoolhouse schools will often need to identify ways to expand the school year for at least some students. Chapter 1 (now Title 1) funds have been used to expand the academic year or school day in numerous districts. A number of states have altered the restrictions on funds for summer school to expand the number and type of students eligible for these programs. Implementing sites that have large gaps between Modern Red Schoolhouse standards and student performance will want to give high priority to expanding the time students have to work at school.

Budget. Within three or four years, all Modern Red Schoolhouse schools should have control over 80 percent of the per pupil funds associated with their school. So if the cost of schooling in a district is $5,000 per student, then a Modern Red Schoolhouse site should have control over $4,000 per student enrolled in that school, including teachers' salaries, building maintenance, kitchen services, and utilities. With this control a school may choose to purchase services, such as building maintenance, provided by the district administrative offices. But it is first and foremost a choice that the school makes. Similarly, though, if a school is able to reduce the cost of utilities, it should be able to reap the benefits of such savings. Budget autonomy should be acquired gradually, simply because the change is often substantial and the ability to manage so many new responsibilities can be overwhelming. Schools begin with areas where there are problems, where autonomy will actually improve conditions. Only then is it worth the effort.

Flexibility and Accountability

Schools should have greater flexibility in deciding how best to accomplish their mission and, at the same time, should be held accountable through regular assessment of student progress.

Decentralized decision making requires clear expectations of every participant in the educational process and requires accountability for meeting those expectations. Benchmarks for measuring the school's success must be available to community members. Modern Red Schoolhouses provide a variety of reports to their stakeholders. A student report, available to individual students and their parents or guardians, is linked to the IEC and contains information about the learning activities the student has completed, the progress the student has made toward mastery of the individual standards, and teachers' comments about the student's strengths, needs, and performance. A school report provides a "snapshot" of the school description, demographic information, unique and identifying characteristics, and other "vital statistics" of the institution. The Modern Red Schoolhouse also produces a community report, providing statistics and details of assessments, standardized measures, and other information that enables the community to determine how successful the school is in reaching its goal of high academic achievement for all students.

The Modern Red Schoolhouse design team and its national task force on standards and assessment faced a critical decision as it began designing this program: Did we want to rely upon existing assessment systems to verify that students have attained the high standards we advocate for all children? It was a question with tremendous cost implications—good assessment systems are expensive. The lessons of the past, though, were equally powerful: Instruction and assessment have to be mirror images. If we were to establish expectations for all students, then we had to have a way to know that students had met those and not some other expectations.

At the time the design team began this initiative, most professional groups were in the initial stages of standards setting. Only the National Council of Teachers of Mathematics had issued of a set recommended standards. (The National Geographic Society had issued a few years earlier some learning objectives that were quite useful.) Few national testing systems reflected these standards, much less those yet to be formed by other professional groups. It became painfully obvious that we would have to build our own standards, carefully keeping track of the work of the national professional groups. Similarly, if Modern Red Schoolhouse was to have high academic expectations, then Modern Red Schoolhouse needed an assessment system that reflected those standards.

Modern Red Schoolhouse's national task force deliberated for almost a year and then sought bids for developing the assessment component of the design. The task force selected from among three bidders Advanced Systems, a testing company in New Hampshire seasoned with experiences from several reform initiatives. Advanced Systems recommended a balanced approach to assessment that included both traditional and authentic methods of assessing students' mastery of Modern Red Schoolhouse standards.

Each division—primary, intermediate, and upper—has what we refer to as a Watershed Assessment which consists of two parts. The traditional component is five subject exams, one in each of the five core academic subjects: each exam has forty multiple choice questions and eight open-ended questions. Capstone units, the second part, incorporate performance-based assessment activities.

The subject exams differ from many standardized tests in that they are constructed as criterion-referenced tests to be administered only when teachers anticipate that a student can demonstrate mastery of a given subject area. If we know that a student is not ready to succeed on the exam, then we do not need to administer that exam just to establish failure. We expect, on the basis of this procedure, that a high proportion of students will pass these high-stakes exams which students must complete before they move to another division in the Modern Red Schoolhouse program. These secured exams are available for students to complete approximately three times a year. Advanced Systems "grades" and maintains the records for the exams. Modern Red Schoolhouse teachers serve on advisory boards that oversee the development and revision of these exams.

Capstone units constitute the authentic portion of the Watershed Assessment. They are both units of curricula and a means of formal assessment. Like the subject exams, students complete them when prior performance suggests they are ready. Typically, they are interdisciplinary units that bring a student to full mastery of a number of standards in a division and require a culminating project that enables the student to demonstrate that mastery. Both learning activities and culminating projects in these units reflect real-world applications of knowledge: building bridges, assessing environmental conditions, reporting on historical events, developing and evaluating solutions to hypothetical or real problems. Developed under the direction of an advisory board composed of teachers at Modern Red Schoolhouse sites, the capstone units are available at any time for teachers to use with students. As many as 12 capstones are needed for each division (primary, intermediate, and upper). Teachers evaluate student performances in the units, an evaluation that is used in assessing whether a student has successfully mastered the material in one or more academic areas. The culminating projects from the various capstone units become the basis of the student's portfolio. Working with the information derived from student performances on the capstones, teachers, in collaboration with students and their parents or adult mentors, decide when students are prepared to be successful in completing one or more subject area exams. The portfolio from the capstone units and the results of the subject area exams together complete the student's Watershed Assessment.

Having chosen this system of assessment, the Modern Red Schoolhouse program remains consistent with research evidence as well as the emerging trends in assessment systems. The more traditional component, subject area exams, will provide highly reliable information grounded in what teachers actually expect of their students, information that is easily understood by parents and the public about what students know. The less traditional component, the capstone units, will provide rich and visual evidence, generally quite compelling, of what a student is able to do. The instructional management systems recommended by the Modern Red Schoolhouse design can store video, audio, and textual information from student projects as part of a student portfolio. With all of this information, students should be able to demonstrate not only their mastery of core academic subjects but also their special talents and skills.

This system of assessment should benefit students in at least two ways. First, they will have a variety of ways to demonstrate knowledge and will have the ability to recall and use that knowledge in a variety of contexts in their adult lives. Equally important, graduates of a Modern Red Schoolhouse school will come to represent something special as they enter the work force or pursue further education. Their portfolios will represent strong assurances of sophisticated knowledge and the ability to use it in real-world situations. We are confident that employers and institutions of higher education will be hungry for graduates of Modern Red Schoolhouses; the assessment system is critical to creating the awareness of what Modern Red Schoolhouse students can do.

Technology Critical

Advanced technology is a critical requisite to attaining high quality education in cost-effective ways.

Success and survival in the 21st century require students to be familiar with today's computers and telecommunications technologies. Schools need to incorporate this technology to operate efficiently as well as to prepare students for the world of work and living.

Over the life of the Modern Red Schoolhouse project, each teacher, administrator, and professional staff member should receive a computer, networked with other computers in the building. Sites should also upgrade telephone, voice-mail, and e-mail capabilities. These arrangements result in improved access to parents and other teachers. For students, the target is a ratio of one computer for approximately six students in the classroom. The number of students per computer, however, may vary according to age. There may be more computers available to upper-division than to primary-division students, for example, because of the older students' greater ability to pursue independent learning. Students and teachers should also have access to a variety of other technologies (CD-ROM or other electronic databases, interactive multimedia, distance learning capabilities, video production and editing hardware) that will enhance learning and facilitate productive use of time. The use of technological resources, like core virtues and work force skills, will be integrated into the academic curriculum, not relegated to isolated classes. Students engaged in active learning and performance activities will use technological resources to create products that demonstrate their mastery of target skills and concepts.

Technology also augments the impact of teachers' efforts and allows for more options in instructional strategies. For example, technology is essential to the objective of abolishing the limits that time places upon teachers and students in most of today's schools. Because communication between teacher and students should be possible at almost any time and from almost any location, productive interaction between teacher and student is not restricted to time in the classroom. Technology allows more individualized instruction by providing systems to track student progress and diagnose weaknesses and by serving as an instructional resource for students.

Taken as a whole, essential technology in the Modern Red Schoolhouse consists of a set of hardware and software "tools," or supports, that are part of one or more of the following: a computer/ data network, a voice system, or a video system. These systems can interact or stand alone and are, in turn, supported by ancillary activities such as training, maintenance, and upgrading.

Such technology systems will help students, parents, teachers, and administrators put Modern Red Schoolhouse design elements into action in an effective and productive manner. While it is technically *possible* for a school to implement the Modern Red Schoolhouse design with only rudimentary and traditional technology (e.g., blackboards, overhead projectors, motion picture projectors), the attempt to do so would, at the least, be a great struggle. For example, although individual education contracts *could* be managed and updated by paper and pencil, this process would certainly prove slow, inefficient, and error-prone. Instead, the proposed technology tools for the Modern Red Schoolhouse are fast, efficient, and secure.

To that end, we encourage schools that become Modern Red Schoolhouse sites to work toward a system that *at a minimum* contains the following types of technological systems and supports:

Data System (Schoolwide Local Area Network and Computer Workstations). Each school is cabled to support a local area network (LAN) that links all instructional, resource, and administrative computer workstations throughout the school and provides access to outside databases through telephone modems.

Each classroom or subject-based instructional area contains at least four networked, student-based computer workstations and one teacher-based multimedia workstation connected to a large screen projection device. In addition, each classroom contains a printer and CD-ROM player networked within the classroom, as well as easy access to VCR and laser disc players.

Each student has a computer-based Individualized Education Compact which can be accessed from any workstation in the school and from the home or community via modem.

A wide array of software and multimedia courseware is available with some loaded on the workstation hard drives (i.e., decentralized), while other pieces are accessed from the network file server (i.e., centralized).

Various management functions, such as attendance and grades, are transmitted electronically from the classroom to the office on the LAN; e-mail is available to school personnel and students.

Telephone/Voice System. Each classroom is equipped with a telephone that has voice-mail and security capabilities.

The school operates a telephone helpline and other voice systems for both school and home communications.

Network modems provide access to outside databases.

Video Capabilities and Distribution System. Each school is cabled and equipped for classroom viewing of cable television and satellite distance learning instructional programming.

Each teacher has ready access to a laser disc player and VCR or is connected to these through a central video distribution system.

Each teacher has ready access to a video camera and each school has in-house video production capabilities: student-produced videos are shown within the school and on local cable stations.

Other Technological Supports. A comprehensive staff development and support program exists, including initial training, as new technological tools are made available, and daily technical assistance; full- or half-time on-site support should be available.

A large collection of software and technology-based courseware is available that supports the attainment of world class standards.

Subject-specific technology equipment and software exist, including probeware and other specialized equipment in science rooms, computer-assisted drafting (CAD) software and tools in vocational arts, MIDI software and tools in music, calculators for math classrooms, and additional computers and productivity tools in business education courses.

Resources such as a fax machine and laser printers are centrally available to teachers, administrators, and students.

A plan for making technology more accessible in homes and throughout the community is developed.

It is tempting to say this technology apparatus is desirable, but unrealistic. We think that position greatly compromises the quality of education any system can provide young people. Schools vary in the speed with which they acquire this technology, the priorities they give to some types of capabilities, and specific elements in the three systems. However, the general capacities are expected to emerge at all schools choosing to become Modern Red Schoolhouse sites.

Attending School by Choice

Schools should be places where students and staff members choose to belong.

Students should attend a school by choice, not by assignment. We expect this opportunity for all students attending a Modern Red Schoolhouse. (Each participating school, of course, complies with any existing court orders regarding racial composition or other features of the student body.) Preferences may be given in ways that allow siblings to attend the same school or ensure that students who live close to the school can enroll there. Beyond those concessions, however, the schools should rely upon a random process for admitting students who want to attend.

Similarly, a strong program is possible only with the support of a vast majority of staff at the school. Teachers at prospective Modern Red Schoolhouse sites must reflect and deliberate carefully. Only with the support of the principal and nearly all of its teachers should a school begin planning for the implementation of the Modern Red Schoolhouse design.

This aspect of the project presents daunting challenges in some locations. As with some of the other design elements, however, small steps provide the basis for significant change. In one Modern Red Schoolhouse district, students may request to transfer from their geographical attendance district into a Modern Red Schoolhouse site. In another district, teachers who did not wish to participate in implementing the design were permitted to transfer to other schools in the corporation.

Implementation

Six elementary schools began implementing the Modern Red Schoolhouse design in 1993. Two middle schools and one high school began implementation in 1994. Four elementary school sites were selected to be May '95 sites, indicating that they would complete implementation of all design elements by May 1995. By the fall of 1996, approximately 25 schools will be at some stage of implementing the design.

Our general approach to initiating and sustaining change, along with the specific experiences and reactions of teachers and students at the initial nine sites, follows.

Training and Organization

At present, many administrators, principals, board members, teachers, and representatives of community agencies are not prepared adequately to assume the kinds of roles and responsibilities required of a truly autonomous organization. The participants in this process receive training and coaching from consultants, Modern Red Schoolhouse design team members, and representatives from sites that have progressed further along the learning curve. For each element of the design, handbooks and personal consultations provide prototypes, specific examples from other sites, and evaluations to task force members as they develop their own plans for implementation. Schools vary in what they do, how they do it, and when they do it. Variations, though, always require that certain general principles are met. For instance, the Modern Red Schoolhouse design provides specific steps for implementing the principle of continuous progress for all students. Schools may vary in the specific practices that they utilize, but all variations must move the school closer to practices that reflect continuous progress.

The general strategy for school change is one we have come to call guided choice. The only fixed and nonnegotiable aspects of the design are the standards and the assessment system. (All other elements are designed to facilitate students' meeting those standards.) A model of guided choice addresses an enduring dilemma of organizational change: Practices that are dictated by a reform agent are seldom sustained because they are not "owned" by the participants. Yet, leaving teachers and administrators free to choose almost anything introduces an unrealistic burden—the time it takes to search for the practice that is best for them. Guided choice reduces the amount of searching that teachers must do before they can make a decision by providing prototypes, evaluations of various software, and examples of how other schools have applied general concepts. By putting teachers and administrators in charge of decisions, the strategy increases the amount of ownership of the design, and thus its sustainability, by placing school staff at the helm (March & Simon, 1958; Senge, 1990). This process is intended, then, to provide a realistic strategy for enduring change.

Interestingly, the issue of sustainability was tested, quite accidentally, at several initial sites. When times were seemingly tough, teachers understandably complained. Often, administrators at participating sites offered them the opportunity to quit and return to their previous practice. In each instance, teachers said, "No, we never want to go back to our old practices." Instead, they voted to continue the process.

Although schools can use different structures or can modify existing structures, sites generally have organized six task forces composed of administrators and teachers at the site to guide the implementation of the Modern Red Schoolhouse. In addition, a leadership team is formed with the principal and the chairs of the task forces (Community Involvement, Curriculum, Organization and Finance, Professional Development, Standards and Assessment, and Technology). Other teachers, staff members, or parent and community representatives also may serve on the leadership team.

This group coordinates the activities of the task forces and assumes general responsibility for implementation of the project. Some districts have identified a Modern Red Schoolhouse project coordinator to assist all the sites in their efforts. Other districts have named a Site Coordinator, who coordinates activities and confers with participants in the various divisions throughout the district. In one district, the Site Coordinator has arranged for leadership teams from the elementary, middle, and high school to meet quarterly to share experiences and discuss common problems and concerns. Two of the most positive results of these meetings have been the increased appreciation for the special challenges and efforts teachers at different educational levels face each day and early recognition of the importance of communication and articulation among the sites.

The Modern Red Schoolhouse design team members and expert consultants provide initial and ongoing training to participants at each site. Leadership and communication skills, coping with change, and strategies for productive and effective meetings are some of the earliest topics addressed by training staff. Week-long summer institutes provide teachers with training in pedagogical strategies and guidance in developing and revising curriculum.

At the end of the second year of the design's implementation, participants were selected from implementing sites for the Modern Red Schoolhouse National Faculty. These people, nominated by their colleagues, design team members, and consultants, have assumed a variety of responsibilities reflecting their individual strengths and talents. One important contribution they have made is to the training of staff at new sites; the national faculty members have been able to provide specific examples of implementation strategies and adaptations made at their sites, thereby enhancing the ability of new Modern Red Schoolhouse teachers to envision design elements in practice at their schools.

Most schools engage in an initial period of preparation and planning; the length of time can vary, based on the readiness of the school to begin implementation. Both a self-evaluation and an audit of the school conducted by a design team member establish the readiness level of the site. Because schools are expected to build upon their previous accomplishments, the paths they take will be different depending on those accomplishments.

The major task for the site during its planning period is, after thoughtful and serious analysis, to prepare a schedule that will bring the site to full implementation of the design, ideally within three years. Both the size and the level of the school affect this schedule; some changes required for complete transformation to a Modern Red

Schoolhouse are more difficult and complex for large schools than for small, for secondary schools than for elementary or primary sites.

Initially, a process of guided choice can be frustrating to teachers, especially those at the elementary level. One teacher, recalling the first year of implementation, said, "I kept wishing you'd just tell us what to do. We'd just do it." Frustration can be high if organizational skills are not developed, one reason for our substantial emphasis on leadership training during the planning phase. By the second year, though, teachers are almost uniformly grateful for the discretion required by this design. Learning curves differ across schools, as do priorities and "baggage." We try to provide training and opportunities for reflection that minimize the growth pains.

Curriculum

In most instances, Modern Red Schoolhouse sites give the development of curriculum their primary attention in the first year of implementation. At sites where the Modern Red Schoolhouse is currently "in process," one of the first changes that marks the beginning of a transformed approach to schooling is the introduction of a new organizational unit for the curriculum, the foundation unit. Teachers at the site, working collaboratively in grade-level teams, subject-area teams, or departments, develop the foundation units they will use.

Conceptually, each foundation unit begins with the identification of content standards that the unit will address. Particularly at the lower levels in a division, foundation units do not lead to *mastery* of specific standards, but the objective of every unit of instruction should be directed *toward* mastery of clearly identified standards. The foundation unit comprises performance objectives for the unit as a whole, learning activities that engage students directly in the content of the "lessons," and assessment activities that enable teachers, students, and parents to determine student progress toward the standards. (See Fig. 6.1 for an overview of a foundation unit.) Successful completion of a foundation unit reflects *accomplishment* rather than *time spent.* Each unit reflects mastery of specific skills and knowledge embodied in the standards of the Modern Red Schoolhouse.

Within certain guidelines, teachers in schools that are implementing the Modern Red Schoolhouse are developing foundation units independently. As more schools join the project, however, and as the technological support systems near completion, a number of foundation units for each subject or set of standards will exist and will be accessible by more teachers and more sites.

Figure 6.1

Components of a Foundation Unit

- Modern Red Schoolhouse standards for which a student is preparing
- Specific performance objectives for unit
- Activities and instructions for the classroom teacher
- Student's plan of work
- Learning Activities
- Culminating Activity
- Self-Assessment
- Assessment objectives and scoring rubrics
- Information and advice for parents or adult mentors
- Essential resources
- Helpful references

Although foundation units may be either single-subject or interdisciplinary, most units will in fact address standards from more than one subject area. A primary unit on simple machines, for example, is essentially a math and science one, but it also pertains to some of the English and language arts standards (selecting and reading a text for information, summarizing it, and connecting new information to prior knowledge). Each learning activity in the unit requires students to manipulate a simple machine and to conduct basic scientific investigations into the nature of the machine, its characteristics, its properties, and its relationships to other simple machines. As a culminating activity for the unit, after learning about each of six simple machines, students must solve a variety of classroom (move an apple from a table to a chair) and real-world problems by selecting and using the machine best suited for a specific purpose. Students explain and justify their choices; others evaluate the effectiveness of the demonstration. In time, multiple units will address any given standard, providing alternative pedagogies. Foundation units, combined with technology, address the fundamental parameters of change for a Modern Red Schoolhouse site: expectations, time, and pedagogy.

Primary sites usually adopt the guidelines of the Core Knowledge Foundation in developing their foundation units. Consistently across all sites, teachers, parents, and students have been highly enthusiastic about the curriculum, materials, and activities used in its presentation. Students were pivotal in this response: Their enthusiasm for learning about ancient civilizations, legends and stories from many countries, and important aspects of American history was contagious. Parents and teachers noticed the new enthusiasm for school and learning. Many parents reported that their children's determination to attend school was at an all time high and their interest in talking about what they were learning in school was almost tiresome. One parent commented that the long explanation of the digestive system delivered at the dinner table may have been somewhat too detailed for the rest of the family.

The enthusiasm and excitement students have carried home with them reflect some of the dramatic changes that have occurred in their classrooms. The Core Knowledge curriculum focuses on a coherent, sequential progression of specific knowledge shared by all children. Students from the Bronx to suburban Indiana have embraced the study of ancient Egypt, myths and legends from African, Asian, European, and American cultures, and topics in measurement, geometry, optics, and astronomy. Much of the curriculum is presented in an integrated, interdisciplinary manner, is conducted in learning groups and at learning centers both in and out of the classroom, requires active student participation in the learning activities, and results in authentic student work derived from the topics of study.

Middle and high school teachers have also begun to discover that the creation of foundation units is not just another sterile exercise in curriculum revision. The thoughtful, goal- and product-oriented thinking and planning necessary for the production of a meaningful and effective unit has led to both increased engagement and increased achievement for many students. Because of a multiplicity of factors, older students, particularly those with a history of failure and noninvolvement and who are not "graduates" of Modern Red Schoolhouse primary or intermediate sites, are less apt to embrace learning as eagerly and joyously as are younger children. The two middle schools currently engaged in implementation, however, have made considerable progress in reviewing their curricula and creating single-discipline, interdisciplinary, and thematic foundation units in all subject areas, addressing the majority of the Intermediate Standards. The first Modern Red Schoolhouse high school began implementation with students entering at the ninth grade and will expand the project annually as the initial cohort of students progresses through the school. Teachers continue to revise and enhance the curriculum throughout the second year of implementation.

Students in Modern Red Schoolhouses are now learning about societies and cultures from around the world, both past and present. They study the early civilizations in the Tigris and Euphrates region; the Ottoman, Aztec, and Incan Empires; feudal civilizations in Europe, China, and Africa; and the modern cultures of Africa, the Americas, Asia, and Europe. Historic and present-day cultures are studied in an integrated fashion. One upper-level history unit, for example, begins with introductory learning activities that lead students to make generalizations about the importance of water as a basic need for individual human survival and for the survival of larger groups and communities. These introductory activities provide opportunities for the development of the main topic of the unit, early civilizations, their location in Eastern Hemisphere river valleys, and their dependence on water resources for their development. References throughout the unit to the importance of water resources in the Middle East as well as to both cities and ranches in the American West today, and to historical struggles for control of warm water seaports, create a context for the study of ancient history that relates it directly to the world of the present.

Another upper-division foundation unit focuses on the American Civil War but also leads students to reflect on all wars. By approaching the American Civil War from the perspective of "How It Came, How It Went," the unit elicits student awareness of both the proximate and the distant causes of the war. Student activities include using primary as well as secondary sources, creating matrices that visually link the well-known events preceding the war with the various attitudes and stands taken by the major participants, and relating skills and knowledge probably gained in their English classes with the historical temper of the times. One of the culminating activities provides the opportunity for students to investigate the distinctions between "just" and "unjust" wars and to relate those concepts and characteristics to the two opposing sides in this particular war.

Implementing sites have made varying progress in their incorporating the work place and character components of the design. One small community using Modern Red Schoolhouse design principles in its schools established a community-wide character education component. As part of that effort, a direct-mail survey to all community residents generated a 15 percent response rate. Of those who responded, most of whom were either parents of school-age children or senior citizens, 95 percent supported all 25 of the traits on the survey (citizenship, cooperation, courage, courtesy, integrity, responsibility, and respect, among others). This Modern Red School-house demonstration district is in the process of incorporating discussions of good character and activities promoting work force skills into individual units of instruction. Students are not evaluated on their mastery of character traits or work force skills; they are, however, provided multiple opportunities, in the context of academic learning, to develop the habits of "heart and mind" that characterize positive, productive, contributing citizens in a democratic society.

Technology

Technology acquisition usually proceeds in an incremental fashion. At the end of the first year, at least one computer, networked with others, was in place in each classroom at the pilot sites. Several sites have now considerably expanded their technological resources: One has placed a networked computer with CD-ROM capabilities in each classroom, and teachers there have access to e-mail; another site has placed a telephone in each classroom and teachers have voice-mail and a homework line; another school has redistributed computers formerly housed in a lab to create minilabs in classrooms. Teachers and the design team continue to work to place foundation units into the instructional management system. Table 6.1 provides an illustration of the implementation schedule adopted at one of the pilot sites.

Students have been quick users of the computers in their classrooms. They have used the computers in preparing reports and illustrations, used special programs for selected subjects, and completed assessment activities on line. Teachers who had developed online testing systems reported that students wanted more exams. Obviously, some of this infatuation with computer technology (and exams) may be a novelty effect. Yet, it is clear that students clearly feel comfortable using the technology and easily maximize its usefulness in learning activities.

A comprehensive instructional management system can hold a student's IEC, generate a calendar of assignments, report performance on previous assignments, "grade" assessment activities stored in the system, record the student's score, and update the cumulative report. As the network and wiring become more sophisticated, the management system can be linked directly with other hardware and software resources, thus connecting the student directly with the specific materials and information designated in foundation unit

Table 6.1

Sample Modern Red Schoolhouse
Technology Implementation Timeline

	Years 1–2	Years 3–4	Year 5
School-based Planning/ Oversight	School-based technology committee formed; teacher usage, equipment inventory, and implementation plan developed	Committee monitors installation, training, and usage	————————>
"Classroom" Equipment	Install LAN including data, voice & video cabling, file server(s), operating software, and network modems/ supporting phone lines	Maintain LAN	————————>
	100% of classrooms receive teacher-based multi-media computer with presentation monitor and printer	Acquire additional needed computers	————————>
	40% of classrooms/subjects receive student computers equaling 1:6 student ratio	80% of classroom/ subject areas receive student computers, 1:6 ratio	————————> 100% in year 5
	Acquire peripheral supports (e.g., video cameras, scanners, laser disc players to equal 1:10 teacher ratio	Acquire additional peripheral supports to equal 1:7 teacher ratio	————————> 1:4 teacher ratio
	Additional phones acquired equaling 1:10 teacher ratio	Additional phones, 1:5 ratio	————————> 1:1 ratio
Other Equipment	Administrative/ office equipment (e.g., fax, laser printer)	Media center collections placed on LAN	General access lab(s) equipped/upgraded and hooked into LAN
		Satellite and cable equipment installed	Acquire in-house video production equipment
	Establish maintenance contracts or other in-district support	Ongoing maintenance contracts/support	————————>
Software	Acquire software: IMS, MIS, e-mail, integrated productivity tools, and instructional packages	Ongoing software review and acquisition	————————>
Training/ Support	Identify funds to hire school-based technology coordinator/trainer	Continue/expand school-based coordinator	————————>
	Provide for initial "basic" training for all school personnel	Ongoing basic and advanced training	————————>

learning activities. One activity in an intermediate-level science unit on plate tectonics, earthquakes, and volcanoes, for example, identifies a laser disk program as an essential resource. In another activity, students use a computer program to locate the epicenter of an earthquake. When networking at this site is completed and the instructional management system fully installed, a student who has called up this lesson can "go" directly to the laser disk player and watch the designated program; "move" on to the computer simulation; complete a comprehension "check quiz," have it graded, and see any errors or deficiencies, all without leaving the workstation.

Four of the six elementary pilot sites have acquired most of the technology needed to support all facets of the Modern Red Schoolhouse design. The foundation units have been entered into the instructional management system and are available in every classroom. The information required to generate individual, school, and community reports is also maintained in the system, although all these reports are not produced on a regular basis as yet (state mandates require other types of reports which at this point would mean duplication of effort). Teachers have received training in using the system to produce IECs, and at least one teacher began last year generating these documents for some students in her classroom. Construction work at this and several other Modern Red Schoolhouse sites has caused delays in bringing all the technology "on line"; in addition, wiring older buildings for local area networks, improving the phone systems, and acquiring the necessary hardware can be quite expensive in many areas. But districts and sites that have joined the Modern Red Schoolhouse project have all made commitments to making these investments in technology. Individual sites continue to implement design elements, even when they do not possess "state of the art" technology to support their efforts; as more resources become available to them, they integrate the advanced technology into their programs.

Assessment

In the mature Modern Red Schoolhouse, students progress from one division to the next only after they have demonstrated mastery of the content area standards for that level. The foundation units are designed to initiate the continuous assessment necessary to verify students' progress toward mastery. Depending on an individual student's pace, but generally near the end of the course of a division-level curriculum (the fourth year), a student will begin completion of *capstone units*. Satisfactory completion of foundation units and capstone units along with the products from the capstones indicates that a student has achieved mastery of the division-level standards and is ready to take the subject area tests, which serve as final verification of the student's mastery of content knowledge. The portfolio of work from the capstones (and other examples of student work if so designated by the student and teachers) and the subject area tests compose the Watershed Assessment, the student's "passport" out of the current division and to the next level.

Teachers at individual sites construct their own foundation units, but both capstone units and subject area tests are produced by testing experts and curriculum consultants. All students will complete the same capstones and subject exams, ensuring consistency and validity of the Modern Red Schoolhouse curriculum. Both capstones and subject tests have been piloted with groups of students in several sites. Teachers and students alike report very positive experiences with the capstones. After completing an intermediate-level capstone entitled "American Originals," students commented that they had both "learned from" and "enjoyed" the unit. These eighth–grade students articulated specifically the skills and concepts they had used: analyzing poems, short stories, and films; comparing social tensions during different periods of American history; realizing that artists are sometimes historians. Seventh graders who had completed "Adaptation or Extinction" felt that the "combination of work and fun" was exciting. A seventh-grade science teacher reported that one boy, fairly disaffiliated prior to beginning his work on this capstone, became so engaged in the project that he ventured back to the public library from which he had been banned because of destructive behaviors, explained why permission to use the library again was important to him, was reinstated as a library patron, and completed his work at a fairly high level of proficiency.

During the third year of implementation, students usually complete capstone units on the basis of their readiness, rather than in the large group settings used for the pilot experiences. Topics covered on the capstones include construction, myths and legends, rain forests, and patterns at the primary level; American originals (in literature, art, film, and music), adaptation, and war at the intermediate level. Curriculum consultants continue to confer with high school teachers about topics, subjects, and administration practices most suitable to these activities in the upper division. Forms of the five subject area tests were piloted in 1994. The process of equating the forms of each exam and of establishing cutoff points for performance levels continues through 1995–1996.

Organization

Implementing changes in the traditional organization of the school has been more difficult to accomplish than some of the other goals sites set for themselves. Each participating school, however, has made some progress in this area. Hansberry Elementary School in the Bronx has developed an exemplary community involvement program, which includes after-school and weekend tutoring sessions conducted by teachers in locations throughout the community, parent fairs and workshops, and community mentors. Hansberry and several other elementary schools have created multiage groupings and have arranged for teachers to stay with the same group of students for more than one year. One of the secondary sites has begun detracking in two of the core subjects and is struggling now with the challenge of providing appropriate learning opportunities for all students in the classes. Teachers in all sites have flexibility in the choice and use of instructional materials and methods. One elementary school in a district which has always operated under the principle of mass textbook adoption has been given control of the funds allotted to it for basal readers and will use the funds to purchase materials suited to the wide range of its students' needs.

Some types of instructors, such as tutors, may work outside of the regular school hours or during the summer. Depending upon the size and type of school, initial transitions may be either dramatic or quite modest in scope. Some elementary schools have made almost wholesale changes to incorporate the Core Knowledge curriculum and materials. At the upper divisions, change is less likely to be so drastic. At an implementing high school, the science department has restructured a class required for current incoming ninth graders. Students meet in a variety of settings (lecture, laboratory, small-group discussion and collaborative projects) on a rotating schedule.

Initial Evaluation

Student, teacher, and parent surveys were administered in the spring of 1995 at all elementary sites and are available to assess the status of implementation of the Modern Red Schoolhouse design.

Student surveys were administered to students who were nine years old or in the fourth grade, depending on the current organization of the school. The student survey included items on school climate, classroom practices, and their engagement with school; 80 percent of the student population responded to the survey.

The teacher survey was administered to teachers at all elementary sites and had a 75 percent response rate. Teachers' items covered their understanding of various Modern Red Schoolhouse concepts, the level of implementation of various aspects of the design, their estimated impact on student achievement, classroom practices, and evidence of students' engagement and learning.

The parent survey was piloted as a convenience sample; we have 184 completed questionnaires from parents at the elementary sites and 52 from middle school sites.

The comments that follow in the sections below are based largely on the surveys completed at the May '95 sites. These four elementary schools were in urban, small town, and suburban settings. Taken together, approximately 50 percent of the students in these sites represent minority groups; most are from moderate- to low-income families; and approximately 25 percent had enrolled in the program just as they entered the third grade. Approximately 80 percent of the teachers have been at the schools since the inception of the Modern Red Schoolhouse initiative.

Understanding the Design

Given the structure of implementation around task forces, teachers initially became experts on one element of the design. After attending a summer institute, nearly all of them had, also, extensive exposure to curriculum development and options in classroom practices. We would expect then, that all teachers should feel comfortable with their understanding of the curriculum component, but that knowledge and comfort of other elements of the design would diffuse somewhat unevenly. Assessment and technology should be second only to curriculum in widely diffused understanding among staff. Community involvement and autonomy are likely to be the last, in that much of that activity progresses with partial staff involvement.

Figure 6.2 shows teachers' responses regarding their level of understanding of various concepts in the Modern Red Schoolhouse design. As the figure indicates, teachers felt most confident about their understanding of Modern Red Schoolhouse standards (70% said "well" or "very well"), Core Knowledge curriculum (80% said "well" or "very well"), and foundation units (80% said "well" or "very well"). Most teachers, then, feel confident in their understanding of the academic goals of the project and the curriculum structure used to achieve those goals.

In certain aspects of curriculum, though, teachers expressed less confidence: approximately 60 percent felt confident of their understanding of the concept of continuous progress, 43 percent of their understanding of the incorporation of work force skills, and

Figure 6.2

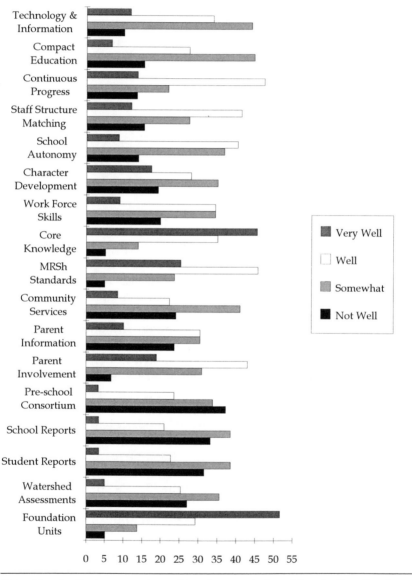

Modern Red Schoolhouse Teacher Survey on Understanding Concepts, Spring 1995

Note: Bars indicate percentage of teachers out of n = 90 selecting the degree of confidence response options.

45 percent in their understanding of the character development component.

Teachers felt decidedly less confident about their understanding of the assessment system—Watershed Assessments, student reports, and IECs. Two factors explain the lower level of confidence. First, only certain teachers at each site have been involved in piloting the Watershed Assessments. For instance, the capstone units and subject exams are most commonly used when students are about nine years old at the elementary sites. In addition, implementation of the reporting systems and IECs were slower than even we anticipated as we struggled not only to get the reports functioning within the larger computerized system, but also, in some cases, to get the technology installed. The student reporting system, in particular, requires that teachers enter data to generate the reports, and in May 1995 most teachers were still learning about the general design of the instructional management system that generates these reports.

As will be evident in the subsequent discussion, these sites will focus on assessment in the 1995–1996 academic year, and the design team is reviewing alternative strategies for implementing these components of the assessment system.

Given the normal apprehensions that teachers have about technology, we were surprised to find that only 10 percent of the teachers felt that they did not have a good understanding of technology and information networks. Approximately 45 percent said they understood this design element "well" or "very well." While all teachers were required to complete basic training on the computer, training in certain areas, such as the instructional management system, has been restricted to approximately one-third or one-fourth of the staff (usually one member from each teaching team).

In terms of school organization, approximately half of the teachers felt that they understood school autonomy "well" or "very well." Those items related to community and parent involvement suggest a similar level of understanding. More than 60 percent felt that they understood the principles and practices associated with parent involvement "well" or "very well." In the case of such things as the pre-school consortium, levels of confidence were decidedly lower (28%).

In summary, then, teachers feel most confident about their understanding of the curriculum component of the Modern Red Schoolhouse design. Their confidence with the assessment system is not strong and suggests an important focus for our future support and assistance. Areas of technology, community involvement, and school autonomy, while lower than the area of curriculum, are not out of sync with where we would expect teachers, in the aggregate, to be at this stage.

Level of Implementation

Figure 6.3 shows the response of teachers at May '95 sites to questions regarding the level of implementation of the various Modern Red Schoolhouse concepts at their respective sites. In large measure, their responses tightly track the level of understanding they reported in earlier items. In terms of standards and curriculum, 80 percent of the teachers say that the standards are fully or largely implemented, and 93 percent say the same about the Core Knowledge curriculum. For other aspects of the curriculum (e.g., work force skills and character development), teachers report less complete levels of implementation. To say that the curriculum is largely completed, though, would be misleading. We view curriculum development as an ongoing process. Developing a curriculum that allows all students to attain the academic standards of the Modern Red Schoolhouse is not a one-time endeavor. Like all professional endeavors, it is a continuing process. Instructional strategies are revised when students appear to falter. Content may change to reflect new discoveries in science or new avenues to illustrate guiding principles. Teachers will find that continuous progress in curriculum requires continued reflection on what students are and should be learning. Collaborative work among teachers and proper technological support make that endeavor feasible and often gratifying.

Continuous progress, an essential element of curriculum structure, has—according to teachers—a modest level of implementation. Forty-four percent perceive it to be largely or fully implemented; 36 percent view it as moderately implemented. Reports from student surveys allow us to triangulate data on the implementation of continuous progress. Two indicators of continuous progress are available from the student survey: reports on how much students think they are learning in school and the degree to which they find themselves bored. The evidence is somewhat contradictory. When students were asked (*yes/no*) whether they were learning a lot in school, 98 percent responded "yes." In terms of specific subjects, mathematics and reading were the areas where a large percentage (81% and 74%, respectively) of students said they were learning "a lot." Yet 35 percent reported they were bored most of the time.

Regardless of the level of implementation of the concept of continuous progress evidenced from either teacher or student surveys, the management team at the Modern Red Schoolhouse considers this goal as yet to be realized. Unlike, though, the

Figure 6.3

Modern Red Schoolhouse Teacher Survey on Level of Implementation, Spring 1995

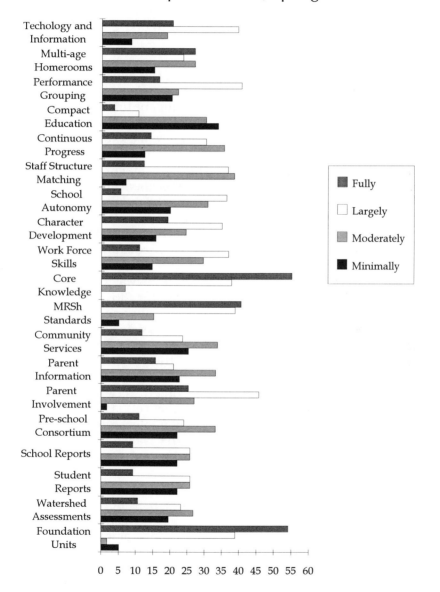

Note: Bars indicate percentage of teachers out of n = 90 selecting the degree of confidence response options.

weakness in the assessment system (which should have been implemented more extensively by May 1995), the weakness we perceive in realizing continuous progress is not, in our mind, alarming. For teachers accustomed to traditional classrooms, continuous progress requires substantial changes in classroom practices. For them, especially, it is important to take steps slowly with high rates of success.

Impact of Design on Student Achievement and Behavior

Just to say that teachers are actually implementing a design is less than satisfactory. (Although considering the time frame in which schools were required to work, the accomplishments of teachers at Modern Red Schoolhouse sites have been remarkable.) It is important to ask: What do teachers think it has done for students? What do state test scores tell us, even at this early stage?

Teachers were asked, for each key element of the design, to evaluate its impact on student achievement: Did it, in their estimation, have a "very positive effect," "some positive effect," "no effect," "some negative effect," or a "very negative effect"? Teachers were most uniform in their conclusion that the Core Knowledge curriculum had had a "very positive effect" on student achievement. Similarly, the development of foundation units was thought to have had a "very positive effect" by 56 percent; another 36 percent thought that they had had "some positive effect." Fifty-one percent of the teachers thought technology had had a "very positive effect." The Modern Red Schoolhouse standards were thought to have had a "very positive effect" by 39 percent of the teachers; another 49 percent identified "some effect." Interestingly, 30 percent of the teachers saw parent involvement as having a "very positive effect," and 54 percent saw it as having "some effect." Understandably, elements of the design that are not fully implemented (Watershed Assessments) or that are external to the classroom (school autonomy) are seldom seen by teachers as having very positive effects on student achievement.

Teachers were also asked about the extent to which certain student behaviors had improved in the past year: attendance, discipline, and engagement. Uniformly, teachers saw improvement in student engagement with learning. Improvements in student behavior (i.e., discipline problems) were more likely to be reported in urban areas (primarily because discipline problems had been initially quite low in suburban and small town schools). Similarly, teachers in urban areas reported improved attendance more often than did others. Statistically, the only significant change in attendance was in an urban school that began with an attendance rate that moved from 83 percent to 89 percent over the two-year implementation period.

In terms of student achievement, the most consistent effect at all May '95 sites was the increase in the proportion of students meeting the essential skills level in state testing: three out of four May '95 sites schools had an increase. The mean achievement scores were consistently improved in the lower grades for all elementary sites; the upper grades were more mixed. At one site, the increases were quite dramatic. Over a two-year period the percentage of students at Hansberry (The Bronx, New York) meeting the essential skills in reading went from 22 percent to 58 percent, and in mathematics that change was from 47 percent to 82 percent. These early data suggest that the Modern Red Schoolhouse design is successful in raising expectations, as well as achievement, for lower-achieving students.

In the spring of 1996, nine-year-old students will complete a modified NAEP exam, providing us with the first comparison data with national reference points. During the baseline year, nine-year-old students at these sites were administered a NAEP-like exam. The results from the spring examination can then be compared to the baseline performances in 1994 as well as to data on national and state-level performances.

Reflections and Anticipations

Two major challenges confronted all May '95 sites: acquiring equipment on schedule and gaining autonomy. Equipment delays were most common in urban areas where decisions in large district bureaucracies tend to be completed in a slow and cumbersome manner. Security considerations in one urban system further complicated installation and support of the required equipment. These delays had further repercussions on two elements of the design in particular: the student reports and the IEC. All of the urban schools lack either sufficient technological resources or sufficient data in their instructional management systems to generate the reports. Most IECs, as a consequence, were merely piloted once before the end of the academic year.

The issue of autonomy remains a difficult element of the design. When one superintendent resigned, we faced special challenges as new administrators considered whether or not they would support the autonomy agreements. Even when there was strong support at the district level, neither district administrators nor school administrators comprehended the full implications of what autonomy could and should be. Thus, it was common to find schools limited to district-wide textbook acquisitions or securing district approval on the content of their professional development proposals and their requests for equipment purchases while the district administration gave honest and full support to the principles of autonomy.

Finally, some challenges were school specific. At one school, teachers and students became so enamored with the Core Knowledge curriculum that teachers decided that nothing needed to be done to prepare their students for the mandated state assessment. Predictably, their test scores dropped. At another school, an entirely new leadership team was selected by an administrator without consideration of the heavy investment in leadership training and team building in the previous year.

A persistent challenge faced by the design team is how to help school staff focus on the general principles (such as continuous progress) rather than on the specific practices that serve as examples. Educators tend, understandably, to gravitate toward specific practices—multiage grouping, cooperative learning, project learning—with too little regard for the larger objective or principle at work. For instance, in trying to provide schools with specific practices that lead to the principle of continuous progress, we have often reinforced the natural propensity to focus on practices, not general principles. Without careful calibration of the training, we can be left with an empty shell of practices and no understanding of the intent, and thus, no capacity to introduce meaningful and adaptive changes. For schools to succeed as adaptive organizations, the staff must be able to evaluate specific practices in terms of larger goals, the type of professionalism that must be embedded in any sustained school change.

Nearly all of the challenges faced in these initial years have remedies in reconfiguring either the design or its implementation. However, two situations that create these challenges seem fairly intractable. First is the instability of district administrators. Second is the cost of technology in older sites. Changes in administrative leadership predictably delay progress in implementation as both community groups and central office officials await endorsement by a new leader. Old buildings with outmoded wiring substantially increase the cost of implementing the Modern Red Schoolhouse design, which requires both new wiring and a local area network.

As part of continued NAS scale-up activities as well as independent initiatives, approximately 40 additional sites have expressed interest in adopting the design. Consistent with the Modern Red Schoolhouse performance to date, the interested sites represent urban, suburban, and rural schools, as well as a broad array of socioeconomic and ethnic populations. As a new design, we seek to expand slowly and deliberately to ensure a high success rate.

References

Adelman, C. (1983). *Devaluation, diffusion, and the college connection: A study of high school transcripts 1964 to 1981.* Washington, DC: U.S. Department of Education.

Bryk, A. S., Lee, V. E., & Holland, P. B. (1993). *Catholic schools and the common good.* Cambridge, MA: Harvard.

Carroll, J. B. (1963). A model of school learning. *Teachers College Record, 64*(8), 723–733.

Coleman, J. S., Hoffer, T., & Kilgore, S. (1982). *High school achievement: Public, Catholic, and private schools compared.* New York: Basic Books.

Cusick, P. A. (1983). *The egalitarian ideal and the American high school.* New York: Longman.

Damasio, A. R. (1994). *Descartes' error: Emotion, reason, and the human brain.* New York: Putnam.

Dreeben, R., & Gamoran, A. (1986). Race, instruction, and learning. *American Sociological Review, 51*(5), 660–669.

Finn, C. F. (1991). *We must take charge.* New York: Basic Books.

Gamoran, A. (1992). The variable effects of high school tracking. *American Sociological Review, 57*(6), 812–828.

Gamoran, A. (1987). The stratification of high school learning opportunities. *Sociology of Education, 60*(3), 135–155.

Gamoran, A., & Berends, M. (1987). The effects of stratification in secondary schools: Synthesis of survey and ethnographic research. *Review of Education Research 57*(4), 415–435.

Glenn, C. (In press). Effective schools. . . and beyond. In R. Ginsberg and D. N. Plank (Eds.), *Commissions, reports, and reforms: Fashioning educational policy in the 1980's and beyond.* New York: Praeger.

Grant, G. (1988). *The world we created at Hamilton High.* New York: Basic Books.

Heyns, B. (1978). *Summer learning and the effects of schooling*. New York: Academic Press.

Jackson, P. W., Boorstrom, R. E., & Hansen, D. T. (1993). *The moral life of school*. San Francisco: Jossey-Bass.

Kilgore, S. B. (1993). The organizational context of learning: framework for understanding the acquisition of knowledge. *Sociology of Education, 66*(1), 63–87.

March, J. G. & Simon, H. A. (1958). *Organizations*. New York: Wiley.

Marshall, R., & Tucker, M. (1992). *Thinking for a living: Education and the wealth of nations*. New York: Basic Books.

National Commission on Excellence in Education. (1983). *Nation at risk*. Washington, DC: U.S. Government Printing Office.

Oakes, J. (1985). *Keeping track*. New Haven, CT: Yale.

Ogbu, J. (1974). Social stratification and the socialization of competence. *Anthropology Education Quarterly, 10*(1), 3–20.

Powell, A. G., Farrar, E., & Cohen, D. K. (1985). *The shopping mall high school*, 233–308. Boston: Houghton Mifflin.

Resnick, L. (1987). *Education and learning to think*. Washington, DC: National Academy Press.

Rosenbaum, J. E. (1976). *Making inequality*. New York: Wiley.

Senge, P. (1990). *The fifth discipline*. New York: Random House.

Sørensen, A. B. (1987). The organizational differentiation of students in schools as an opportunity structure. In M. T. Hallinan, (Ed.), *The social organization of schools* (103–129). New York: Plenum.

Sørensen, A. B., & Hallinan, M. T. (1977). A reconceptualization of school effects. *Sociology of Education, 50*(4), 273–289.

West, T. G. (1991). *In the mind's eye: Visual thinkers, gifted people with learning difficulties, computer images, and the ironies of creativity*. Buffalo, NY: Prometheus.

Reform at All Levels
National Alliance for Restructuring Education

Robert Rothman
National Alliance for Restructuring Education

The National Alliance for Restructuring Education is dedicated to transforming the American education system so that all young people reach high standards of achievement. Although that statement may seem simple, it represents a profound challenge.

At its heart, the challenge is twofold. First, it means transforming the system from one that sorts students onto divergent tracks to one that sets high expectations for all and enables all but the most disabled youngsters to perform at levels as high as those expected anywhere in the world. Second, it means redesigning the system— school, district and state, as well as community and public support— to make such a transformation possible.

The idea of common high standards for all students is a new one for American education. For decades, the United States has operated an insidious tracking system, one that sets high expectations for performance for some students and low expectations for the rest. This system has to change if all young people are to lead fulfilling, productive lives in the 21st century.

Time was when young people could get a job that paid well with a minimal level of literacy, but that time in many places is long past. This trend, moreover, threatens the American democratic system. In recent years, the gap in earnings between those who are well educated and those we have failed to educate has been accelerating fast. If this continues, the stage will have been set for the kind of social division that could end our democracy altogether. None of this is hyperbole. More than ever before, a great deal depends on abandoning the idea that only a few can learn and then building a society that expects high levels of achievement for all its members—and does what it takes to enable young people to meet those expectations (Marshall & Tucker, 1992).

The National Alliance is dedicated to bringing about such a transformation. Formed in 1989 by the National Center on Education and the Economy, the Alliance is a partnership of states, school districts and national organizations that work together to change the education system at all levels—school, district, and state. The Alliance is helping by providing tools and models, professional development, and technical assistance to educators, local leaders, and policymakers for implementing changes in their community.

These changes affect virtually every aspect of the way people at each level do business, from the standards they set for students and the way they measure progress toward achieving the standards to the way learning and teaching takes place, to the services and supports available to children and families, to the way parents and the public support schools, and to the way school systems are organized and managed.

This agenda is broad, but the Alliance partners believe that achieving the goal of enabling all young people to meet high standards of performance takes rebuilding the entire system. As reformers are well aware, the United States education system has tried many kinds of reforms. The literature over the past two decades alone is replete with examples of well-intentioned programs and policies, from computer-assisted instruction to finance equalization to vouchers and much, much more. But little seemed to change. The system seemed to swallow change as easily as a child swallows ice cream. The schools that were successful with the students who needed them most were the work of brilliant, dedicated renegades. The system, endlessly patient, would eventually wear them down and spit them out (Odden, 1991).

Moreover, as reformers have found, factors outside the education system also have a profound effect on student and school success. Students spend most of their day outside of schools, and many of them face problems—such as poor health and nutrition, violent environments, and lack of parental engagement in their schoolwork—that impede their ability to achieve in school. At the same time, the public, which pays the taxes and elects the school boards and sends children to schools, also has a strong voice in deciding what happens within school walls.

Where to begin? The Alliance is convinced that reform begins and ends with standards—what we expect students to know and be able to do. The hallmark of its agenda is the Certificate of Initial Mastery (CIM), a credential that will be awarded to students who demonstrate they have met certain high standards of accomplishment in academic subjects and applied learning. These standards are derived in part by determining which countries' 16-year-old students perform the best in various subject areas and then by making sure the standards match those of the high-performing countries. The CIM takes the abstract idea of high standards for all and turns it into a concrete proposal. All Alliance partners have embraced the notion of a CIM being developed by the Alliance and its sister organizations, New Standards and the Workforce Skills Program of the National Center on Education and the Economy. By establishing a CIM system and committing themselves to ensuring that all students attain a Certificate by the time they leave high school, Alliance partners are reshaping their entire systems—the curriculum, the instructional program, the accountability and assessment system, the school organization and structure, the supports they provide students, and just about everything else (Workforce Skills Program, 1994).

Thus, the Alliance is looking at changes beyond the school. To be sure, the Alliance is deeply concerned with changing what happens in classrooms and in schools; that is where children are educated. But the Alliance is equally concerned about what happens in district offices and state departments of education. Changing schools without changing the central offices is like changing a company by retooling a factory without addressing headquarters. It will not work.

In addition, the Alliance is deeply concerned about community factors as well. It is interested in creating a web of supports and services for children and families, and in engaging parents, guardians and the public in the education of their children. Because the problem is larger than the schools alone, the solution must encompass entities outside of schools, as well.

Finally, the Alliance has been committed from the outset to a strategy for bringing its restructuring effort to scale. The Alliance partners never merely intended to create a few good schools; the United States already is home to some of the finest schools in the world. The challenge is to create systems in which good schools are the rule, not the exception. There is no example of a state or large school district where that is the case, as far as the Alliance partners are aware. So the Alliance is committed to creating systems in which large numbers of schools routinely produce students who achieve at high levels. As New American Schools enters Phase III, which is focused on scaling up the reform effort, the Alliance has assumed a special role. The goals the Alliance had from its inception become important when the focus is on going to scale.

A New Organization for a New Type of Reform

Starting with the point of view that what was needed was creating a system of high-performing schools, the National Alliance in its initial proposal to New American Schools set out an agenda that was comprehensive in breadth and scope.

The substantive breadth of the Alliance work is represented by five design tasks. These tasks (spelled out in detail in the next section) represent the unifying conceptual structure within which the work of all the Alliance's participants is organized:

Standards and Assessments

The Alliance is setting common high standards of achievement for all students in the core subjects and using the most advanced assessment techniques available to assess accurately progress toward those standards. The standards emphasize basic skills and go beyond; they demand mastery of academics but also require that students be able to apply what they learn to complex, real-world problems.

. . . but high standards and new forms of assessments will only result in more sophisticated ways to measure student failure unless something changes in the classroom, so . . .

Learning Environments

- The Alliance is giving teachers the curriculum building blocks they need—tied directly to the new standards—so they can design engaging, demanding instructional programs that will enable every one of their students to reach the new standards.

  . . . but new curriculum will make no difference unless teachers have access to professional development resources to develop the skills they need to deliver that curriculum effectively, so . . .

- The Alliance is building a national and regional professional development system around the new standards and new curriculum ideas.

  . . . but if instructional technology continues to be tied to the old curriculum and ways of teaching, students will not benefit, so . . .

- The Alliance is enabling students to use the new information technologies as powerful tools for getting information they need, analyzing it and displaying it in ways that greatly extend their learning power. The application of technology is harnessed directly to the curriculum, which in turn is tied to the new standards, all working in harmony to make sure that students can reach the new standards.

    ... but if schools continue to pay attention only to students who are headed for four-year colleges and ignore the others, then we will continue to fail more than half of all youngsters, so . . .

- The Alliance is involving the schools, colleges and employers in collaborative development of opportunities for young people to develop the skills they will need to pursue rewarding careers and go on to further education and training when school is finished.

    . . . but many of our children are growing up in circumstances that make it all but impossible for schools by themselves to get these children to the high standards they will have to meet, so . . .

Community Services and Supports

The Alliance is redesigning the way health and social service programs work so they can more effectively support youngsters in trouble and their families, enable the people responsible for those programs at every level to work hand in glove with the schools so that every community can make better use of the scarce resources these youngsters so badly need.

. . . but it is dreaming to believe that all these changes could be made if nothing changes in the state department of education and the school district central office, so . . .

High Performance Management

The Alliance is restructuring the organization and management of schools, school districts, and state departments of education and the policy systems in which they do their work by adapting state-of-the-art, high-performance management and organizational practices developed by the best American firms.

. . . but we can do all of these things and still fail miserably if the American public does not support these changes, so . . .

Public Engagement

The Alliance is helping its members find better ways to reach out to the public, listen hard to what people are saying, and engage the public in dialogue about what the goals of schools should be and how they should be achieved. Only when this happens, and when parents are fully engaged in the education of their children, will the public be there when it counts.

These five design tasks can be thought of as the horizontal dimension of the Alliance's conceptual structure. But there is also a vertical dimension—it extends from the school through the district and community to the state. District and state structures and policies must change radically to ensure that large numbers of schools, not just a relative few, routinely produce high levels of student performance. Only if the goals, policy structures and practices of these three levels of government are mutually reinforcing can the job be done.

The Alliance partners represented a set of states and school districts already committed to the agenda laid out in the 1986 report of the Carnegie Forum on Education and the Economy, *A Nation Prepared: Teachers for the 21st Century.* Marc S. Tucker, the president of the National Center on Education and the Economy, who had directed the Carnegie Forum, in 1989 invited these jurisdictions— the school districts in Rochester, New York; Dade County (Miami); San Diego; Pittsburgh; New York City and White Plains, New York, as well as the states of New York, Washington, Arkansas, and Vermont—to work together, because they all agreed they could make more progress together than any one could on its own. By the time the Alliance submitted its original proposal to New American Schools in 1991, New York City and Dade County had withdrawn, and Kentucky—a state whose reform law was written with the strong influence of David Hornbeck, director of the National Alliance— joined the partnership. The first director of the Alliance, Michael Cohen, meanwhile, left to serve as an advisor to Secretary of Education Richard Riley, and wrote the Clinton Administration's Goals 2000: Educate America Act.

In the first year, the Alliance agreed to work with 12 schools in three jurisdictions: 3 in Kentucky, 3 in Vermont, and 6 in Rochester. In 1993–1994, the Alliance added an additional 44 schools: 3 in Arkansas, 12 more in Kentucky, 4 in Pittsburgh, 6 more in Rochester, 5 in San Diego, 9 more in Vermont, 8 in Washington state, and 2 in White Plains.

In 1995, the Alliance expanded dramatically. The Alliance jurisdictions chosen to be part of Phase III of New American Schools— Kentucky, Pittsburgh, San Diego, and Washington state—have selected 10 percent of the schools in their jurisdictions, with the goal of transforming 30 percent of their schools over three years. The jurisdictions vary; in Kentucky, the Alliance is working in 11 school districts; in Washington, 5 school districts, including Seattle and 4 neighboring districts; in San Diego, 2 clusters of schools; and in Pittsburgh, the entire city school district. In addition, the Alliance will also work with the non-New American Schools jurisdictions of Arkansas, Rochester, and White Plains, as well as the Milton Hershey School, a K–12 school in Hershey, Pennsylvania, and new jurisdictions. In all these sites, the Alliance is working with schools that represent a broad range of social, economic and school conditions—urban, suburban, and rural, from preschool to high school.

The Alliance organized itself to help ensure that all of the design tasks were addressed and truly implemented at each level. Each school designated a leadership team, whose members were responsible for each design task. These team members became the school's representatives to Alliance workshops and conferences, thereby helping to ensure that each professional development opportunity builds on the previous ones. The school design task leads, in turn, designated network leaders who would be responsible for the program at the district level, and a site coordinator was named to oversee the program at the site level.

In addition to lining up state and district partners and designating lead schools, the Alliance also enlisted a broad range of national organizations whose contributions are essential to the outcome. No single organization could possibly amass all of the skills and capacities needed to address the full range of this agenda under one roof. The Alliance has not tried to do so. It has asked instead what organizations have established leading reputations in their respective fields in the areas addressed by the Alliance agenda and sought them out as "non-site" partners. These partners work along with the Alliance central staff in Washington, DC to develop tools, models, and strategies in the various design tasks, to prepare conferences and workshops, and to deliver technical assistance on site.

The Alliance nonsite partners are: Apple Computer, Inc.; Center for the Study of Social Policy; Harvard Project on Effective Services; Jobs for the Future; High Performance Management Program of the National Center on Education and the Economy; Learning Research and Development Center (LRDC) at the University of Pittsburgh; National Board for Professional Teaching Standards; New Standards; Public Agenda; Texas Industrial Areas Foundation; University of Southern California; Workforce Skills Program of the National Center on Education and the Economy; and Xerox Corporation.

Bringing together these partners has proven beneficial both to the schools, districts, and states in the Alliance and to the national organizations themselves. The site partners gain access to the extraordinary expertise and experience the nonsite partners can offer, and the nonsite partners can work together to accomplish far more than any could alone. For example, the Alliance has combined the instructional technology resources of Apple with the research on student learning produced at LRDC and is developing a powerful tool for assisting teachers in creating standards-driven instructional units that employ technology as a means of enabling students to learn.

With this structure in place, the Alliance formed a strategy for implementing its design. Unlike many other school reform efforts which are focused on one or two "lighthouse" schools, the National Alliance from the outset sought a way to reach large numbers of schools and systems. That meant that it was not possible for the Alliance staff to essentially live in the schools, as lighthouse efforts can afford to do. Nor could the Alliance rely on the each-one-teach-ten trainer of trainers model, which tends to result in the degradation of the ideas two steps away from their source. In place of those approaches, the National Alliance sought a new way, which would employ lighthouse techniques on a mass scale (Little, 1993; McLaughlin & Marsh, 1978).

With that goal in mind, the Alliance employed a number of strategies, all centered around what is commonly called professional development. In essence, all of the Alliance work is professional development, but not in the way the term is customarily used. Rather, the idea is to build local capacity to lead and implement the design.

To accomplish this goal, the Alliance's professional development strategy contains a variety of elements. One key component is a series of national conferences to provide awareness and knowledge of the five design tasks and to get commitment to the broader agenda. These national conferences are supplemented with on-site technical assistance by the Alliance staff and helping partners.

The conferences do not simply present information to partici-pants. Each meeting is preceded by a concept paper intended to ground the participants in an overall conceptual framework that will guide the work to follow. In many cases the nonsite partners prepare tools or strategies, such as New Standards portfolio systems or school-to-work resource kits, that focus the work of the conference. The meetings begin with a presentation on the materials. Then the teams from the sites meet to discuss the materials and divide up their members so that all the concurrent working sessions will be covered. In some of the concurrent sessions, teams are asked to send a representative other than the person who has lead responsibility for that topic. After the concurrent sessions, the teams reassemble to pool what the members have learned. At other times, concurrent sessions are organized by role type—teachers, principals, central office people, state level staff, business leaders and so on.

All the sessions are organized as work sessions, though there are plenty of opportunities for teams from different places to share their approaches with one another. Mostly, though, each session is organized around a task, something that must be accomplished for the teams to take a next step that they view as important. Every meeting concludes with the teams' creating a plan for what they will do for the next two to three months, a very specific plan, with assignments. Among other elements, the plan indicates how the site will use the information from the concept paper and tools and strategies to provide professional development for their colleagues at their schools and sites.

One example of this series was a conference on school-to-work, held in Seattle in April 1994. For that conference, the Alliance brought together school and business people from each Alliance site, and had presentations from virtually all of the leading programs in the field from around the country. The conference put special emphasis on the role of elementary and middle schools in this area by providing numerous models of elementary and middle school school-to-work efforts to show educators from those levels, who often feel that they have no part in school to work, that their role is essential. To take one example, Sally Hampton, then of the Fort Worth Independent School District in Texas, outlined the effort of a school there in which primary grade students plan and organize a class project, including application for "grants" from the district for supplies. (Hampton is now the New Standards managing director for English language arts.)

The meeting really opened many people's eyes. They began to see the way school to work can be infused throughout a school career and beyond, and the relationship to standards. One example illustrates the point: Following the conference, at least two different local business groups—from San Diego and Washington state—went ahead, on their own, and forged new coalitions to help coordinate and govern all the school-to-work activities in their communities. The conference helped them appreciate that only a coordinated effort would be effective, and they agreed to form such efforts from scratch.

As the Alliance moves into Phase III of New American Schools, with a focus on scaling up the design, the professional development strategy will necessarily shift. Because of the expanding number of schools with which the Alliance is working, and because the Alliance recognizes that implementation of the design can only take place in schools and districts, the center of gravity will move from large national gatherings to professional development focused at the site itself. The new strategies are discussed next.

Organizing Framework: The Five Design Tasks

To provide a framework for its ambitious reform agenda, the Alliance divided the work of restructuring education into five design tasks. These five tasks—standards and assessments, learning environments, community services and supports, high performance management, and public engagement—represent the full scope of activities needed to change a system (see summary in Table 7.1).

Yet at the same time, the five design tasks—not ten, not fifteen—provide a focus for the restructuring effort. Alliance partners have found that concentrating their work on these five elements enables them to coordinate their efforts and move forward more quickly. To take one example, when the Woodland Middle School in Taylor Mill, Kentucky, began its restructuring effort in 1992, the school staff formed a total of 35 committees to take on nearly every conceivable task. In practice, however, only a few teachers and parents actually did the work of the committees, and they soon became overworked. Regrouping, the school team streamlined the structure by creating eight committees, renamed task forces, and aligned them with the Alliance design tasks. Teachers were each assigned to only one task force, and they divided their responsibilities so that staff members would be aware of what a broad range of their colleagues were doing. As a result, the school has been able to make great strides in transforming its curriculum, instruction, and school organization, and these changes have paid off in large gains in student performance.

Standards and Assessments

If the goal for the Alliance is to enable all students to reach high levels of performance, then standards—the level of performance we expect—and assessments—how we determine if students have met the standards—are critical. If done properly, though, standards and assessments do more than measure student performance. By setting clear, visible targets for performance, standards can help students achieve at high levels by providing them with models of what good performance looks like. Likewise, stimulating and engaging assessments can improve student learning, not just measure it, by providing students with tasks that challenge them to use their knowledge (Rothman, 1995).

Table 7.1

The Alliance Design Tasks

Design Task	Major Components
Standards and Assessment	• Performance standards—what students should know and be able to do in core subjects
	• Performance assessments, portfolios
Learning Environments	• Redesign of curriculum and instruction around standards for performance
	• Incorporation of technology into instructional program
	• Integration of applied learning (skills for workplace) into academic program
Community Services and Supports	• Collaborative governance, including schools, community agencies, parents, elected officials and others
	• Outcomes for children, youth, and families
	• Identification and development of services and supports to achieve desired outcomes
	• Creation of financing methods based on achieving desired outcomes
	• Professional development for workers across systems
High Performance Management	• Leadership development
	• Redesign of school districts and state departments of education
	• Results-based strategic planning
Public Engagement	• Assessment of community goals and expectations
	• Strategies for communication and enlisting support
	• Strategies for engaging parents in the education of their children

In carrying out the Standards and Assessments task, the Alliance has relied on the partner with whom it has a particularly special relationship, the New Standards Project, now called New Standards. New Standards was created by Marc Tucker, the president of the National Center on Education and the Economy and the founder of the Alliance, and Lauren B. Resnick, the director of the LRDC at the University of Pittsburgh. It is a national partnership that currently includes 17 states and six city school districts.

New Standards has moved rapidly on its agenda. In the fall of 1994, a reference examination in mathematics, which asked students to solve complex mathematical problems and communicate their results, was administered to some 50,000 elementary and middle school students. A portfolio assessment in math and in English language arts, in which students' classroom work during the course of a year will be judged against high standards for performance, was piloted in the 1994–1995 school year. And in June 1995 New Standards produced draft performance standards in English language arts, math, science, and applied learning that indicate what students should know and be able to do, how well they should know it, how they can demonstrate that they know it, and samples of student work that exemplify these standards.

The Alliance has played an integral part in the development and implementation of the New Standards system. Teachers from all Alliance schools took part in New Standards task development and scoring workshops. Their participation helped New Standards by providing a cadre of able professionals committed to their agenda. The workshops helped advance the Alliance agenda as well. By all accounts, these were valuable professional development experiences, since they gave teachers the opportunity to study high-quality student work, discuss it with their colleagues, and consider how to reorganize their own instructional program to enable students to produce similar work.

Likewise, all the Alliance elementary and middle schools administered the New Standards reference examinations in mathematics in 1994, and all piloted the portfolio assessments in math and English language arts in 1994–1995, thus providing a substantial base to enable New Standards to demonstrate that these assessments could be carried out on a large scale. But these experiences, too, have done more than most workshops to transform teachers' practice in these schools. In many ways portfolios are as much instructional tools as assessment instruments; they allow teachers to enable students to engage in a variety of tasks, all geared to high standards for performance. Participating in New Standards has provided opportunities for hundreds of teachers in Alliance schools to have this experience and learn about it.

The Alliance will play a key role in refining the performance standards that New Standards produced in draft form in 1995. A key element of the refinement process is the collection of student work, in order to determine if the draft performance statements omit important elements or expect too much or too little of students. Teachers in Alliance sites will provide samples of such work and gain much in their understanding of the standards as a means to guide their own instructional programs.

At the same time, Alliance sites will continue to pilot and implement the New Standards assessment system. The second field trial of the English language arts and math portfolio assessment will take place in 1995–1996, and a field trial in applied learning and one in science will take place the following year. In addition to administering and scoring the assessments, Alliance sites will also provide student work for use as benchmarks.

Other parts of the New Standards system are also scheduled to be developed over the next few years, and Alliance sites will play a key role in their development. Exams that could be used to produce individual student scores—important to measure the performance of students eligible for Title I assistance—will be ready in 1996–1997; New Standards is also developing an examination in science and a linking system that will enable states and districts to link their standards with the national system.

Learning Environments

Enabling students to meet high standards of performance demands a redesign of the environment in which students learn. The standards require students to demonstrate a deep understanding of core content, the ability to use their knowledge to solve problems encountered in the real world, and the ability to communicate their understanding and knowledge. Such abilities are not developed solely in classrooms in which students passively receive knowledge from teachers and textbooks (Resnick & Klopfer, 1989).

A learning environment aimed at developing high levels of student knowledge and skills extends far beyond the classroom. It includes links to the community and the workplace to smooth the path between school and work. It includes technology that can link students and teachers with peers and information well past school walls. But it also includes a fundamental redesign of the learning and teaching in the core subjects.

Curriculum and Instruction. The Alliance approach to curriculum and instruction rests on two fundamental pillars: an understanding of how students learn and the standards embodied in the CIM. These two pillars have strong implications for the way classrooms and schools are organized. They imply an environment in which students are known as people and as learners, in which they are engaged in meaningful projects, in which they know the criteria for good work and take responsibility for meeting those criteria, and in which they draw on a variety of sources of expertise, often outside the classroom.

The redesigned environment is one in which teachers become coaches, encouraging students to succeed. The teachers, who are knowledgeable in the content of their subject area, serve as expert learners, modeling and providing opportunities for students to serve as apprentices by making authentic products and giving performances that demonstrate their understanding and knowledge. In this redesigned learning environment, standards are clear and assessment is continual. Teachers and students—as well as parents and the public—are aware of the expectations and of how close students are to meeting them (Resnick, 1995).

Teachers may recognize these characteristics for what they are—good practice—and many schools in the Alliance are well on their way toward integrating them into their instructional program. For example, the Eminence (Kentucky) Middle School is designing its instructional program around complex, engaging units of study that are explicitly tied to standards for student performance. With close guidance from teachers, students work in teams to prepare products and performances they will present to the public to demonstrate they have attained the knowledge and skills the state standards call for. Other schools that are part of the Alliance are redesigning their curriculum and instructional programs toward the same end, albeit in different ways. But to enable all students to reach high standards of performance, learning environments based on sound learning principles and tied to high standards must be the rule, not the exception. Students need consistently good instruction across the school day and across school years.

To achieve that goal, the Alliance is proceeding on a number of fronts. First, it is working with schools to assist them in developing standards-driven units of study. Structured workshops and tools, known as HELPS, or High Expectations Learning Process for Standards-Driven Units of Study, are aimed at arming teachers with the ability to develop complex, engaging instructional units that are explicitly tied to standards for student performance. Eminent teachers took part in a preliminary version of HELPS training. The process goes a long way toward bridging state and national standards and the activities teachers perform in classrooms. At the same time, the HELPS matrix ensures that the units incorporate applied learning competencies (the types of abilities needed in the workplace). In that respect the HELPS process plays an important role in the school-to-work area.

A second element in the Alliance strategy in curriculum and instruction is its partnership with the LRDC at the University of Pittsburgh, a leading source of expertise on learning and instruction. In 1995, Lauren Resnick and the LRDC formed the Institute for Learning, which will work with Alliance jurisdictions and others to help schools redesign their curriculum and instructional programs to match what research suggests about student learning. The emphasis is on good practice: The Institute's associates will study effective methods of enabling students to learn at high levels, develop tools to help teachers institute those practices, and work directly with schools to reshape their instruction and curriculum.

A third element in the Alliance strategy in this area is help in identifying curriculum materials that will assist teachers in enabling students to meet high standards of achievement. In partnership with the Institute for Learning and New Standards, the Alliance produced three volumes of essays, written by teachers and curriculum specialists, that offer guidance on appropriate materials in English language arts, mathematics, and science.

School to Work. The vast majority of American youths—more than 70 percent—do not earn postsecondary degrees, yet they leave high school ill-prepared to enter the workforce directly. They have neither the skills needed for good jobs nor the knowledge of occupational and training opportunities necessary to plan their careers wisely, and as a result move from one low-paying job to another until well into their twenties. School-to-work transition programs make learning meaningful to students and equip them with the skills and knowledge to be successful in the workplace or as they pursue further education and training (Tucker, 1994).

In the Alliance view, school-to-work is not a collection of isolated programs or occasional employer visits to schools, but a coordinated effort tied to a system of standards and integrated work and school-based learning experiences. This effort, moreover, takes place at all levels of schooling—from the beginning of elementary school through high school and beyond. The Alliance envisions a system that will help prepare young people to make informed choices—after meeting an internationally benchmarked standard at around age 16—about the future path of their education and training, help young people master academic and work skills based on standards defined by industry and schools, offer opportunities for all students to acquire the technical skills they need to pursue rewarding careers, and encourage a broad set of career pathways, including entry into college degree programs from any point in the system.

Making this happen takes partnerships—at the district, state, and national levels and among secondary schools, employers, labor leaders, policymakers and higher education. Without far reaching partnerships, school-to-work programs will never be available for the majority of young people. The primary strategy in the Alliance, working with its partner Jobs for the Future, has been to help educators identify their partners and understand their priorities, and then to help them open up the channels of communication. The Alliance has taken an active role in the field helping local communities create formal compacts, consisting of education, industry, labor, and government, to coordinate school-to-work activities. Federal funds from the School-to-Work Opportunities Act have helped by providing resources for convening meetings and hiring staff to plan, where they are available. This is the case in Kentucky.

At the same time, the Alliance is working with high schools to develop innovative options for students who have earned the CIM. Alliance partners work with schools in Washington state to enable students to enter community colleges early. They have worked with a number of schools to form career academies, which combine advanced academic studies with occupational training. They have worked with schools and businesses in San Diego, Washington, and Rochester, N.Y. to develop apprenticeships that enable young people to train on the job. They have worked with schools in Kentucky and Rochester to develop systems that enable high school students to attend community college while still in high school. And they have worked with business partners across the Alliance to develop meaningful learning opportunities for students in their workplaces.

Technology. Modern technologies—computer-based devices, advanced communications systems, video cameras, scanners, copy and fax machines and books—have the potential for greatly improving the efficiency, productivity and quality with which every one of the Alliance design tasks is performed. From the use of modern database technology in management and administration to the use of electronic kiosk ideas in opening up public access to community services, these technologies can transform the way school systems do almost everything (Office of Technology Assessment, 1995). The Alliance is aggressively exploring all of these possibilities. As it does so, though, the object is not to advance technology or its applications per se, but to find ways in which technology can be used to advance the work within each design task.

Thus far, the Alliance has concentrated largely on using technology to advance instruction. The Alliance has not been interested in using computers and related technologies to substitute for the teacher, as devices that deliver instruction, nor has it been interested in making the technologies the subject of instruction. These technologies are, first and foremost, powerful tools to be put in the hands of students and teachers to help them get their work done in a more powerful way than they could without them.

To that end, the Alliance developed a two-pronged strategy. First, the Alliance's partner, Apple Computer, Inc.'s Apple Classroom of Tomorrow (ACOT) program, joined with those working on curriculum and instruction and those working on the school-to-work transition to form the Learning Environments Group. The task for the group is to find ways to integrate the constructivist learning approaches that the LRDC at the University of Pittsburgh are pioneering with the applied learning strategies developed by the school-to-work transition group, and to do so through technology.

The approach the group developed was the Unit of Study process. In that process, teachers develop complex instructional units that are intended to produce expected outcomes for children. They share information on the units, including the activities, the pedagogical strategies and methods of assessment, with their colleagues in the Alliance and with the ACOT staff through an electronic network. In fact, ACOT reserves a "room" on America Online, an electronic mail and bulletin-board service to which all Alliance schools subscribe, to enable teachers to post Units of Study and comment on them.

The Unit of Study process produced some positive results. According to teacher and principal reports, several of the units resulted in outstanding performances by students. At Calloway County Middle School in Murray, Kentucky, for example, students themselves devised a six-week Unit of Study on the 1960s. The eighth graders decided how to meet the outcomes set by teachers, how to organize the unit, how to assess their progress, and what assignments students should complete in each subject area. The final product was a newspaper, produced on computers, with student articles on space, the environment, politics, and fashion.

To ensure that examples like Calloway's could be found across the partnership, the Alliance developed the HELPS process, described above. The HELPS process takes the Unit of Study process a step further by ensuring that the instructional units are explicitly linked to standards for student performance.

The second major strategy to integrate technology into the Alliance design is the use of Teacher Development Centers (TDCs). As designed, TDCs are technology-rich sets of classrooms where students and teachers use a wide range of hardware and software—from computers with Internet access to CD-ROMs to video and much more—in ways that are fully integrated into instruction that is linked to high standards for performance. In one example, a physical education teacher used video to compare students' motor skills with those of expert models.

The TDCs do more than serve as exemplary classrooms. They also serve as models and training sites for teachers throughout the school and the area. The Alliance and Apple in 1994 established four sites in strategic locations: Morrisville (Vermont) Elementary School; Calloway County Middle School; Linda Vista Elementary School in San Diego; and Lynnwood High School in Edmonds, Washington (The state established three additional TDCs in other districts). Teachers from these schools and other nearby schools spend a week at the TDCs attending practicums, where they observe the centers in action and work together to plan units of study tied to high standards that incorporate technology. The TDCs are aimed at addressing the problem of scale: rather than require Alliance and ACOT staff to work intensively with all schools in the expanding network, the TDCs created a central professional development site where teachers can learn in an actual working model of effective practice.

In its next phase, the Alliance is redesigning the TDCs to ensure they model integration of all the design tasks, including the way technology can enhance their implementation, and to enable more teachers to take advantage of the professional development opportunities they offer. To that end, Centers are being renamed School Development Centers (SDCs), and all the partners have agreed to establish an SDC in an elementary, middle, and high school. The Alliance is also developing ways to integrate technology in all design tasks connected by a telecommunications network, AllianceNET.

Community Services and Supports

Students who come to school hungry, tired, and abused (or who don't come to school at all) cannot take full advantage of curriculum reforms, no matter how diligently the teacher tries to engage them in learning. Teachers cannot solve all these problems, yet until they are addressed, students are unlikely to make sufficient progress in achieving their education goals (Schorr, 1988).

Therefore, the Alliance, working with its nonsite partners, the Center for the Study of Social Policy and the Harvard Project on Effective Services, created the Community Services and Supports (CSS) task as an essential element of the goal to create systems and schools where children learn at high levels and are prepared for a productive, successful adulthood. The CSS contribution to this goal is to ensure that children arrive at school, every day, ready to take advantage of the education being prepared for them through the other design tasks. This requires that children be healthy, safe, and supported by their families in their learning and in their overall development.

To arrive at these goals, the design task consists of a five-part strategy. First, schools and communities determine the outcomes they want to achieve for children, youth, and families. The desired outcomes depend on community needs—one might focus on reducing teenage pregnancies, another on ensuring safety in the school area—but they all relate to ensuring that students are able to learn at high levels. Second, the schools and communities form collaborative groups—consisting of social service agency heads, parents, teachers, policymakers and others—to oversee the provision of the supports and services needed to achieve the outcomes. These groups then survey the community to determine the supports and services available and find ways to fill in the gaps. Fourth, the schools and communities redesign the way they fund services and supports to match the outcomes, and finally, they provide professional development to enable professionals from various systems to provide the appropriate services.

A number of schools and systems in the Alliance have used this framework to improve the services available to students and families. In Shoreline, Washington, for example, a program council developed a set of outcomes for children's health and well-being, and surveyed the community to determine the services they would need to achieve those outcomes. As a result, the community now has English classes and day-care for non-English speaking parents, a mental health case worker, and a wellness clinic.

High Performance Management

Just as the mass production economy helped form the basis on which the education system was created at the beginning of this century, that economic system also helped shape the way the education system organized and managed itself. And the management methods and organizational form of our schools and districts are very little changed since the time they were formed. The state systems and the district central office typically run things in detail, producing seemingly endless rules and regulations describing everything from what must be taught to how the minutes of the day will be used. The rhetoric is that teachers are professionals and the principals are instructional leaders, but the reality most often is that teachers are treated like blue collar workers, any one of whom can easily be substituted for any other, and the principal's job is construed as keeping order and making sure the central office's directives are faithfully implemented—in other words, as being very much like the job of the factory foreman.

Yet while the education system seems stuck in a mass production style of organization, businesses and industries—and, increasingly, public agencies—are moving to new ways of organizing and management, aimed at high performance. The approaches of such organizations can be adapted and applied to education systems.

In high performance organizations, common high standards and results are the focus. They set clear goals and expect results, not compliance with rules. They also align their systems to support high performance, by redesigning the central office to provide service, rather than monitoring compliance, and by collecting and disseminating information that can enable people at every level to make informed decisions.

High performance organizations also create strategic plans to assist them in assessing their status and improving continuously. They push authority and flexibility down to the lowest level possible and hold those with authority accountable for results. They invest in people and treat those with authority like true professionals—responsible for achieving success and intolerant of poor performance. The organizations provide those professionals with the kinds of incentives that will motivate them to achieve their goals and take away disincentives that impede high performance (Marsh, 1995).

It will be impossible to reach the Alliance's goal of having all but the most severely disabled students meet internationally benchmarked standards of performance unless the American education system makes these kinds of fundamental changes in the way it is organized and managed. We cannot get high quality results without organizing and managing to produce them. To help Alliance schools, districts, and states make such organizational changes, the Alliance has worked with its nonsite partners, the Xerox Corporation and the National Alliance of Business, to incorporate the principles of high performance into its work. It has included a leadership strand in every Alliance workshop to provide school and site leaders with professional development around leadership issues. It has provided technical assistance to particular sites to guide them in adapting the principles of total quality management to their systems.

The Alliance also has created a National Academy for Restructuring to bring together superintendents, central office staffs and teachers' union leaders to study ways to reorganize school districts and develop tools to help bring about such a reorganization. And the Alliance has cosponsored, with its partner the University of Southern California, an International Principals' Institute to enable principals from Alliance schools to discuss issues of common concern with counterparts from Australia and Great Britain.

The Alliance also has worked with schools and sites to develop and hone strategic plans, to analyze where they were and to develop a coherent plan for achieving their goals. As part of this process, national experts analyzed the strategic plans and determined if they made a "strong case" or not, thus enabling schools and sites to redo their plans, so they become tools for continuous improvement.

Through the leadership of the National Center on Education and the Economy's High Performance Management program, the Alliance also has created a concentrated program of work at the district level, assisting central offices in their efforts to push resources and authority to the school level and holding schools accountable for results. One district with which the HPM program is working is Everett, Washington. There, Jackson Elementary School saw the budget for which it was responsible shoot up from $100,000 to $1.7 million in one year, and with it a corresponding jump in autonomy over staffing, curriculum and much more. The school is now able to make decisions based on what is needed at the site.

Public Engagement

The Public Engagement design task was born from the idea that without public support, systemic change would be extremely difficult, if not impossible. The Alliance knew from bitter experience that educators who haven't yet discovered the power of public support may soon discover the power of public opposition.

It also knew that the traditional way schools went about seeking support for change—making a change and then asking the public to back it—would fail. Schools cannot change if the community doesn't want them to, and the community won't ask for change until they are convinced that the old way of educating children is not working and that a new way of educating will help children succeed.

Thanks to the Alliance's partner, Public Agenda, the Alliance knew, too, that schools have not listened well to the public. Public Agenda's highly acclaimed *Crosstalk* and *First Things First* (Public Agenda, 1991, 1994) reports showed both the enormous extent and the nature of the gulf between the world view of the education reform community and the world view of the public.

Thus the Alliance set out in the Public Engagement task to listen carefully to communities, understand their concerns and address them in a way that engages the community in the reform effort. For example, the Alliance found in the Public Agenda reports that a primary concern of the public's was safety. It knew that, unless schools provide a safe environment for students, none of the other reforms could take place. In response, the Alliance has focused efforts on helping schools ensure safe climates.

At the same time, the Alliance has also embarked on a strategy focused more specifically on parents. While support from the public at large is essential, finding ways to involve parents in their children's education is integral to the success of the Alliance's work. Parents support high standards, and they want to be involved in their children's education. And involvement means more than sitting on governance councils. The research is clear: Parents need to support their children's learning if children are to achieve at high levels.

Alliance schools and systems have developed a variety of approaches to engaging parents and members of the community. In San Diego, the district has strengthened the community's understanding of portfolios by devoting a segment of a district-run television program to the subject. At the same time, local schools have bolstered that understanding by forging strong relationships with parents and listening to their concerns. Richard Camacho, the principal of Linda Vista Elementary School, has been particularly effective at engaging parents who might be reluctant to come into the school: He makes a habit of taking "community walks" to meet parents "on their turf."

Implementing the Design

Results to Date

Implementing a design as sweeping as the National Alliance's has proven to be every bit as challenging as the Alliance anticipated—and then some. Not only is the Alliance trying to accomplish as broad a reform agenda as any organization has undertaken, it is also trying to do so in many diverse settings, and to scale up the reform as quickly as possible.

The Alliance has learned a lot in the past five years, and it is still learning. The program of the Alliance is still being developed. Important parts of the Alliance are just now in the design stage, such as the HELPS tool for developing instructional units, while others, such as much of the New Standards assessment system, are fully in place. Above all, the Alliance has learned a great deal about what it takes to organize and maintain a partnership.

Alliance sites have made the most significant progress in implementing a state policy framework that supports student achievement to high levels. The state partners of the National Alliance—Arkansas, Kentucky, and Washington state—have all adopted comprehensive legislation or policies that focus on student performance standards. These states have developed or are in the process of developing standards and a related performance assessment system, and have adopted statewide policies that tie curriculum frameworks to the standards, that hold schools accountable for meeting student standards, and that provide strategies for engaging the public in the standards-setting and performance system. The states also have adopted policies to integrate social services and education.

The Alliance state partners are actively considering policies to devolve resources and authority to schools and to hold districts accountable for results. Two states—Arkansas and Washington—have adopted the Certificate of Initial Mastery as state law, and others are considering such a policy. The Washington law is well on its way toward implementation: By the year 2000, to graduate from high school, students in Washington state will have to earn a CIM, demonstrating high levels of achievement in core subjects.

The experiences in these states demonstrate that state policy frameworks can indeed support reform efforts at the school level. In Kentucky, the dramatic improvements in student performance (see the following discussion) and the widespread implementation of reforms in learning environments, community services, and other areas show that state policies have had a strong influence on local practice. The Alliance anticipates similar results in Washington state and Arkansas, where state policies have only begun to take hold.

Reforms at the district level, meanwhile, have also moved forward. One area where districts have made substantial progress is in investing in the development of employees at all levels. A survey of seven Alliance districts found that nearly all have implemented systems to hire and train competent workers and to enable all staff members to learn and grow professionally, and have given managers the authority to coach their employees and take corrective actions when needed.

Several districts in the Alliance also are undertaking major initiatives to shift resources and authority down to the school level, while holding schools accountable for results. In Pittsburgh, following work with the National Center's High Performance Management program, the district increased the share of funds over which the school had direct authority from 5 percent to 55 percent, and plans to shift even more to the school level in the future. Other Alliance districts have devolved greater amounts of resources to local schools.

The reforms at the school level also have taken hold. The schools that have shown the most significant progress appear to be those that have made standards for student performance the focus of all of their efforts. This is evident in Kentucky where the state reform law places high stakes on achieving student performance standards. Elsewhere, schools are welcoming the draft performance standards adopted by New Standards, which are expected to provide an anchor for the performance systems the schools seek.

The Alliance schools are also using training and tools supplied by the Alliance and its partners to align their instructional practices to the standards for student performance. The HELPS workshops conducted thus far have been well received; teachers in San Diego, Washington state and Rochester have used the process to develop instructional units tied to student performance standards. Likewise, teachers in Washington state and Kentucky have worked with the TDCs in those sites to develop standards-driven instructional units. In developing and implementing these units, moreover, the teachers are shifting their classroom practice from a teacher-dominated style to one that allows students to construct their own knowledge.

Schools also have shown rapid growth in the use of technology. A survey of eight Alliance schools shows that most have implemented a plan for technology that incorporates a variety of media, not just computers, and the intelligent use of these technologies. Schools also have shown surprising progress in the area of public engagement, an area that was new to many schools with the advent of the Alliance design. Most schools in the survey said they have established a public engagement team to listen to the public and build public understanding of the need for change, and that the teams produce a variety of materials and events to engage the school staff and the public in the schools' efforts.

More than half of the schools reported that they have begun to implement processes to improve community services. In many cases this has meant analyzing the problems facing young people and developing outcomes they want to attain, and identifying the resources available to help achieve those outcomes.

Additionally, schools have moved on the High Performance Management agenda. Most of the eight schools in the survey said they have developed a leadership team and a long-range strategic plan, and all but one reported that they have the flexibility and authority to make decisions and to allocate resources necessary for improving student achievement.

The Alliance's efforts to roll out the design—through professional development and the use of strategic planning—have earned high marks from the partners. In general, the conferences and workshops have been very well received. Participants said consistently that the quality of the presentations was quite high, and that the sessions were relevant and applicable to their work. Participants at an Alliance conference on parent and family engagement in February 1995 were particularly enthusiastic about the sessions. Participants said the sessions addressed their concerns and that the information will be helpful to them in their schools and districts.

The strategic planning process, meanwhile, has shown an impact. Schools have developed plans that include all of the elements identified as critical to effective strategic plans. Perhaps more importantly, these plans are now seen as means of continual improvement; they are documents schools are using to assess their progress continually and place resources in areas that need additional attention. The Alliance is also refining the tools in Phase III. The goal is to link more tightly the strategies schools undertake with the outcomes they expect to achieve.

Did all of the changes in state policy, district structure, school practices, professional development and strategic planning pay off where it counts, in improved student achievement? The best available data to answer that question come from Kentucky, where the state assessment system is tied to high standards and where the state annually reports results from individual schools. The Kentucky Education Reform Act also includes a strong incentive system that rewards significant improvement. Under that system, schools in which student performance increased substantially earned cash bonuses equal to about $2,000 per teacher; schools where performance declined became eligible for assistance from a state-appointed "distinguished educator."

The Kentucky results suggest that the Alliance work is paying off. Of the 15 Alliance schools in Kentucky, 13, or 87 percent, earned cash awards in 1995, the first year of the program, compared with 38 percent of schools statewide. These results exceeded those of any other reform effort in the state, according to the state Department of Education: As a result, in 1995 the department agreed to expand the

Alliance work in Kentucky to include schools in 11 districts, including a district where performance declined.

Scaling Up the Next Three Years

The Alliance's objective is to show how the concepts and tools it is developing can be used by schools, districts and states to improve student performance dramatically on a wide scale. To do that, the Alliance must (a) finish developing the needed concepts and tools; (b) demonstrate their effectiveness in at least two to three jurisdictions in an unmistakable way; and (c) develop the capacity to deliver needed assistance on a much wider scale to be able to meet the needs of many more sites without any diminution in the quality of the assistance.

As a first step toward those ends, the Alliance is redesigning its professional development program. While the Alliance will continue its national professional development efforts, it also will be building strong professional development programs directly in the jurisdictions—states and school districts—in which the Alliance is concentrating the next phase of its program. Transforming 30 percent of a jurisdiction's schools within three years—the goal of Phase III of New American Schools—means that hundreds, in some cases thousands of state policymakers and administrators, school board members, central office staff, principals and lead teachers, among others, in each jurisdiction must experience the same kind of knowledge and awareness their peers took part in last year. Unlike the national programs, however, these local programs will be tailored to the specific needs of each jurisdiction.

There also will be a strong need for a locally based professional development program that goes beyond orientation to the development of the kind of advanced skills and knowledge needed to support deep implementation of the Alliance program. This is true both at the district and school levels. To accomplish that, three of the four Alliance jurisdictions chosen as Phase III New American Schools sites—Kentucky, Pittsburgh, and San Diego—will have a field team of a half dozen people working on the Alliance design. Each of these people will be responsible for one of the design tasks. Collectively, the team will attempt to do in their jurisdiction what the Alliance central team has done for the Alliance as a whole: coordinate professional development and technical assistance and help local schools as they go through the change process.

For the future, the Alliance will be exploring additional strategies to help transform even larger numbers of schools. As a major part of its plans, the Alliance is seeking ways to use technology as an aid in the delivery of resources to the field, supplementing that technology with more conventional professional development and technical assistance resources.

High quality tools, systems, databases and communications facilities—all seamlessly integrated into a single system—could provide the basis for continuous skill and knowledge updating that is the goal of every designer of professional development systems for the education community. It would not suffer from the degradation of the quality of the "signal" so characteristic of conventional teacher training systems, because the signal would go directly from the source to the ultimate user. In that way, the Alliance design can spread even more widely, and the Alliance goal—enabling all young people to reach high standards of performance—can move that much closer to reality.

References

Carnegie Forum. (1986). *A nation prepared: Teachers for the 21st century.* Washington, DC: Carnegie Forum on Education and the Economy.

Little, J. W. (1993). Teachers' professional development in a climate of educational reform. *Educational Evaluation and Policy Analysis,* 15(2), 129–151.

Marsh, D. D. (1995). *Restructuring for results: High performance management in the Edmonton Public Schools.* Washington, DC: National Alliance for Restructuring Education.

Marshall, R., & Tucker, M. (1992). *Thinking for a living: Education and the wealth of nations.* New York: Basic Books.

McLaughlin, M. W., & Marsh, D. D. (1978). Staff development and school change. *Teachers College Record, 80*(1), 69–94.

Odden, A.R. (Ed.). (1991). *Educational policy implementation.* Albany, NY: State University of New York Press.

Office of Technology Assessment, (1995). *Teachers & technology: Making the connection.* Washington, DC: U.S. Government Printing Office.

Public Agenda. (1991). *CrossTalk: The public, the experts, and competitiveness.* New York: Public Agenda.

Public Agenda. (1994). *First things first: What Americans expect from the public schools.* New York: Public Agenda.

Resnick, L. B. (1995). From aptitude to effort: A new foundation for our schools. *Daedalus, 124*(4), 55–62.

Resnick, L. B., & Klopfer, L. (Eds.). (1989). *Toward the thinking curriculum: Current cognitive research.* Reston, VA: Association for Supervision and Curriculum Development.

Rothman, R. (1995). *Measuring up: Standards, assessment and school reform.* San Francisco: Jossey-Bass.

Schorr, L. B. (1988). *Within our reach: Breaking the cycle of disadvantage.* New York: Doubleday.

Tucker, M. (1994). *A school-to-work transition system for the United States.* Washington, DC: National Center on Education and the Economy.

Workforce Skills Program. (1994). *The certificate of initial mastery: A primer.* Washington, DC: National Center on Education and the Economy.

Roots and Wings:
Universal Excellence in Elementary Education[1]

Robert E. Slavin
Nancy A. Madden
Barbara A. Wasik
Johns Hopkins University

At Lexington Park Elementary School in a small town in Southern Maryland, 10-year-old Jamal rises to speak. "The chair recognizes the delegate from Ridge School," says the chairwoman, a student from the local high school.

"I'd like to speak in favor of House Bill R130," Jamal begins. "This bill would tell farmers they couldn't use fertilizer on land that is within 200 feet of the Chesapeake Bay. Fertilizer goes in the bay and causes pollution and kills fish. Farmers can still grow a lot of crops even if they don't plant close to water, and we will all have a better life if we can stop pollution in the bay. I yield to questions."

A hand goes up. The chairwoman recognizes a delegate from Carver School.

"How does fertilizer harm the bay?" she asks.

Jamal explains how the fertilizer provides nutrition to algae in the bay, and when too much algae grows, it deprives the larger creatures of oxygen. When he finishes, a delegate from Green Holly School is recognized.

"I'm a farmer," says 11-year-old Maria. "I can hardly pay all my bills as it is, and I've got three kids to feed. I'll go broke if I can't fertilize my whole field!"

---

[1] Portions of this chapter are adapted from Slavin, Madden, Dolan, and Wasik (1994).

The debate on the bill goes on for more than an hour. Student delegates who are playing the role of watermen speak about how their way of life is disappearing because of declining catches due to pollution. Business owners talk about how pollution ruins the local economy. Finally, the committee amends the bill to prohibit farmers from planting near waterways unless they are poor. The bill passes and later on is voted on by the whole House of Delegates.

What is happening at Lexington Park and three other schools in St. Mary's County, Maryland, is a revolution in elementary education. These schools are piloting a school restructuring program called Roots and Wings. Roots and Wings is one of the "break the mold" school designs being funded by New American Schools (NAS) to create the schools of the 21st century.

Roots and Wings has two primary objectives. One is to ensure that *every* child, regardless of family background or disability, achieves world class standards in reading, writing and language arts, mathematics, science, history, and geography. In Roots and Wings, the school, parents, community agencies, and others work in a coordinated, comprehensive, and relentless way from the birth of the child onward to see that children receive whatever they need to become competent, confident, and caring learners. In previous work at Johns Hopkins University on a program called Success for All, we have shown in high-poverty schools across the U.S. that by combining prevention, research-based curriculum and instruction, tutoring for at-risk children, and family support, nearly every child can succeed in the elementary grades (Madden, Slavin, Karweit, Dolan & Wasik, 1993; Slavin, Madden, Dolan, & Wasik, 1992; Slavin, Madden, Dolan, & Wasik, 1996; Slavin, Madden, Dolan, Wasik, Ross, & Smith, 1994). This is the "roots" of Roots and Wings: the guarantee that every child will make it successfully through the elementary grades, no matter what this takes.

It is essential to ensure that every child can read, compose, and understand math, science, history, and geography; yet this is not enough for children today. Children need to be able to creatively and flexibly solve problems, understand their own learning processes, and connect knowledge from different disciplines. To build these higher-order skills, Roots and Wings provides daily opportunities for students to work collaboratively to solve simulated and real life problems using the skills and information they are learning in class. This is the "wings" of Roots and Wings: engaging students in activities that enable them to *apply* everything so that they can learn the usefulness and interconnectedness of all knowledge.

These are the main components of Roots and Wings:

WorldLab

The debate in the "House of Delegates" illustrates one of the most distinctive and innovative elements of the "wings" of Roots and Wings. This is an integrated approach to science, social studies, and writing called WorldLab. In WorldLab, students take on roles as people in history, in other countries, or in various occupations. The students in the "House of Delegates" have been studying the Chesapeake Bay, focusing on sources of pollution, watersheds, tides, the rain cycle, and the life cycle of aquatic plants and animals. They have also been learning about government, economics, geography, and politics. Their work on these topics is done in preparation for a model state legislature, in which students write, propose, and debate many bills relating to cleaning up the Bay. In other WorldLab units, students take on roles as inventors, as delegates to the Constitutional Convention, as advisors to the Pharaohs of Ancient Egypt, as explorers in the 15th century, and so on. In these simulations students work in small, cooperative groups to investigate topics of science and social studies. They read books and articles about their topics, write newspapers, broadsides, letters, and proposals, use mathematics skills to solve problems relating to their topics, and use fine arts, music, and computer, video, and other technology to prepare multimedia reports. Students ultimately learn all the usual content of elementary science and social studies (plus much more), but they do so as active participants in the scientific discoveries, historical events, and other systems they are studying.

The idea behind WorldLab is to make the contents of the entire elementary curriculum useful and relevant to children's daily lives by immersing them in simulations in which knowledge and skill are necessary. One key problem of traditional elementary schooling is that the content students are learning is not immediately useful to them. It is entirely possible to be a happy and successful 10-year-old with no knowledge whatsoever about the American revolution, or the rain cycle, or how to add fractions, or how to write a persuasive letter. Students may work to please their teachers or parents or to get a good grade, or they may be interested in some parts of the content they are studying, but motivation, curiosity, and insight are certain to be much greater when students need information or skills to solve problems that have meaning to them.

Simulations provide an ideal opportunity to make information immediately useful. In a well-designed simulation, students fully identify with the roles they take on. Maria, in the House of Delegates example, is a farmer with serious responsibilities: three children, a mortgage, bills and taxes. She is also an elected representative to the

Maryland House of Delegates. As a real-life kid and as a simulated farmer and delegate, Maria cares about the ecology of the Chesapeake Bay. However, she cares about it from a particular perspective. She pays great attention to information about the effects of fertilizer runoff because this has direct relevance to her role. To participate intelligently in the debates she has to have a deep understanding of watersheds, erosion, eutrophication, the needs of sea life for oxygen, tides, economics and the economic impact of the Bay, government, laws, and many other topics. She has used math to solve real economic problems, has written impassioned letters to support her views, and has read books relating to the Bay to build her understanding of the issues she confronts in her simulated roles. The Bay unit is not only an interdisciplinary thematic unit. Because of its use of simulations, it is an opportunity to make knowledge and skills not only integrated but also useful.

Simulations can give students an emotional investment in the material they are studying. In a unit called Rebellion to Union, fifth graders received a distressing note from their principal. The note announced taxes (against the classes' simulated economies) on certain activities, such as using the pencil sharpeners, to help support the costs of WorldLab. The students in each class assembled their class governments, wrote back notes of protest, and decided to boycott the pencil sharpeners. After a while additional notes taxed the use of desks. Classes moved their desks into the hall and sat on the floor. Exasperated, the principal dissolved the class governments. At this, classes decided to "secede," and wrote a declaration of independence to explain and justify their reasons.

Even though they knew it was a simulation, the students were deeply emotionally involved. They wrote letters, picketed the principal's office, and took great pleasure in defying her authority. When they then read the various drafts of the real Declaration of Independence, they could identify not only with the framers' words and logic but with their emotions. They were really there, not acting out a script but wrestling with similar questions, fears, and uncertainties. Later, the students became delegates to the Constitutional Convention and debated positions appropriate to the interests of their states and occupations. These children will never forget the American Revolution or Constitutional Convention. They were *there*, in their hearts and minds. They participated in the debates, stood up for their points of view, heard, saw, and felt what it was like. Everything they had learned in a two-month unit was relevant and important to them.

Our intent in Roots and Wings is to develop integrated simulations to address the entire content of social studies and science in grades one through six, and to integrate reading, writing, math, fine arts, and other content with WorldLab topics. Other WorldLab units include the following:

- "Encounters" (grades 4–5) is a unit that helps students understand how the interactions among three major cultural groups— African, European, and Native American— shaped the development of our nation. Instead of merely memorizing a litany of facts about the origins of our nation, students become historians and scientists-in-training. They explore the methods historians use by studying a local historic site. They become scientists as they investigate how scientific discoveries impacted on early American societies. Students recreate Ben Franklin's Traveling Electrical Show using Franklin's original experiments in static electricity. The unit includes authentic experiments to replicate and primary historical documents to investigate. Later in the unit, teams experiment with methods for growing crops typically grown during colonial times. They collect data to help them decide how to produce the most bountiful harvest for their family. Ultimately teams harvest and enjoy their crops. Students develop their roles as Africans, Europeans, or Native Americans during specific historical periods by composing "Day in the Life" stories about a typical day in the life of the character they are role-playing. This personalizes learning and helps students appreciate what people were thinking and feeling as historic events unfolded. Students use WorldLab computer software to research and publish their "Day in the Life" stories and assemble them into class books. At the conclusion of the unit, students plan and present an Encounters Fair to share their learning and insights with the local community.

- "Body Networks" (grades 4–5) is an investigation of the nervous system that focuses on the role of the brain in controlling body functions. Students take the roles of consultants who develop public health announcements focused on safety procedures that prevent head injury and protect the brain. For example, students design, build, and test bicycle helmets and then produce commercials to persuade children to use them.

- "Inventors" (grades 4–5) consists of four components: (a) reviewing inventions that have made an impact on modern society; (b) learning about the creative process and entrepreneurship by reading biographies of famous inventors; (c) engaging students in identifying a need for a product, designing a product to meet this need, and creating a campaign to sell the product; (d) using the "World in Motion" program developed by the Society of Automotive Engineers to assist students in taking on the roles of an engineering design team as they experiment with the laws of motion and apply what they have learned to create the speediest vehicle in their class.

- "Adventures" and "Africa" (grade 3) are units designed to be taught consecutively. They focus on geography, economics, physical and earth sciences. "Adventures" prepares students for world-wide explorations by exploring their own school community first. As students prepare a visitor's center and guide to their school, they apply newly mastered map making and research skills. They identify elements common to all communities. Next, students conduct experiments about buoyancy and navigation as they prepare to simulate a ship's crew on a voyage of discovery. They apply their findings as they make critical design decisions and build a clay ship that carries cargo and floats. They learn about the economic concepts of scarcity, opportunity cost, and supply and demand as they choose what to bring along on their expeditions. Finally, they set sail for Africa, using the stars to plot their course. When they arrive a simulation of life in an African community begins. They investigate the same aspects of community they identified earlier in their school. They compare and contrast government, communication, infra-structure, use of natural resources, foods, customs and tradi-tions, among other factors. Students find that communities exist to satisfy peoples' wants and needs. Students also discover a problem in this community. There has been a drought and water is scarce. Students work in teams to design a new irrigation system and apply water conservation methods to solve the problem. Students pack their bags and set sail for their next destination. New units that will take students on adven-tures in Japan, Brazil, and finally a futuristic community in space are currently in the development process.

- "Trees" (grades 1–2) involves students in a study of the life cycle of trees throughout the year. Students become botanists as they identify what they already know about trees, and decide what they need to find out. The unit offers them a variety of opportu-nities to explore and investigate their questions with activities such as adopting a tree, observing it throughout the school year and writing about it in a journal, planting seeds and observing their growth, conducting experiments, and recording their findings in lab reports. Students "branch out" and investigate the roles trees play in other parts of the world, such as South American rain forests. They build thinking, reading, and writing skills as they discover that trees are not only beautiful, but play an important role in providing food, shelter, recreation and employment. The unit culminates with creative and dramatic performances designed to entertain and educate.

- "Harvests" (grades 1–2) lets students take the trip of a lifetime in search of harvest celebrations around the world. In this multi-cultural, multi-disciplinary unit, students compare and contrast different customs, traditions, and farming methods all related to the foods people eat in many diverse lands. The unit increases cultural awareness, respect for diversity, and an understanding of what we all have in common. Students receive passports, prepare itineraries, and take on the role of the international traveler in order to complete their investigation. The unit culminates with an international celebration of the harvest featuring student projects, cooking, and creative dramatics.

- "Eggs" (grades 1–2) is a unit that transforms young students into zoologists as they classify all phyla of living things that develop from eggs. Students learn how and why farmers candle and incubate quail and chicken eggs. When the eggs hatch, the students compare and contrast the chicks, observe their behavior, and chart their growth. Each team of zoologists investigates a different phylum of organisms in order to become experts on the subject. They conduct numerous experiments and record data. Teams observe tadpoles to learn about the life cycles of amphibians. They compare this to another wonder of nature as they wait and watch expectantly for the metamorphosis of a butterfly to occur. The unit culminates with each team teaching the class about their specialty.

Early Learning Programs—Preschool and Kindergarten

Both the pre-kindergarten and kindergarten programs in Roots and Wings use a thematic approach to learning. The core of the thematic unit is based on either a science or social studies topic and the literature, writing, math, and literacy activities that correspond with and are integrated with each specific theme. For example, in a unit on plants, understanding the scientific concepts about plants is the general theme and the daily activities focus around this theme. The class may read a children's book about planting carrots (emphasizing concepts of print in this reading), plant a seed during center time, record the progress of plant growth in their plant journal, and sing "The Farmer Plants the Seed" as a finger play activity. The goal is to teach the children about plants and how they grow through meaningful activities that are interrelated around a common goal.

Six units have been developed: Plants, Environment, "Special Me," Community Helpers, Multicultural Awareness, and Space. The units are designed to be resources for teachers as well as allow teachers the flexibility to input their own ideas in creative ways. Each unit contains a section on theme learning, literature, writing, math, center activities, cooking activities, music and motor activities, and phonemic awareness instruction. The theme learning sections contain the learning objectives that are presented in each unit. In the literature section, an extensive list of books along with a brief summary of each book is presented. This section also includes activities from the STaR program. The STaR (Story Telling and Retelling) emphasizes oral language and memory skills as well as concepts of print. Teachers read books to children and then give them the opportunity to retell or act out the story, predict story outcomes, and answer questions about story structure. Writing activities are designed to be implemented both during center time as well as a special writing time which is integrated in the daily schedule. The math activities emphasize basic concepts such as counting, grouping, and matching, as well as problem-solving activities including measuring and estimation. The center activities are designed to give the children the opportunity to have "hands on" experience. Suggestions for a variety of centers include a dramatic play center, a reading center, a writing center, and a water activity. Cooking activities integrate math, reading, and writing activities. The music activities correspond to the theme and provide opportunities for the children to sing and do finger play activities. The phonemic awareness activities are frequently related to the music activities and include opportunities for playing with language and sounds.

In addition, each unit has a section on home activities and an individualized student assessment. A letter is sent home to parents when a new unit is beginning which explains what the unit is about and how the parents can help participate in home activities that are related to the unit. The purpose of this is both to inform parents and to provide concrete suggestions for ways they can be involved in their child's learning. At the end of each unit, there are assessments that the teacher uses to determine the strengths and weaknesses of each child's performance in different areas of the unit. For example, the teacher can evaluate how well children understand the learning objective, how their writing has progressed, and how well they comprehend what is read to them.

All of the activities are developmentally appropriate and considerable emphasis is placed on child-initiated and cooperative activities. The goal is to encourage children to think and problem solve with the guiding hand of the teacher.

Reading Programs

Roots and Wings uses a modification of a beginning reading curriculum originally developed for Success for All. In this model, reading teachers begin the reading time by reading children's literature to students and engaging them in a discussion of the story to enhance their understanding of the story, listening and speaking vocabulary, and knowledge of story structure. At the early stages, the program emphasizes development of basic language skills with the use of Story Telling and Retelling (STaR), which involves the students in listening to, retelling, and dramatizing children's literature. Big books as well as oral and written composing activities allow students to develop concepts of print as they also develop knowledge of story structure.

Reading Roots is introduced to students when they are ready, usually at age six. This program uses as its base a series of easy but interesting minibooks and emphasizes repeated oral reading to partners as well as to the teacher. Letters and letter sounds are introduced in an active, engaging set of activities that begins with oral language and moves into written symbols. Individual sounds are integrated into a context of words, sentences, and stories. Instruction is provided in story structure, comprehension monitoring using specific comprehension skills, and integration of reading and writing. The family support coordinator works to ensure that parents know how to reinforce this learning at home.

When students reach the primer reading level, they use Reading Wings, an adaptation of Cooperative Integrated Reading and Composition (CIRC; Stevens, Madden, Slavin, & Farnish, 1987), with novels, trade books, anthologies, and other materials integrated with content that students are studying in other subjects. Reading Wings uses cooperative learning activities built around story structure, prediction, summarization, vocabulary building, decoding practice, and story-related writing. Students engage in partner reading and structured discussion of the stories or novels, and work toward mastery of the vocabulary and content of the story in teams. Story-related writing is also shared within teams. Cooperative learning both increases students' motivation and engages students in cognitive activities known to contribute to reading comprehension, such as elaboration, summarization, and rephrasing (see Stevens et al., 1987).

In addition to these story-related activities, teachers provide direct instruction in reading comprehension skills, and students practice these skills in their teams. Classroom libraries of trade books at students' reading levels are provided for each teacher, and students read books of their choice for homework for 20 minutes each night. Home readings are shared via presentations, summaries, puppet shows, and other formats twice a week during "book club" sessions.

Reading Tutors

One of the most important elements of the Roots and Wings model is the use of tutors to promote students' success in reading. One-to-one tutoring is the most effective form of instruction known (see Slavin, Karweit, & Madden, 1989; Wasik & Slavin, 1993). The tutors are certified teachers and paraprofessionals with experience teaching Title I, special education, or primary reading. In addition, a large number of volunteers have been recruited to provide tutoring. Tutors work one-on-one with students who are having difficulties keeping up with their reading groups. The tutoring occurs daily in 20-minute sessions. The tutoring model has been adapted from that used in Success for All. In general, tutors support students' success in the regular reading curriculum, rather than teaching different objectives. For example, the tutor works with a student on the same story and concepts being read and taught in the regular reading class. However, tutors seek to identify learning problems and use different strategies to teach the same skills and teach metacognitive skills beyond those taught in the classroom program.

Initial decisions about reading group placement and the need for tutoring are based on informal reading inventories that the tutors give to each child. Subsequent reading group placements and tutoring assignments are made based on curriculum-based assessments given every eight weeks, which include teacher judgments as well as more formal assessments. Six- and seven-year-olds receive priority for tutoring, on the assumption that the primary function of the tutors is to help all students be successful in reading the first time, before they fail and become remedial readers.

Writing and Language Arts

The Roots and Wings writing and language arts program has two stages. Writing from the Heart teaches writing using invented spelling with six- and seven-year-olds. It emphasizes helping students take on a role as authors to describe their perceptions, feelings, and ideas. Beginning with eight-year-olds, Writing Wings then presents a more elaborate approach to writing emphasizing the use of four-member peer response groups. In this program, students help each other plan, draft, revise, edit, and publish compositions. Language arts instruction is woven into the context of composition, with special lessons in style (e.g., "grabbers" and "avoiding and disease"), mechanics (e.g., capitalization, punctuation), and usage (e.g., complete sentences, subject–verb agreement). These lessons are presented according to students' needs, and are immediately integrated into the editing process as soon as they have been taught.

The writing program in Roots and Wings is closely integrated with the other subjects students are studying. It may be taught during a combined reading/language period or during WorldLab. When students are reading *Treasure Island*, they also write adventure stories. When they are studying the Civil War, they write broadsides against slavery or for states' rights.

Mathematics

Math Wings, the Roots and Wings mathematics program for grades one through five, is based on the standards of the National Council of Teachers of Mathematics. A program to prepare students for mathematics in the 21st century needs to actively involve students in the conceptual development and practical application of their mathematics skills. The Math Wings program balances solid mathematical conceptual development, problem solving in real world applications, and a maintenance of necessary mathematics skills.

Students enter school with a great deal of mathematical knowledge. They know about combining and separating, halves and wholes, and so on. What they need is a bridge between their pre-existing knowledge and the formal representation of this knowledge in mathematical symbols. This requires the use of manipulatives, demonstrations, and discovery to help students build mathematical understanding. Math Wings uses cooperative learning at all age levels as its vehicle while incorporating problem solving in real situations, skill practice and reinforcement for efficiency in application, calculator use, alternative assessments, writing, connections to literature and other disciplines, and application to the students' world and personal experiences. Students will always be individually accountable for their own learning, and are frequently assessed on their progress in understanding and using math.

Three main components form the Math Wings structure: (a) a daily routine of problem solving, facts, homework check, logbook and team organization; (b) a series of Whole Class units that include a project (performance-based task) as the introductory lesson and span three to five weeks; and (c) a two-week Individual unit between most whole class units when the students are working appropriately on remediating or refining skills, or accelerating into other mathematical topics. The Whole Class units and Individual units each have three lesson components, Check-In, Action Math, and Reflection, to ensure that a balance of problem solving, skill building, and conceptual development is constantly maintained in the classroom. Connections between the WorldLab and mathematics are strong and are continually being developed. What the students learn in mathematics is integrated into the WorldLab simulations.

All students should not only be given the opportunity to establish a solid foundation in mathematics, but also the opportunity to extend and stretch their knowledge and experience in mathematics. Thus, a program of mathematics should include a structure to accommodate a diversity of abilities and background mathematical knowledge, while ensuring that *all* students experience the depth, breadth, and beauty of mathematics. The Math Wings curriculum incorporates this philosophy into its development.

Professional Development

A key objective of the Roots and Wings program has been to develop fully the potential of every teacher. This is being accomplished by means of an ambitious, systematic, professional development program. The idea of training was expanded beyond regular classroom teachers to include special educators, Title I, Gifted and Talented, media, physical education, art, music, principals, central office staff, paraprofessionals, volunteers, substitute teachers, nurses, and community members. Our goal is to model "teamwork"— everyone plays an important role in the total education of each child.

The training design includes direct instruction of program components, adult simulations of student processes, and "teams" of educators offering suggestions to modify, adapt, and connect the program elements to meet their student needs. Training sessions for the program components are followed up by expert coaching from the project staff and program facilitators. Peer coaching within and among the schools, based on research by Joyce, Hersh, and McKibbin (1983), allows teachers to refine implementation and make decisions regarding which additional program components to adopt. The best advocates for program expansion are teacher and student enthusiasm coupled with positive attitudes of knowing that needed support and materials are readily available. The teachers continue to decide what training, follow-up, and other assistance (e.g., demonstration lessons) will assure quality implementation. Opportunities are provided for staffs to visit other Roots and Wings schools and to share videos of what teachers in each school are doing.

The pilot and replicating schools phase in all curricular elements of Roots and Wings over a period of two years. Training is provided for one subject area, and then teachers have several weeks or months to try out, adapt, and internalize the new method with assistance from the facilitator and project staff. After this component is well under way and the teacher's comfort level is secure, the next subject area is introduced, and so on. In this way, high quality implementations of all project elements can be ensured over time. We continue to model the "teamwork" approach to professional development through a collaborative decision-making process in which everyone's efforts can guarantee the success of each child.

Facilitators

From our experience with Success for All, we have learned that for a school to effectively implement a complex and closely coordinated set of changes in all aspects of school organization, curriculum, instruction, special services, family support, and other elements, there must be a highly qualified individual whose only responsibility is to help make certain that all programs are well implemented and that all staff members are working cooperatively to achieve the same broadly shared vision of what the school should be.

Each Roots and Wings school has a full-time facilitator whose job is to help the school's staff implement all the changes needed to make the program successful. The facilitator has many responsibilities. One is to visit classes as a nonevaluative coach to help teachers implement the Roots and Wings curricula. Facilitators give teachers feedback on what they are doing and may teach demonstration lessons or cover classes to allow teachers to observe others' classes. They organize meetings to provide opportunities for teachers working at the same age levels to help each other solve problems. Facilitators conduct workshops and coordinate training sessions on elements of the program, class management, family support, and other topics provided by Johns Hopkins staff. Facilitators manage the eight-week assessment program, including student placements. They use assessment information and teacher recommendations to identify students in need of adult or peer tutoring, family support services, or other services, and monitor the services provided to make sure they are making a difference. Facilitators organize meetings among teachers, tutors, family support staff, and others to coordinate services to students and to make sure that open and frequent communication among staff members working with the same students occurs. In short, the facilitator's role is to make certain that no child "falls between the cracks," that every child is moving as rapidly as possible toward attainment of world-class standards, and that resources are used effectively and efficiently.

Family Support and Integrated Services

Family Support and Integrated Services is designed to achieve three goals in the Roots and Wings project. It is the component which works to ensure (a) success for every child, (b) the empowerment of parents through partnership, and (c) the integration of services to children and families. Each school has a site-based team of school personnel who are concerned with four areas: attendance, school-based intervention, parent involvement, and creating and maintaining effective connections with community service providers. In addition, there is a network of community service providers who provide a broad range of necessary services for children and families.

Roots and Wings schools adapt community services and supports to their local needs and resources. Examples of activities from the pilot sites are illustrative of the goals we have in this area:

Attendance. Family Support Teams in Roots and Wings schools monitor attendance, create incentive programs, and make home visits along with district pupil personnel workers (PPWs) for children with chronic attendance and tardiness problems.

School-Based Intervention. Many Roots and Wings schools have a full-time family support coordinator. This coordinator manages the family support team meetings. She or he is in charge of ensuring that agendas are developed, notification of meetings is timely, case managers are assigned, parents are invited, and follow-ups are scheduled. School staff receive a series of workshops on Family Support and are aware of the mechanism and procedures for referral. This team is designed to be an early intervention team so the referral process is easy and can be used quickly by teachers. In addition, schedules may be changed in order to provide better access of services to families. Guidance counselors may have some evening hours, and the family support coordinator may work a flexible shift.

In addition to early intervention, the Family Support Team plans and develops classroom-based prevention efforts. Social skills lessons are used to augment the development of cooperative teams in the classroom. These units include basic lessons in listening skills, empathy skills, and team building skills. Lessons on conflict resolution and social problem-solving skills are being integrated with the World Lab curriculum. Novels and books that highlight these areas are available for the reading segment so that social skills are woven into the curriculum and school day. All schools review discipline procedures in order to ensure that children use a social problem-solving model. Class councils are often set up to enable classes to brainstorm solutions to ongoing student- and teacher-identified problems. In addition, parenting skills classes and in-services for parents are often made available so parents can help encourage their children to use the same problem-solving strategies at home that they use in school.

Family Support Teams have also developed school buddy programs, peer tutoring programs, and volunteer listener projects to ensure that the school offers a wider variety of support mechanisms for students who may need them. The goal of school-based intervention is to be preventive as well as providing early intervention. Teams continue to assess the specific needs of their sites and develop projects accordingly.

Parent Involvement. Broadening parent involvement is a main focus for Family Support. The family support coordinator has the implementation of a wide range of parent involvement projects under her purview. In particular, schools may develop a Welcome Wagon for new families. Parents have been recruited to be volunteer listeners at school and participate in a wide range of activities. Schools have planned a wide array of parent activities. In particular, many schools have parent activities that are designed to help parents understand and support the new school curriculum at home. One example of this is a program called Books & Breakfast in which parents learn how to support literacy in the home setting.

Service Integration. The Family Support Team is the mechanism that consistently links community services to the school. In particular, the family support coordinator is the main contact person for community providers. This team works to broaden business partnerships and develop partnerships with local organizations.

A major focus of Roots and Wings is to integrate community services into schools. The goal is not only to provide better access and linkage but to really coordinate service delivery. The goals of Roots and Wings go beyond co-location of services. Better service delivery to children and families by better coordination is the goal. Duplication of effort and poor communication often limit the success of service delivery. By using a team approach, services should be provided in a more timely and unified fashion. Each school has specific connections to local health, social service, and mental health agencies. Several specific projects have been implemented and a more thorough discussion of each one is provided.

After-School Programming

Roots and Wings schools may organize after-school programs. The initial goals are primarily academic. For example, schools may have enrichment tutoring and a homework club. Certified teachers are usually the main source of tutors. Another form of after-school tutoring is the use of cross-age peers. Students in the intermediate block are given special instruction in how to tutor younger children and then assigned to work with children having difficulty in basic skills in the lower grades. Peer tutoring is provided for students with less severe problems. Finally, tutoring is provided by adult mentors who are local volunteers. In addition, there may be a range of recreational, cultural, and arts activities at each site.

Special Education

Roots and Wings incorporates an approach to special and remedial education called "neverstreaming" (Slavin, 1996). What this means is that special education resources will be directed toward prevention, especially for children ages birth to five, and early intervention. These programs are closely coordinated with the Roots and Wings early childhood program, described earlier.

For most students at risk of being categorized as learning disabled or mildly to moderately mentally retarded, early intervention takes the form of one-to-one tutoring in reading at ages six or seven, but students may also receive family support services, social skills training, behavioral interventions, speech or language assistance, or other services closely integrated with their progress in the regular school program. Special education teachers and resources provide these preventative and early intervention services to all at-risk students, whether or not they have IEPs.

Thus, nearly all children who would ordinarily be in special education are instead maintained in the regular classroom programs and served flexibly by any of these supplementary services. However, for those students who still require special education and related services, their IEP clearly specifies special services that enable them to participate as fully as possible in the regular classrooms.

Implementation Process for New Schools

The implementation process for Roots and Wings is patterned on one we have used successfully to disseminate Success for All, the program that forms the basis of many of the elements of Roots and Wings, such as reading, writing/language arts, preschool and kindergarten curricula, tutoring, family support, facilitators, and other program elements. As of fall 1995, Success for All is being implemented in more than 300 schools in 70 districts in 25 states throughout the U.S. and in Canada. Initially, much of our dissemination effort is directed toward adding to existing Success for All schools the new program elements developed for Roots and Wings, especially WorldLab and Math Wings. When schools express interest in becoming Roots and Wings schools, our recommendation is that they first become Success for All schools and then add WorldLab and Math Wings in the second year of implementation.

The implementation process we use for Roots and Wings is designed to ensure that each school meets the highest standards of quality and fidelity to the model. We always adapt to local needs, interests, and resources, but key elements of our design we expect to see in place in all Roots and Wings schools. In the early phases of program adoption we are trying to see that the conditions for effective implementation exist, that schools have the district support, resources, and staff support to ensure a quality implementation. Considerations for implementation of Roots and Wings appear below.

1. *All School Staffs Must Have Made an*
   Informed Choice to Use Roots and Wings
Our most important requirement is that schools implementing Roots and Wings have clear district support for this decision, a clear commitment on the part of the principal, and a vote by secret ballot of at least 80 percent of the teaching staff. We strongly recommend that district administrators, principals, and representatives of teachers and parents arrange to visit existing Roots and Wings or Success for All schools. We also strongly recommend that key decision makers read this document and other publications describing the program in detail. There is an awareness videotape on Roots and Wings that all school staff should view. Roots and Wings involves

change in almost every aspect of elementary school organization, instruction, and curriculum. Everyone involved needs to know what the program is and to make a free choice to implement the model. Johns Hopkins staff are available to arrange visits, to negotiate with district administrators, and when the district and principals have decided they would like to move forward, to present the program to school staffs, parents, and community members.

2. District Administrators Must
Clearly Support the Program

Because it affects so many aspects of the schools that adopt it, we have found that it is essential that district administrators unequivocally support the implementation of Roots and Wings in their districts. This means more than that the superintendent approves. Roots and Wings almost always becomes the school's Title I program (and is usually funded primarily from Title I funds). It should become an important part of the school's special education program. It involves substantial curriculum changes in every subject. As a result, district administrators in charge of Title I, special education, curriculum and instruction, and other relevant areas should be informed and supportive from the beginning.

3. The Main Program Elements Must
Be Implemented

We are always willing to negotiate with districts about adaptations of Roots and Wings to meet the needs and resources of individual schools. We are also willing to discuss implementation of elements of Roots and Wings in schools that are interested in some but not all components. However, for schools that intend to become full-fledged Roots and Wings schools, several key elements must be included in a school's implementation plan. These are as follows.

- *One-to-one tutoring* will be provided by certified teacher-tutors. There should be at least one tutor for every 50 Title I eligible students. Tutoring will be delivered in 20-minute blocks every day to each eligible student. (Range of tutor/student ratio is 1:5 to 1:10.) While certified teachers are best for students with the most serious reading problems, well qualified paraprofessionals may serve as tutors for other at-risk students. Other cost-effective means of providing adequate tutoring include paying teachers to stay after school to tutor, hiring retired teachers, or having special education or ESL teachers do some tutoring.

- A full-time *facilitator* who works with the teachers in a Roots and Wings school is needed to implement the program successfully and provide ongoing assistance to teachers. The facilitator will need to be supported with a budget for training and travel to Baltimore once each year.

- A *Family Support Team* needs to be established to help support parents in ensuring the success of their children. It will focus on attendance, coordination of outside social services, parent involvement, and student behavior. If the school has less than 95 percent attendance, a schoolwide *attendance program*, usually including a half-time monitor, should be established. Additional staff for family support, such as social workers or counselors, are recommended. Family Support Team meetings should be seen as a priority within the school as indicated by release time for administrators and teachers to attend meetings that involve their students.

- A *full-day kindergarten or half-day pre-kindergarten* is desirable. The pre-kindergarten and kindergarten program use thematic units, Story Telling and Retelling (STaR), and a variety of curriculum supplements. The focus of the program is on language development. In January of the kindergarten year, students may start the Reading Roots curriculum if district policies support the teaching of reading in kindergarten.

- In grades one through five or six, schools ultimately must commit to *implementing Reading Roots* (grade 1), Reading Wings (grades 2–6), Roots and Wings Writing/Language Arts, Math Wings, and WorldLab. These curricula are generally phased in over a two-year period beginning with reading programs, but sequence and pace are negotiated with each school.

- Students will be grouped heterogeneously for homeroom and most of the school day *but regrouped across grade lines* (grades 1 through 3) so that each reading class contains students at one reading level. Tutors are used as reading teachers during reading time to reduce class size. Groups will be re-evaluated every eight weeks for the purpose of making reading group and tutorial placements.

- *School and classroom libraries* may need to be supplemented to address the needs of the reading curriculum.

- The schools involved should have a commitment to significant *reduction or elimination of the numbers of special education referrals and a reduction or elimination of the use of retention* as an intervention.

- A *Building Advisory Committee* should be established to help shape program policy and guide program development. At a minimum, this committee should consist of the principal, the facilitator, and representative teachers and parents. Existing committees of this type can assume this function.

- *Scheduling adjustments* to accommodate 90-minute reading periods and 10 to 12 tutoring slots per tutor need to be made.

- Time and resources for *staff development* prior to and during the program need to be identified. During the first year of the program, at least six and as many as ten staff development days will be necessary.

- Time for *grade-level team meetings* at least every two weeks needs to be built into the teachers' schedules to allow for the faculty to problem solve and support one another.

- Schools that teach reading in Spanish may use the Spanish version of Reading Roots and Reading Wings. Schools with many limited English proficient (LEP) students that do not teach reading in Spanish may use the English version with adaptations to the needs of LEP students.

- If schools have significant technology resources available, technology can be integrated into the Roots and Wings program, especially in WorldLab at the upper grade levels.

- Schools may implement after-school programs to provide opportunities for enrichment and for individual or group tutorial or homework assistance.

4. Districts Must Adequately Staff Roots and Wings
   Schools and Provide Funding for Training
   Materials and Other Expenses

The Roots and Wings curriculum and instructional program could be used without tutors, family support staff, and other staff, but at present we are emphasizing dissemination to districts able to implement something close to our vision of a school in which very few students fail or require special or remedial education, and this requires tutors and other staff. Based on our experience with Success for All, we believe that most high-poverty schools can implement Roots and Wings using existing Title I, local, and special education resources, especially if Title I dollars are not required to fund preschool or extended-day kindergarten programs. Schools with fewer disadvantaged students and, therefore, fewer Title I dollars, often require funds from elsewhere: desegregation funds, state funds, Goals 2000 or Eisenhower funds, bilingual education funds, foundation or government grants, and so on. Costs generally diminish over time as the need to provide remedial services for older children diminishes. The resource requirements for staff development, staff, and nonpersonnel for implementing Roots and Wings are detailed in Table 8.1.

Outcomes

There are many early indicators of program outcomes in Roots and Wings. First, in our pilot schools, students are performing substantially better in reading, and assignments to special education for learning disabilities have been significantly reduced. This should not be surprising; studies of Success for All in nine districts around the U.S. have consistently found similar outcomes (Slavin, Madden, Dolan, & Wasik, 1996), and the Roots and Wings reading, tutoring, and special education approaches are adapted from Success for All. However, we have also begun to see improvements in our Roots and Wings pilot schools on the Maryland School Performance Assessment Program (MSPAP), a state-of-the-art performance-based test, in social studies, science, math, and writing (as well as reading). This is particularly important; the MSPAP is the kind of performance-based assessment that many states are moving toward in their accountability testing programs.

Figures 8.1 and 8.2 show gains over three years in MSPAP scores for third and fifth graders, respectively. The figures show substantial gains over that time period in the percentage of students scoring satisfactory or above on all six MSPAP scales. The overall State of Maryland also increased over this time period, but far less than the Roots and Wings schools. Averaging across the six scales, the percentage of Maryland third graders scoring satisfactory or better increased in 1993–1995 by 8.6 percentage points, in comparison to a gain of 18.9 for Roots and Wings schools. For fifth graders, the state gained an average of 6.4 percent while Roots and Wings schools gained 13.0. This was true despite the fact that the Roots and

Table 8.1

Resource Requirements for
Implementing Roots and Wings
Implementation Years 1–3

	Quantity	Price	Cost	Comments
STAFF DEVELOPMENT REQUIREMENTS				
Teacher Time	25 teachers x 6 days			released time; costs vary by school
Trainers	20 days per year	$800 per day	$16,000	on-site training conducted by R&W staff
PERSONNEL REQUIREMENTS				
Facilitator	1.0 FTE			provided by school; usually reallocation of existing staff
Tutors	3 to 4 teachers			usually reallocated Title 1 teachers
Central Office Coordinator	0.1 FTE			provided by jurisdiction; to support ten schools/jurisdiction implementation
NONPERSONNEL REQUIREMENTS				
Instructional Materials			$20,000	includes all duplicating costs
Travel/food/ accommodations for R&W staff	10 two-day trips	$900 per trip	$ 9,000	includes travel expenses to/from site for R&W trainers to conduct training & follow-up sessions
Site Planning Fee			$ 2,000	one-time fee for first year only; to plan implementation and offer awareness programs in community

Note. Requirements are for planning purposes only; they are meant as a starting point for further discussions with the Design Team. All or most of these requirements may be met by reallocating existing resources. These are per school costs assuming the following: at least five schools in a jurisdiction; school size equals 500 PK–5 or PK–6 students; staff of 25 teachers; schools are Title 1 schools.

Figure 8.1

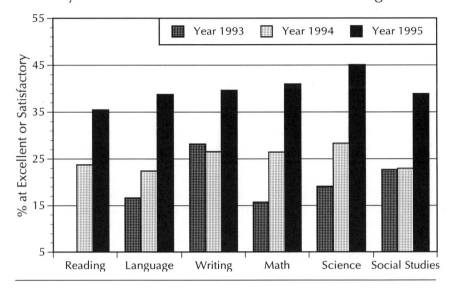

Roots and Wings, *Third Grade*, St. Mary's County
Maryland School Performance Assessment Program

Figure 8.2

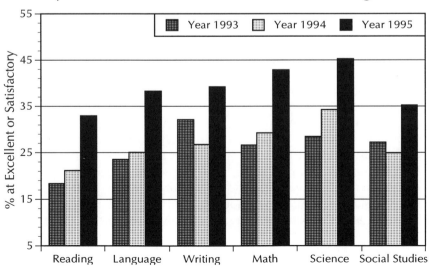

Roots and Wings, *Fifth Grade*, St. Mary's County
Maryland School Performance Assessment Program

Wings schools served many more children in poverty, had three times as many Title I students, and had mobility rates twice the state average.

As of this writing, the dissemination of Roots and Wings is just getting under way. Beyond its pilot sites in St. Mary's County, Maryland, Roots and Wings programs are beginning in Memphis, Miami, Baltimore County (MD), Cincinnati, Aldine (TX), Flint (MI), and other locations. However, the parent of Roots and Wings, Success for All, is currently being implemented in more than 400 schools in 95 school districts in 28 states throughout the U.S. Success for All schools use the early childhood, literacy, tutoring, family support, and school organization elements of Roots and Wings, and as we add WorldLab and MathWings to this base, we will have a broadly disseminated alternative to traditional elementary school programs. In particular, we expect changes in Chapter 1/ Title I to cause schools to begin looking for comprehensive, proven models of fundamental reform keyed to new forms of performance assessment soon to be emphasized in state and Chapter 1/Title I accountability programs. By the year 2000, we hope to have more than 1,000 Roots and Wings schools.

In the next stage of school reform we must have effective, replicable, and comprehensive designs for total school restructuring capable of being adapted to a wide range of circumstances and needs. Roots and Wings provides one practical vision of what elementary schools could be like if we were to decide to give *every* child the academic grounding and the thinking skills, creativity, and broad world view we expect today of only our most gifted children.

Notes

Roots and Wings is a collaborative project of the John Hopkins University, the Maryland State Department of Education, and the St. Mary's County (MD) Public Schools funded by the New American Schools Development Corporation. Key design team members have included Cecelia Daniels, Stan Bennett, Coleen Furey, Pat Baltzley, Kathy Simons, Mary Alice Bond, Irene Waclawiw, Margaret Livingston, Laura Rice, Anna Marie Farnish, Carolyn Gwaltney, Barbara Haxby, Sam Stringfield, Alta Shaw, and Robert Petza of Johns Hopkins University; Lynn Linde and Joan Palmer of the Maryland State Department of Education; and Joan Kozlovsky, Kristin Berryman, Elfreda Mathis, Janice Walthour, Mary Blakely, Janet Kellam, Ron Thomas, and Pat Richardson of the St. Mary's County (MD) Public Schools.

References

Joyce, B. R., Hersh, R. H., & McKibbin, M. (1983). *The structure of school improvement.* New York: Longman.

Madden, N. A., Slavin, R. E., Karweit, N. L., Dolan, L. J., & Wasik, B. A. (1993). Success for All: Longitudinal effects of a restructuring program for inner-city elementary schools. *American Educational Research Journal, 30,* 123–148.

Slavin, R. E. (1996). Neverstreaming: Preventing learning disabilities. *Educational Leadership 53*(5).

Slavin, R. E., Karweit, N. L., & Madden, N. A. (Eds.) (1989). *Effective programs for students at risk.* Boston: Allyn & Bacon.

Slavin, R. E., Karweit, N. L., & Wasik, B. A. (Eds.) (1994). *Preventing early school failure.* Boston: Allyn & Bacon.

Slavin, R. E., Madden, N. A., Dolan, L. J., & Wasik, B. A. (1992). *Success for All: A relentless approach to prevention and early intervention in elementary schools.* Arlington, VA: Educational Research Service.

Slavin, R. E., Madden, N. A., Dolan, L., & Wasik, B. A. (1994.). Roots and Wings: Universal excellence in elementary education. *Educational Leadership 52*(3), 10–13.

Slavin, R. E., Madden, N. A., Dolan, L. J., & Wasik, B. A. (1996). *Every child, every school: Success for All.* Newbury Park, CA: Corwin.

Slavin, R. E., Madden, N. A., Dolan, L. J., Wasik, B. A., Ross, S., & Smith, L. (1994). "Whenever and wherever we choose . . .": The replication of Success for All. *Phi Delta Kappan, 75*(8), 639–647.

Stevens, R. J., Madden, N.A., Slavin, R.E., & Farnish, A.M. (1987). Cooperative Integrated Reading and Composition: Two field experiments. *Reading Research Quarterly, 22,* 433-454.

Wasik, B. A., & Slavin, R. E. (1993). Preventing early reading failure with one-to-one tutoring. In R. E. Slavin, N. L. Karweit, & B. A. Wasik (Eds.), *Preventing Early School Failure* (pp. 143–174). Boston: Allyn & Bacon.

Community Learning Centers

Wayne B. Jennings, Designs for Learning

The Community Learning Centers (CLC) program describes a comprehensive, top-to-bottom school design to dramatically increase the school achievement of all students. As such, the design is complex and exacting to implement in its entirety given long-standing school traditions, beliefs and policies. However, it is our conviction that only a systemic model for school change will raise American education to the level required for a sophisticated democratic society and the competitive world of the 21st century.

In the past most of the changes installed in schools didn't last even when they were proven effective practices. In one of the most telling reports, Nachtigal (1972) and other researchers visited sites where the Ford Foundation, over the period of a decade, had made "comprehensive school improvement" grants totaling $30 million. They found little remained of the promising efforts to reform education. The problem was that the rest of the system didn't accommodate the innovation. In most cases, the innovation had withered or disappeared without a trace. Most institutional change is piecemeal and fragmented. Educators toil to bring about changes in the present system of education and many have been successful at introducing new practices. We don't disparage this type of incremental change as many organizations develop this way. But in most cases, isolated incremental changes do not come to fruition or endure. Instead, they give an illusion of progress through a facade of activity. According to Sizer (1983, p. 674), most of the problems that beset education ". . . are obvious, well understood, and of long standing. Educators and their critics have been rhetorically hammering away at them for

Figure 9.1

Community Learning Centers Features

several decades. It is the remedies that seem problematic. None seems to stick. Why? Things remain the same, because it is impossible to change very much without changing most of everything. The result is paralysis."

The CLC design is meant as a systemic change model because it addresses the major aspects of schooling: staffing, instructional methods, curriculum, allocation of resources, technology, parental roles, training, governance, outcomes, assessment, and partnerships (see Fig. 9.1 for an overview). In addition, the design confronts the suffocating barriers to institutional change with the mechanisms of choice, contracts, and charters. The design probably best fits school districts that consciously and deliberately choose to make major advances in one or more of their schools. However, most districts work at incremental change and are unable to propose systemic change for political or other reasons.

The CLC design was created during New American Schools (NAS) Phase I by a team of researchers and practitioners at Designs For Learning, a school transformation consulting firm in St. Paul, Minnesota. Once the design was published, the team solicited interest for implementing the design for NAS Phase II. Over 80 preliminary proposals were received from throughout the nation. These were winnowed to the 21 strongest, and a team from each was funded to attend a conference to review what was involved in preparing a final proposal on comprehensive school change. As requested, each team attending the conference included school staff, parents, community members, and students, if possible. The teams were told of the complexities of implementing the design during the next two years. This was done in the spirit of full disclosure and to reduce the carrot factor of applying primarily to obtain the additional funding for start-up training and technology acquisition. Submission of a final proposal would be judged, in addition to the usual criteria, on the diversity of the team preparing the proposal and degree of community support for their plans. Twenty proposals were received and ten were chosen as CLC sites. In the spring 1993 NAS ran into funding problems and was unable to assure teams of the implementation phase. This meant the CLC sites could not be told if they should proceed. As a result, sites were unable to shape budgets and staffing for the new design during the normal time of year for finalizing budgets and notifying staff about the following year's employment. The massive training planned for the summer preceding fall implementation to prepare staff, parents, and community was scrapped. In addition to the delay in supporting Phase II, the expected level of funding was cut 60 percent. The number of sites was reduced to seven, all in Minnesota, to save on transportation and other costs.

The final school sites were diverse: urban, rural, tribally controlled, charter, and conventional schools. Training took place as the year progressed. As could be expected there was huge variation in the progress of the schools. Some were new charter schools with inexperienced staff hired just a week before school began. Many staff at the sites had virtually no knowledge of CLC expectations. It took a major effort to bring everyone to a state of understanding of the CLC design and then to confronting the issues of implementing the design. During the second year, an evaluation firm was employed to visit all sites and conduct a careful appraisal of these factors:

1. How well the design had been implemented.

2. Feasibility of the design as viewed by stakeholders at each site.

3. Student performance data.

The evaluation report found some sites had made excellent progress at implementing the CLC design and that all sites, in general, found the design feasible (Miller, 1995). Problems were found in differentiating staff in one school because of union issues, and in another, small rooms limited an increase in class size. Other difficult to implement features included lump sum budgeting in conventional school districts, the freedom to select appropriate and remove inappropriate staff in conventional schools districts, a reluctance to substantially reallocate budgets differently, and issues around integrating community social services. Sites also reported that teachers and aides had difficulty making the many paradigm shifts inherent in the design. For example, the design called for basing curriculum at least in part on student questions about themselves and society. With few exceptions, teachers found this outside their training and experience. These problems were not unexpected by the CLC design team who felt that the lack of initial training and the less than two years for implementation were inadequate for most of the sites to implement the complex design. Nonetheless, sites became committed to the design and stated their desire to continue implementation with or without additional assistance. They particularly continue to want technical assistance and training.

The CLC design was established to cost no more than conventional schools beyond a startup amount for training and technology of about $200,000 for a school of 500 students. Beyond this, design costs were to be reallocated within the school budget by changing many of the usual expenditure items. For CLC sites, this required building a base of understanding about school revenues and expenditures and an unwavering commitment to the bottom line of student achievement versus protecting past practices and positions.

An implementation guide has been developed by Jennings (1995) to pilot a school or school district on the path to establishing CLCs. It recommends beginning by developing a broad base of understanding which can lead to support by all stakeholders. This takes time but creates the foundation for a robust and enduring structure. The guide provides details for implementing the various elements of the CLC design.

Key Elements of the Design

The following principles and elements define the CLC design and guide its approach to reinventing American schools:

1. CLC sites represent systemic or comprehensive change. All assumptions about education are open to examination for the end result of greater student achievement by all youth and the establishment of the Centers as headquarters for lifelong learning in their communities.

2. Each CLC site must negotiate with the local governance authority to become a charter or contract school in order to overcome barriers to systemic change. CLCs can be organized as charter schools (provided for in some state statutes) or the equivalent (as provided by authority of the state superintendent in some states or under tribal governance) or as a tightly drawn contract between the Center and the school district. The contract authorizes broad site decision-making powers in the areas of program, staffing, and budget. Each Center must have the local, state, and federal revenues students earn and the authority to shape the program, staffing, and budget to accomplish its mission and organization.

3. CLCs have well articulated missions, beliefs, and assumption statements to guide their development. The foundation of these statements lies in the increased achievement for all students.

4. Standards for attainment of major outcomes must be of a caliber that exceeds traditional levels in preparing students for their major roles in a complex, changing society. Assessment of achievement is in part embedded into daily work and evaluated through competency expectations, exhibitions, portfolios, or presentations, and checked against nationally normed tests. Community input is essential in establishing standards.

5. Curriculum is designed from outcomes. Sites design powerful learning experiences that assure development of skills, knowledge, and attitudes for success in life. *Curriculum* is defined as all the learning experiences of the student irrespective of place, time, or person.

6. Learning experiences are based on modern learning principles and are child-centered, experiential, life-centered, and brain-

based, that is, compatible with the power of the brain to assimilate and organize learnings.

7. Each learner has a Personal Learning Plan (PLP) in which goals, experiences to reach goals, and progress toward goals are recorded. The PLP defines each student's schedule of learning activities. Each learner has an advisor who meets periodically with the learner and parent to build and review the PLP. Computer software aids in recording PLP goals and activities.

8. Resources are reallocated to accomplish program ends. More is spent on instructional materials, instructional equipment, field trips, staff development, and community-based learning than in most schools. Large technology expenditures are capitalized over time. School budgets are lump-sum based and include all revenues students earn from all sources.

9. CLCs elevate the position of teachers to "facilitators of learning" and a variety of support staff augment the work of teachers for specialized functions. Teacher productivity is increased with the assistance of paraprofessionals, clerks, technology specialists, community resource linkers, and volunteers. Levels of teaching are compensated on the basis of responsibility, skill, productivity, and other factors. Staffing includes others: parents, community resource people (citizens, seniors, business employees, agency staff) and students. All teachers agree to three fundamental roles: teaching, advising, and participating in continuous improvement, both professional and school-wide.

10. Staff development occurs the equivalent of 20 to 30 days a year, every year. Staff development is based on a Professional Growth Plan each staff member maintains stating goals, strengths, areas for improvement, professional growth activities, and progress reviews.

11. Maximum effective use of technology empowers learners and staff. All students routinely use word processing, electronic mail, spreadsheets and databases. Many use desktop publishing, graphics, music, multimedia, and other programs.

12. Students are viewed as powerful resources and become an integral part of staffing. Their active participation in decisions

about the school and their own program contributes to cognitive development and adds a considerable measure of deep connection. Their contributions of ideas and actions increase the pool of creative thinking for problem solving and their school service responsibilities lighten the workload for all.

13. Stakeholders, defined as those affected by decisions, participate in making key decisions about program, staffing, and budget. Teachers make curriculum decisions and are accountable for student learning outcomes. Decisions are data-based and checked against outcomes and results.

14. The program vigorously involves parents in their child's education in several ways: participating in student-advisor conferences for goal setting; helping determine paths to goals; reviewing progress regularly; sharing skills and experiences; providing home-based learning reinforcement, and participating in governance. The program assists parents with the development of family learning plans.

15. Partnerships with other units of government, public and private agencies, early childhood programs, and post-secondary education are maximized to share community resources, reduce fragmented services, and decrease duplication. Social services are integrated with education through agreements for collaborative services and shared costs, revenues, and location.

16. Program choice is provided to students and parents. No one is required to attend or work at the CLCs. Parents and staff have a choice of the conventional programs. The student body represents the pool of applicants and reflects the racial, socioeconomic, and academic makeup of the community. Outreach efforts are made to recruit underrepresented groups.

17. CLCs are headquarters for lifelong formal and informal learning for the entire community. As such, they are open year round with extended hours (24 hours a day electronically). Richly stocked collections of learning materials are available on site or electronically for all ages. The costs of this feature are defrayed with community education programs, another part by overlapping staff shifts, and by expanded definitions of the school day and what constitutes faculty.

18. CLCs de-emphasize typical double-loaded corridors of class-rooms and support active learning environments such as media centers, production studios, discovery centers, theaters of learning, labs, community-based learning and work stations for computer applications. The learning environment must be inviting, convivial, and accessible to the community.

19. Support mechanisms must be in place to sustain change such as: funding stability, broad site-based decision-making authority, feedback on progress, and staff rewards and recognition. Attention must be paid to staff mental health to increase productivity and to avoid burnout and stress.

Certainly, this is a challenging list of changes. Many of these features won't work or make sense without a systemic view. Most of the 19 items are a system themselves within the system of a school. Most have proven themselves in limited settings but have not endured or flowered because the remainder of the system did not accommodate the innovation. What makes this design compelling is that it addresses all aspects of school operation, thereby standing a chance of creating real reform and of substantially boosting achievement of all students. It's as though a 1940 model Remington typewriter was being improved incrementally with a motor, a type wheel, and a correcting ribbon. On such a course, the typewriter will never be a word processor. The design team believes that schools will not achieve the breakthroughs thought necessary to raise all students' achievement without a systemic approach. The history of school reform doesn't support piecemeal and incremental change as sufficient to produce the change necessary to reach all youth and to adequately prepare them for citizenship and work.

Vision or Mission Statement

The following basic beliefs about learning govern CLCs. These ideals furnish a foundation for building the program and procedures.

Mission

All learners will enjoy school and will become effective people and responsible citizens. Basic beliefs comprise the following:

- Students are talented, precious, and special.

- Differences are to be prized and supported.

- Students are eager, curious learners.

- Parents are indispensable partners.

- Staff care deeply about providing a high quality program.

- Learning means active engagement, exploration, and inquiry.

- Schools control the conditions for learners' successes.

- Schools strive for continuous improvement.

Absolutes

- Choice of programs is provided to staff and students.

- Inappropriate staff are moved from the program.

- Decisions about program, staffing, and the total budget are made by program stakeholders.

Educational innovation is often short-circuited by a failure to follow up or to determine the implications of the noble statements above. To maintain the momentum of reform efforts, CLCs confront the following questions:

1. What usual school practices violate our beliefs and must, therefore, be discontinued?

2. What present practices support our beliefs and should be continued or extended?

3. What new practices must be initiated to support the beliefs?

Standards and Assessment

Learning Outcomes

The learning outcomes at CLCs focus on bringing students to a high level of competence as workers, citizens, family members, and consumers in a complex, diverse, and rapidly changing society. Learning outcomes must be explicit, meaningful, and measurable to students, parents, and the community. *Explicit* means that students and parents understand the outcome and are able to gauge their status in relation to it, knowing precisely what remains to be learned.

Meaningful means that students and parents see the sense of the outcome, recognize it as valuable for life, and accept the challenge of accomplishing it. *Measurable* means staff, students, and parents understand the criteria and assessments used to determine progress toward outcomes and know when a performance standard has been met. The outcomes take the form of complex behaviors or roles. These five suggested outcomes require that each student become a:

- productive worker,

- responsible citizen,

- problem solver,

- self-directed lifelong learner,

- creative, healthy individual.

After a school and its community have established their major outcomes, each is expanded with a definition and more specific outcomes. For one example of the next step, consider the first outcome, *productive worker*. The Department of Labor in a recent significant publication described the expectations by employers for employees at all levels of compensation (SCANS, 1993). Figure 9.2 shows their condensed list.

The outcomes apply at any grade level and provide a framework for developing curriculum. Most teachers at the fifth grade would desire students to have or be developing all of these competencies and could plan learning experiences to aid students to grow in these areas.

Assessment

Creating challenging standards for outcomes requires at least three important steps.

1. Stakeholders establish a short list of clear outcomes related to life roles including, for example, the five outcomes listed above.

2. Stakeholders define the outcomes by elaborating on their meaning. This could be accomplished, for example, using the SCANS material to elaborate the productive worker outcome.

3. Standards and benchmarks are established as measures for student attainment, for example, stating a level of attainment that students of a certain age are expected to achieve.

Figure 9.2

Competencies for the Workplace

A Three-Part Foundation

➤ Basic Skills: Reads, writes, performs arithmetic and mathematical operations, listens, and speaks

➤ Thinking Skills: Thinks creatively, makes decisions, solves problems, visualizes, knows how to learn, and reasons

➤ Personal Qualities: Displays responsibility, self-esteem, sociability, self-management, and integrity and honesty

Five Competencies

➤ Resources: Identifies, organizes, plans, and allocates resources

➤ Interpersonal: Works with others

➤ Information: Acquires and uses information

➤ Systems: Understands complex interrelationships

➤ Technology: Works with a variety of technologies

Benchmarks or standards help transform assessment from strictly a norm-referenced to a criterion-referenced measurement. For example, staff might expect 10-year-olds to be able to produce a school newsletter using desktop publishing and meeting predetermined standards of clear expression and grammatical correctness. The primary mode of assessing student attainment of learning outcomes are performance-based tasks, portfolios, and demonstrations or exhibitions of competence. To the extent that they are available, state or national performance assessments are used. Examples are tests developed in connection with subject areas or those used by the National Assessment of Educational Progress, as they become available for local use. In addition, to ascertain how well students are doing in comparison to others nationally, CLCs use norm-referenced tests.

Other areas of student assessment include teacher observations, student self-assessment, and work samples. The Centers also obtain valuable information for program decision making through these kinds of data: parent and student satisfaction surveys, attendance and graduation rates, numbers and types of books read, behavior reports, and types of learning experiences.

Curriculum and Instructional Strategies

Modern Principles of Learning

The educational approach is brain-compatible. This means learning that accelerates with large amounts of input and with many opportunities for students to learn by doing, inquiring, and discovering. Learning must be active, engaging, and immediately applicable. Brain-based learning is a systems approach and encompasses many practices known to advance permanent learning. Another compatible source of learning theory is found in the Presidential Task Force on Psychology in Education of the American Psychological Association (1993) publication, *Learner-Centered Psychological Principles*.

Leslie Hart (1983) developed the Proster Theory of Human Learning and popularized the term *brain-based* learning, which postulates four basic building blocks of the brain's functioning:

Patterns or Understandings. Patterns are structures in the brain that represent recognition or understanding. Patterns develop from experience, most efficiently in a rich and stimulating environment which contributes large amounts of input to the brain.

Programs or Instructions. Programs in the brain enable one to walk or jump, button a shirt, solve problems, or to speak or write the word *hot*. Speaking, for example, requires a massive number of instructions from the brain to facial muscles, vocal cords, lungs, and other regions of the body. Programs are learned largely through trial and error, with refinement through practice. Humans develop and deepen thousands, perhaps millions, of programs through the reinforcement of carrying out activities many times in various ways.

Feedback or Assessment. The brain requires feedback to refine patterns and programs. In the practical sense, this means learning how well one did and receiving suggestions and coaching at all stages of development. Feedback applies, not only to physical actions, but also to thinking patterns, responses, and habits.

Safety and Security. Downshifting is a condition that occurs when a person feels threatened or in danger. The brain's focus involuntarily shifts from use of higher faculties to use of lower faculties (older in evolutionary time) to prepare for fight or flight. This explains why a child needs to feel safe and secure to learn.

Experiential Learning and Learning by Application

To implement brain-based learning our sites increased the use of field trips and involved greater numbers of community resource persons, thereby increasing input to the brain. They learned that brain-based learning supports experiential learning and learning by application. These types of learning activities engaged the energy and enthusiasm of youth. Examples of how these concepts were manifested at our sites included: participating in community service projects, working with a poet from the community, serving apprenticeships at local businesses, preparing television or theatrical productions, researching pollution levels of local waterways, peer teaching and cross-age tutoring, coaching, using technology, establishing democratic classrooms, and implementing a thematic curriculum that addressed the academic, career, cultural, and personal needs of students. Learners at CLC projects worked on real products (such as newsletters or models) and services (such as teaching word processing or helping in a day care center). Ideally, the entire world in all of its richness and reality becomes part of the school campus and plays a vitalizing role in expanding the program's learning experiences.

CLC sites view the community as a gold mine of people, events, and activities for learning. Students can create databases of the deep reservoirs of community talents: cooks, storytellers, trappers, clergy, doctors, miners, foresters, gardeners, travelers, hobbyists, artisans, business people, government agents, judges, policy analysts, and clinicians. Such resources are the sparks that bring life to topics being studied.

Learner-Centered Approach

Learner-centered approaches involve attention to student interests and learning styles. Content is made meaningful when students are involved in goal setting, determining paths to reaching goals, and appraising progress toward goals. At our sites, students, with the help of parents and faculty, design a personal learning plan (PLP). This procedure developed ownership and understanding of the learning process by students, teachers, and parents. Goals stated in the form of realistic and useful outcomes or results heightened motivation, energy, and commitment by students. Most former "problem" students, when viewed through the youth-as-resource paradigm, exhibited totally different behaviors and became successful learners. Diversity among learners becomes an opportunity, not a problem.

The role of the teacher must be that of collaborator and team leader and guide, rather than boss. The teacher monitors the academic and social growth of students, leading each into new areas of understanding and competence.

Curriculum

James Coleman (1972) pointed out that for youth growing up in 1900, society was information poor but responsibility rich. There were few newspapers and magazines and no television or radio. Nonetheless, youth had many chores and duties. Today's society, for youth, is the opposite: information-rich, but responsibility-poor. People are flooded with media and data, but youth have few responsibilities that clearly, visibly, and immediately benefit the well-being of their family or community. Schools must act on this societal change or run the risk of a curriculum seen as irrelevant to youth and the needs of society.

For CLC sites, curriculum isn't defined as just those experiences controlled by the school. It's all experiences of the student irrespective of time, place, or people. Education takes place in and out of school buildings, during and outside of school hours, from teachers and others. CLC sites recognize the power and educational value of family experiences, television, the grocer, clergy, playing, and other persons and activities in the student's life. The advisor, parent, and child consider past and present outside-the-school experiences in building a program.

A student's program is based on achieving high levels of performance toward major outcomes. Where assessments indicate unacceptable levels of achievement of content and skill outcomes, the program is modified to increase activity aimed at improving the weak areas. For example, take a case of weak writing skills. Imagine that the student's program includes working in the day care center part of the day and preparing a stage performance another part of the day. The advisor and learning facilitator could adjust the program to include additional writing such as writing in a journal each day, work on a computer program for capitalization and punctuation, and a short course on writing. The decision about each of these activities would be based on the student's needs and learning style.

For ease of access, record keeping, making revisions, and printing reports, each student's PLP is maintained with a software program. The program is used to catalog progress toward performance and content outcomes.

The PLP yields important information about the child's progress toward performance and content outcomes. Results of assessments indicate strengths and weaknesses. As students work on projects alone or in groups, skill and knowledge deficiencies become obvious to the student and staff members associated with the project.

The Advisor

Each student has an advisor and the success of the entire program resides fundamentally on how well advisors do their work. Thorough and ongoing training of staff in the advisor–advisee system must be provided. While many schools have established advisor programs, most fall far short of their potential by not maintaining a quality training program and following through with all aspects of advisor performance. The advisor is an educational broker, friend, helper, guide, counselor, suggester, appraiser, record keeper, facilitator, expediter, and arranger. The advisor must be able to plan with students rather than for them, to help the student grow in all areas, intellectual, social, and physical, and to develop talents and uniqueness. Our sites made good progress in establishing the rudiments of an advisor program. Much polishing of the role remains to be done to ensure a complete understanding of the purpose and operations of this program and its essential contribution to the success of the school's mission.

Professional Development

Necessity for Intense Staff Development

CLCs require intense amounts of effective staff development because of the design's exacting requirements. At our sites, traditionally trained staff had considerable difficulty understanding and implementing the design. It seemed they had to acquire new mind-sets and skills. Program success will be limited without training on an ongoing basis, follow-up coaching, and data-driven feedback to discern progress and to determine what remains to be done to achieve the full program design.

The dominant teaching paradigm is an enormous hurdle to school reform. Teachers grow up in a system of schooling that is much the same everywhere. Goodlad (1983) and Sizer (1984) found that courses, textbooks, and teaching methods are surprisingly similar across the United States in public and private schools. Teachers are trained, often urged, to depart from traditional practices that are dysfunctional for many children and youth. However, teachers are quickly socialized into the dominant system and discouraged by institutional traditions from adopting progressive teaching practices.

The paucity of good staff development and training is well known. Most schools schedule about five days a year, which is seriously inadequate to the task of transforming schools, particularly where high staff turnover occurs. The challenge of training staff in better ways of organizing and delivering learning must cope with the realities of life in schools. Staff training must be thorough and ongoing at the rate of 20 to 30 days a year, forever. To accomplish this degree of staff development, the total design contributes through such means as these:

• Teaming for joint planning,

• Releasing a member of the team to attend a conference or visit another program,

• Banking time so that a day of staff development can be scheduled periodically (accomplished by extending the number of minutes of instruction each day, thereby accumulating a pupil-free day),

• Extending the work day periodically for curriculum development,

• Reviewing videos and other professional materials.

Each staff member maintains a Professional Growth Plan as a condition of employment and as a means of assuring an orderly progression of increasing competence. The Professional Growth Plan includes an assessment of strengths, areas for improvement, short- and long-term goals, plans for accomplishing goals, a time line for accomplishing goals, and provisions for periodic progress reviews. The school's stakeholders (staff, parents, students, and community members) help evaluate all staff annually.

Technology

Schools are largely in the print age, while students and the world are moving rapidly to the electronic age. This dilemma creates serious problems for teachers struggling to maintain student engagement. Problems befall graduates when they enter the world of word processing, spreadsheets, databases, and multimedia work stations, where jobs go to those comfortable with such tools.

Just as the right tool in the hands of a carpenter multiplies productivity and quality of work, students and staff must be empowered with modern tools to multiply learning, increase productivity, and reduce tedious and repetitious actions. Such tools as desktop publishing, graphics programs, music software, and computer-aided design provide for the flowering of talents and abilities.

Funding Technology Acquisitions

Instructional equipment and materials are not one-time purchases; nor it is necessary to pay for all of it within one budget year. A huge initial investment can be capitalized over its useful life, three to five years for example. Consequently, the initial expenditure can be reduced by a factor of approximately two thirds. Maintenance costs, replacement costs, new products, and software must also be included. Our sites allocated about 10 to 15 percent of the total budget to technology instead of the more usual figure of 2 to 5 percent. Our experience showed that less than 10 percent would be inadequate for a school serving under 400 students. Above this enrollment number, economies of scale operate and the 10 to 15 percent allocation is sufficient to obtain threshold levels of a technologically enriched learning environment.

Schools must acquire about $1,000,000 of instructional equipment to enter the technology era. This level of funding will purchase, for example, computer labs, a television studio, a short-wave radio station, an electronic response classroom, a publishing center, take home laptop computers, drama equipment, science lab equipment, practical arts equipment, telecommunications equipment, and wiring. To do this with usual school budgets requires proceeding differently:

- Fewer staff can be funded. A reduction of staff makes sense only when coupled with systemic reform and won't work if all else remains the same.

- Equipment is capitalized over time so that the cost doesn't fall entirely in one year's budget.

- Leasing, renting, bonding or time payments provide means for spreading costs over the life of equipment.

Figure 9.3 compares some key budget areas between a conventional school (old school) and the recommendations for a CLC (new school). Fewer regular teachers would be employed. The number of paraprofessionals would increase substantially to about a 1:1 ratio with teachers (at about half the cost). Technology expenditures

Figure 9.3

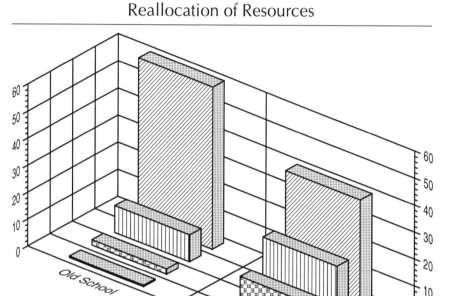

Reallocation of Resources

would move from about 2 to 10 percent of the total budget. Staff development would increase from about a 0.5 percent to 2 percent.

School Organization and Governance

A New Model for Staffing

Education is labor intensive, much like agriculture was in 1890. While education is a people-intensive activity, a correction must be made to recognize new thinking about how learning occurs and to provide powerful tools for learning. Maximum effective use of technology makes it possible to more efficiently allocate staff resources. There would be an essential core of the most expensive people, experienced teachers, elevated in status to facilitators of learning. The reallocated dollars would train and employ a greater number of paraprofessionals and provide funding for training, materials, and technology much as other modern institutions have done. Instead of being equipment poor, students and teachers must be empowered with technological tools. This is the equivalent of capitalizing employees in business to increase productivity. One of our sites ran a 1:1 ratio of teachers with paraprofessionals. Another came close to this figure. The conventional schools had great difficulty changing even slightly from the equivalent of a 1:20 ratio of paraprofessionals to teachers.

Because typical school district budgets spend heavily for personnel, 80 to 90 percent, reallocation of budget items must of necessity reduce the percentage for personnel. An exciting school with engaged students needs fewer teachers spending major portions of time monitoring assignments and managing behavior. At a CLC, students assume important responsibilities in teaching and school operations, not for the goal of saving money, although that occurs, but to gain valuable learning experiences, experiences that schools usually deny youth in the mistaken assumption that those activities carry little learning significance.

The paradigm shift that the CLCs represent can be accomplished if the right staff are in place. This means employing a small core of highly trained, highly motivated, and dedicated teachers. Such teachers already exist, but are often unappreciated in schools that are not involved in advanced practices of education. These teachers must be recruited to organize powerful learning experiences. They must be given relief from the overburden of tasks requiring less expertise. Paraprofessionals can accomplish many duties that teachers now perform and that currently take them away from more direct, high skill tasks of organizing learning experiences.

Because the personnel budget of CLCs is similar to, or smaller than, other schools (because of reallocating resources to other educational costs), an alternative staffing model has been devised. The student-to-teacher ratio must increase to accommodate employing other types of personnel. This means increasing the student–teacher ratio from 1.5 to 2 times the normal level. Few schools believe that they can manage such changes. Yet, in Minnesota such conventional schools (non-CLC sites) as Stonebridge Elementary School (Stillwater), Hillcrest Elementary (Bloomington), and the St. Paul Area Learning Center (at-risk high school) have operated at these ratios for years.

As unrealistic as the CLC staffing specification may seem, the CLC design needs to be seen in its entirety: It departs from standard classroom models, conventional subject-matter mastery curricula, and students in largely passive roles. Money released by having fewer professional teachers can be allocated for various specialists to assist teachers. The design aims to produce higher achievement by all students with the same resources schools now have. It might be well to consider the present level of resources. According to the Digest of Education Statistics (1993), on average, American schools have a licensed educator for every 15 students, an employee for every 9 students, and spend $5,700 per student. From the view of CLC researchers, these considerable resources led us to consider their redeployment. In the CLC design, teachers become facilitators of learning and supervisors of a team, a position of higher responsibility than in most traditional schools. Our sites wrestled with these concepts and some made excellent progress with this part of the design.

Teachers in this program must be top professionals, experts about learning, and managers of learning systems. Assistants handle many functions and assignments essential to the learning process, but that require less training and experience than the professional teacher. Compensation can be adjusted on the basis of experience, productivity, and responsibility (e.g., teaching, advising, participation in school improvement, organizing curriculum, and staff development), skill (e.g., content knowledge, application of learning principles, teaching methods, and relationships) and outcomes (e.g., learning results, engagement of learners, and success with all students).

A significant shift in staffing can occur when schools enlist students, parents, and volunteers in delivering instruction under teacher supervision. Kurth-Schai (1988) found students an essential and untapped resource that must become an integral part of staffing by assisting in many functions of the school. She felt that to do less undercuts youth development and strips adults of the creativity, spontaneity, and energy of youth. Because learning results from engagement with issues and problems that are real and meaningful to students, the operation of a school offers many opportunities for student involvement. CLC sites involved students with such duties as teaching, tutoring, operating educational technology, touring visitors, peer counseling, devising public information materials, building maintenance, program decision making, discipline, hiring and evaluation of personnel, and every aspect of school operations. Sites saw students in a different light—as a resource and an opportunity, not as a problem.

Tiered Salaries and Responsibilities

Salary tiers are based on degree of responsibility for the program, experience, training, and productivity. We suggest several levels of compensation for instructional staff: administrative aides, learning facilitators, teachers, specialists (e.g., technology), and teaching assistants. The highest level of teacher is as a learning facilitator. These staff members are experts about learning. They arrange, organize, and orchestrate learning experiences. They remove barriers to learning. They direct the remainder of the staff in the mission of a learning community.

Learning facilitators are licensed teachers who must be compensated well enough to ensure their continuation with the school. This means competitive salaries for this small group. The same is true for administrators. Learning facilitators are employed on a student–teacher ratio of between 30 and 40 to 1. This is well above normal ratios because differentiated staffing involves others in teaching and tutoring relationships. The others include specialists, teaching assistants, elders, volunteers, parents, mentors, business people, agency personnel, and most important of all, students. CLCs publish student-to-adult ratios in addition to student-to-teacher ratios.

Included in CLC staff are part-time employees and contracts with firms to provide services, programs promoted by a relatively new professional group, The American Association of Educators in Private Practice. Contracted services may involve delivering aspects of the educational program as well as other services, such as transportation and food services. Contracted services build in flexibility. In contrast to hiring full-time employees, contracts are for just the amount of service necessary. Contract control remains with the Center, so specifications are written to match needs and renewal is based on needs and performance. Part-time staff enable the program to hire the exact number of staff needed for a particular service, say, a Russian specialist.

CLC schools comply with federal and state mandates for special education students. The program serves these students in a rich mainstream education learning environment in almost all cases. This means less labeling, less separation by pull-out programs, and less decontextualized drill in workbooks. A licensed special education teacher oversees the program, evaluates its progress, and facilitates its services.

Site Management and Shared Governance

School-based shared decision making, a form of school district decentralization, makes the individual school the unit where decisions about the educational program, staffing, and budget take place. School governance involves stakeholders (principal, teachers, other school staff, parents, students, and other community members) as participants in vital decisions about their program. To provide for the governance function, CLC sites organized site councils to develop policies, establish budget items, determine the configuration of staff, and to monitor program progress. For most sites, these were difficult (even agonizing, as in the case of terminating a colleague) decision areas, particularly for members used to having decisions made by the school district's central office. In these decision areas, staff, parents, students, and community members spent many, many hours, usually admitting far too much time weighing all sides of a decision. As experience and trust accumulated, efficiencies emerged with the decision-making processes, or, if for no other reason than sheer weariness. Nonetheless, the design team found that CLC sites developed a deep understanding of critical school issues and a grassroots ownership that is believed will result in long-term systemic school change.

Community Services

One of the continuing dilemmas for educators in traditional systems is accessing needed services for children who struggle in classrooms, not for lack of ability, but for lack of nurturing, lack of nutrition, lack of consistent support at home, family problems (unemployment, chemical use or abuse), and other difficulties. Standard, fragmented approaches have not been effective in tackling these tough issues affecting children's lives and their well-being. Social service providers, government agencies, and nonprofit organizations providing services to children and families have recognized the problem but have taken few steps toward integrating services, usually without involving schools.

Integration of Services

Integration of social services has been in vogue in some communities in the last few years. One CLC site co-located programs like Big Brothers/Big Sisters in the school building. However progressive this may seem, the real challenge goes beyond physical presence and access. Even the most successful efforts at co-location do not assure access, information sharing, and true participation.

Ironically, traditional middle-class families take advantage of service integration more than those with even greater needs. Focus groups (organized by the CLC project) of parents, service providers, and community members representing unserved and underserved populations have expressed anger over the lack of sensitivity in existing systems. Parents and community members want an active role in determining what services are needed and how those services should be delivered. Some communities of color consider the action of integrating psychological and counseling services with education to be intrusive and disrespectful. They express concern about confidentiality and misuse of information. Other communities are comfortable with these services being provided through the school even to the point of surrendering decision making to the staff and service experts.

CLCs promote and support a new paradigm for service integration and delivery. Sites worked at engaging social service partners sharing a vision of family-centered, child-focused services respectful and supportive of the families and cultures. Sites approached service integration with these criteria:

• Service integration partners must share CLCs' values.

• Service integration partners must work cooperatively to design services that include family orientation and respect for culture as well as creating new paradigms for service delivery.

• Services must involve a more holistic family-based strategy as the foundation. *Family* may need to be individually defined for each child.

All services contracted or accessed through Centers are required to do the following:

• emphasize strengths, not deficiencies;

• change the concept of *client* to *customer*;

• move to a valued partner orientation;

• eliminate duplication of services;

• use proactive rather than reactive approaches;

• work to achieve universal rather than single-targeted services; and

• honor families' culture, heritage, language, and ethnicity.

Service providers must work toward greater collaboration. Most services have been at best consultative, exchanging information periodically and often only reactively when a major incident or transition occurs for the student. Coordinated services can remove duplication and uncomplicate processes for families and students and can involve clients as full partners in the development and delivery of services. This was one of the most difficult aspects of the CLC design to implement. It required meetings of diverse agencies in the community who were busy with their own battles of understaffing and budget. Enough progress was made to see the goal of service integration as worth pursuing, though, at times, people wished for some kind of czar to cut through the endless sessions, conflicting procedures and Byzantine diversity of organizations.

Other Design Elements

Parent Involvement

Parents have crucial roles in their children's learning and in the functioning of the school. They bring essentially one item to the school agenda: They want a good education for their children! They cling tenaciously to this point. Their commitment is authentic since responsibility to their child's welfare is foremost.

Bringing educators, parents, and students to the decision-making table results in less blaming and finger-pointing and more genuine problem-solving behavior by all parties. It's too easy for parents to blame teachers for not motivating their child or for teachers to blame parents for not providing proper guidance when parents and teachers are in separate groups. The solution is to work together, sharing problems and answers while recognizing and supporting each other's best efforts and intentions. The result is always sharing ideas and increased respect for diversity, fundamental ingredients for the child's success.

Headquarters for Lifelong Learning

By disseminating information on local community services, CLC sites contributed to the total effort at broad-based community education programs. CLC sites began the process of compiling a database of community resources to inform people of learning opportunities for people of all ages, from early childhood to senior citizen. Formal state-funded and locally funded community education programs, early childhood, and parent education programs were vehicles for making the school a headquarters for citizen learning programs. Some sites remained open for student and community use of the computer labs and other facilities. CLC sites fully subscribe to the idea of becoming a community headquarters for lifelong learning but made little headway in this area, immersed as they were in many other school change efforts.

Program Choice

For the CLC design to succeed, a choice of programs must be provided for students, parents, and staff. School programs, no matter how good, attract both supporters and detractors; the latter can halt or reverse progress. CLC sites found that their new programs were strange to some. Parents will cite many reasons for reservations about a new program. Some parents want the new program to mature or to prove itself. Some people prefer a classic or traditional education, perhaps because they did well in such a program. Some fear the new program will not prepare their children adequately for higher education. Some see the lessened use of textbooks as "soft" education and not rigorous. Some think if children and youth enjoy school, something is wrong because school should be hard.

It would not be unusual to find that when faculty hear of a new program, particularly one that departs radically from the familiar, some will be early adopters, others more reserved, and some can be counted on to dislike the program even to the point of harsh resistance or sabotage. Many a fine new program has been terminated because a vocal, vociferous minority of staff and parents made it their mission to oppose the program. People do this for various reasons: philosophical differences, honest differences of view, misunderstanding, professional jealousy, and so on.

Choice provides a remedy. There must be more than the new program to choose from. No one should be required to attend or to serve in the new program. Failure to provide choice can prematurely end a program.

The Facility

CLC facilities need to be congruent with their innovative programming. Their buildings must be visually stimulating and less classroom-bound. They need to serve student project work (working alone or in small teams), orient outward to the world and nature, and contain a variety of work spaces. Small, medium and large group multipurpose rooms are needed. The main activities take place in "doing" spaces: labs, studios, workshops, exploration and discovery centers, theaters of learning, carrels, kitchens, shops, craft centers, and media centers. There should be a greenhouse and animal center. Equipment and facilities must be integrated with community-based learning experiences, inviting to the community, and controlled for extended hours usage. The building needs to be wired for the 21st century to accommodate changing technology. Display units and walls are needed for student creations with ample storage space provided for student projects.

Few of our sites met many of these criteria, as most were housed in traditional school buildings. Almost all, however, created special computer labs and engaged in extensive wiring for network-ing computers or phones; two sites gave classroom teachers cellular phones to avoid the wiring expense in old buildings; one site created a television production studio; two sites provided parent and volun-teer meeting rooms; one site rented community space for physical education and theater productions to augment their facility; one site is housed in downtown rented storefront space that they modified into studios or learning labs, and one is considering building a greenhouse extension on the existing building.

Implementation Process for New Schools

The degree of change from conventional practice that CLCs represent makes their establishment difficult to understand and accept for people accustomed to traditional schooling. To negotiate systemic change in a traditional school runs high risks of compromise and resistance. Complicating the establishment of the CLCs during NAS Phase II was the need for their almost instant installation. In effect, the Centers needed to accelerate from 0 to 60 in one second. Because the agenda for school reform feels so urgent in many places, uncommon measures may be necessary.

As vehicles for bypassing school reform barriers, charters as provided for by statute in some states can speed implementation of CLCs. Statutes for chartered schools greatly reduce the number of regulations, policies, and laws governing schools, thereby freeing participants to try innovative approaches without constant remind-ers of being in violation of the rules. Charters require learning results or the charter is terminated, the ultimate in accountability.

Where a charter is not available or feasible, a contract between the school wishing to implement the CLCs design and the local school district can provide many of the provisions of a charter, if it is coupled with waivers from state rules and employee bargaining unit contracts. In some cases, a school-within-a-school becomes the unit for change rather than the entire school. The contract must insulate the site from the usual energy-draining, time-consuming negotiations over staffing, budget, and program development. Trust becomes the basis of the contract. The school board and superintendent say, in effect, "We trust that you will exercise sound professional judgment in the execution of the program. Therefore, we will give you wide ranging authority over your program."

Summary

The CLCs' design addresses the challenge of increasing the achievement of all students using the same resources granted other schools. For the CLC design team, this mission required a substantial departure from conventional practice on almost all dimensions of schooling. The CLC design, tested in a diverse group of schools, shows promise of being effective and feasible, though difficult to implement in conventional school climates.

Notes

Wayne Jennings, PhD, president of Designs For Learning, Inc., spent 40 years as a teacher and administrator creating new schools. He heads a New American Schools design team charged with reinventing education.

References

Coleman, J. (1972, February). The children have outgrown the schools. *Psychology Today*, 72–76.

Digest of Education Statistics. (1993). Washington, DC: U.S. Department of Education, National Center for Education Statistics.

Goodlad, J. (1983). *A place called school.* New York: McGraw-Hill.

Hart, L. (1983). *Human brain and human learning.* Kent, WA: Books for Educators.

Kurth-Schai, R. (1988). The roles of youth in society: A reconceptualization. *The Educational Forum, 52*(2), 113–130.

Miller, G. (1995). *Evaluation report on the CLCs Project.* St. Paul: Designs for Learning.

Nachtigal, P. (1972). *A foundation goes to school: The Ford Foundation Comprehensive School Improvement Program.* New York: Ford Foundation.

260

Presidential Task Force on Psychology in Education of the American Psychological Association. (1993). *Learner-centered psychological principles: Guidelines for school redesign and reform.* Washington, DC: American Psychological Association.

SCANS (The Secretary's Commission on Achieving Necessary Skills). (1993). *Learning a living.* Washington, DC: Department of Labor.

Sizer, T. (1983, June). Editorial. *Phi Delta Kappan.*, 674.

Sizer, T. (1984). *Horace's compromise: The dilemma of the American high school.* Boston: Houghton Mifflin.

Los Angeles Learning Centers
An Initiative of Los Angeles Unified School District, United Teachers Los Angeles, and Los Angeles Educational Partnership

Judy Johnson
John McDonald
Los Angeles Educational Partnership

The design for the Los Angeles Learning Centers (LALC) was created to address the realities of public education in Los Angeles and other urban communities across the nation.

In the Los Angeles Unified School District (LAUSD), schools are multiethnic and often multilingual. More than a third of the students come to school speaking little or no English. Students represent a range of ethnic backgrounds, primarily Latino and African American, the majority of them poor. More than 60 percent live in families with incomes below federal poverty guidelines. Transiency rates are very high as families move for work or other reasons.

Many students and their families live in neighborhoods that often lack basic services and offer little economic opportunity. There is a dire need for access to health care. High crime rates and violence are a reality, as are the other social and emotional problems associated with the impacts of poverty.

The schools themselves are often very large, yet in spite of their size, tremendously overcrowded. The majority of schools in the Los Angeles Unified School District (which has more than 640,000 students) operate on a year-round basis to accommodate the demand created by the overwhelming number of students. In spite of this, in some neighborhoods students must ride a bus for more than an hour to school, simply because there is no room at their neighborhood school site.

The schools are underfunded (California ranks 42nd in per-pupil funding) leading to labor strife, poor morale, and the decay of school facilities. (The LAUSD has had to cut more than $2 billion from its budget in the last five years.) Quality instructional materials are often in short supply and resources for planning and professional development are scarce.

Like many large urban schools systems, at the time the Learning Center design was developed, schools in the LAUSD were managed primarily by a central administration. School site administrators and teachers had little authority over management, governance and instructional issues. Budget decisions were made by a central administration. (The LAUSD/Los Angeles Education Alliance—Restructuring Now [LEARN] plan for School Reform now calls for a decentralized management and governance system with school site autonomy and budget authority.) Because of lack of funding and other issues, school sites have had insufficient access to expertise and training on assessment and instructional issues, little time for planning and professional development to improve educator skills and knowledge, and few resources to address school management and governance or to develop strategies for resolving the health and social service needs of students and their families.

Given this context, the challenge facing the design team for the Los Angeles Learning Centers was not to create an unreplicable educational utopia but rather to forge a learning community where students could thrive in the urban school environment. In doing so, we sought to create a center with high expectations for learning for all students. We envision the Learning Center as a place where students, parents, educators and community members can establish a strong sense of community with access to much needed health and social services, as well as learning and recreational opportunities. Our intent is to create a place where educators will be continual learners, with time to plan and prepare for quality instruction and where they have the opportunity, authority, and responsibility for making instructional and governance decisions (including budget); and where the learning community—students, parents, educators, and community members have the opportunity to participate in an autonomous and collaborative system of governance. If our design has any major flaw, it is that it suffers from a bad case of ambition.

Learning Center—Design Overview

The design for the Los Angeles Learning Centers represents a vision for the development of a K–12 learning community to meet the needs of the children of the urban neighborhoods of Los Angeles and their counterparts in urban communities across the United States. The Learning Center design calls for significant changes in instruction and curriculum, school management and governance, and how schools address the health and well-being of students.

The goal of the Learning Center design is to create a learning environment in which all graduates are expected to meet high standards of scholarship and be productive citizens and lifelong learners. It is expected that every student will obtain a solid understanding of the basic subjects of history, geography, science, mathematics, and English, as well as the arts. Learning Center students are also expected to develop critical thinking and problem-solving abilities; to be able to use new technologies to access, use, and produce information; and to be prepared for work or postsecondary education.

Operating at one site, or across a K-12 family of schools, the Learning Center design envisions the school as a safe, active hub of community life where students and parents know and are known by Learning Center staff, and all participants in the learning community are invested in and responsible for student learning. Developed by the Los Angeles Unified School District, United Teachers Los Angeles, and the Los Angeles Educational Partnership, with support from corporate and community organizations, the Learning Center design is a plan for development of an urban learning community.

Implementation of the design is strongly supported by the advanced use of technology.

The Learning Center design is built around three primary and complementary components:

- An *instruction and curriculum* component designed to ensure that all students are taught in a community of learners using the most effective educational practices (includes collaborative teaching, an in-depth thematic, interdisciplinary curriculum built around high standards and a constructivist orientation to learning).

- An *enabling* component designed to restructure and integrate school community resources to address barriers to student learning (includes comprehensive school-based programs and services for enabling learning; multiple interveners, advocates, and social supports for students and families).

- A collaborative *management* and *governance* component designed to ensure that all participants are represented in decision making and that there is an effective infrastructure upon which the Learning Center can build and evolve (includes shared governance, administrators as leaders for systematic change, effective communications, infrastructure maintenance and renewal, responsive and flexible management).

The First Learning Centers

In crafting the Learning Center design and in efforts to implement the Learning Center model, the Learning Center team intentionally set out to work in schools facing some of the most difficult challenges Los Angeles has to offer. As in many urban schools, our first sites are overcrowded, multiethnic, and multilingual. Virtually all the students are poor; many are immigrants from Central America and Mexico.

The Learning Center design is currently being implemented in two sites, the Elizabeth Street Learning Center in Cudahy, an area of Southeast Los Angeles, and the Foshay Learning Center, in South Central Los Angeles. Together the two sites serve more than 5,000 students in K–12 learning communities. The schools operate year-round and offer services from early morning to the late afternoon.

Elizabeth Street Learning Center (ESLC) began implementation in July 1993. ESLC originally included preschool through eighth-grade students. In 1994–1995, ninth and tenth grades were added. In 1995 and 1996 respectively, eleventh- and twelfth-grade students will be added to the ESLC. The school is open year-round, with approximately 2,500 students assigned to one of three alternating calendars or tracks. The population is made up almost entirely of Latino students from low-income families, many of whom are recent immigrants. More than half the students speak limited or no English. Test scores perennially rank among the lowest in the school district and state, and student transiency rates are high.

Foshay Learning Center (FLC) became the second LALC site in July 1994. Like ESLC, Foshay is an overcrowded urban school with over 2,500 students on a three-track year-round schedule. Foshay students are about two-thirds Latino and one-third African-American. One-third of the students have limited proficiency or do not speak English. Family incomes are low (75% of the students qualify for Chapter 1 support). With a transiency rate of more than 80 percent, the students are coming and going constantly. The school was targeted in 1989 by the state for potential loss of Chapter 1 and bilingual education funding because the achievement of its students was so low. A new principal was assigned, new teachers and administrators joined the faculty, and a wide array of programs were adopted by the school. The dropout rate has plummeted from 20 percent to 5 percent, and test scores have improved slightly.

Prior to becoming a Learning Center, Foshay was a junior high serving grades seven through nine. During the space of five days in the summer of 1994, it became a K–10 school on one calendar track and a 6–8 school on the two remaining calendar tracks by adding 200 elementary students and 275 high school students. Grade eleven was added in fall 1995 and grade twelve will be added during 1996.

The Design Components:
Instruction, Enabling, and Management

Each of the three design components are comprised of key features that guide the development and operation of the Learning Center.

The Instructional Component

The instructional component calls for significant changes in standards, curriculum and instruction. The Learning Center design sets high standards for student learning and establishes a common set of expectations for what students should know and be able to do. These standards are intended to help organize the curriculum, instructional practices and assessment of LALC students and their performance:

Literacy. Read with fluency and comprehension and can flexibly change their reading style for different purposes. They are well-read across a variety of genres, at or above grade level. They comprehend, analyze, and appreciate text and non-print media (e.g., speech, movies, video).

Numeracy. Conversant with fundamental mathematical concepts, operations, and strategies. They apply their mathematical knowledge strategically, for different purposes. They understand a variety of mathematical representations, such as the textual, algebraic, geometric, and graphic.

Identifying and accessing resources. Know how to identify and locate information or resources for a range of purposes, using an array of technological tools. They effectively process and evaluate information. The information and resources they use include those from literature, mathematics, social science, technology, kinesthetics, the arts, and daily life.

Important knowledge. Good basic understanding of science, mathematics, language arts and literature, social sciences, technology, physical education, and the arts.

Complex thinking. Creative and sophisticated reasoning to address real-life issues and problems. They apply complex thinking to science, technology, mathematics, language arts and literature, social sciences, the arts, physical education, and interdisciplinary issues, and can make important connections within and across disciplines. Students can define problems, identify relevant information and resources, come to reasonable solutions, and implement them.

Communication. Communicate clearly and effectively with a variety of audiences. They speak and write well. They can also convey their ideas effectively in other modes, such as numeric, symbolic, graphic, video, and artistic. When they participate in public discourse, they are good listeners and speakers.

Interpersonal skills. Work well independently and collaboratively in a variety of settings, with people of diverse backgrounds, in a range of roles. They can monitor their own behavior, exhibit self-control, evaluate their progress, and set personal goals.

Habits of mind. Display responsibility, self-esteem and confidence, integrity, eagerness and curiosity, and respect towards learning, others, and self. They view themselves as continual learners and show personal investment and pride in their work. They function as active, constructive participants and responsible decision makers in our democratic society and as world citizens.

Teachers and other stakeholders participated in teams from each Learning Center to reach consensus on the core LALC standards for student learning. They met to discuss what they wanted their students to know and be able to do by the time they graduated from each level of schooling. These teams are now engaged in defining levels for these standards and how they can be assessed in their schools.

The design calls for classrooms to be organized into multiage or nongraded classes and for teachers to use team teaching and collaborative instructional strategies. Instructional methods reflect current cognitive theories of learning, intelligence, motivation and individual differences. The curriculum addresses the five core subject areas of history, geography, mathematics, science, and English, as well as the arts, health and fitness, self-discipline and social and emotional growth. Much of the curriculum is organized into thematic and interdisciplinary units. Teachers have experienced some frustrations trying to create substantive, engaging themes and make a theme fit each discipline equally well. As one teacher said,

> The theme my cluster chose was "Immigration: Its Causes and Consequences." It was easy coming up with connections between my English class and social studies, but it was difficult finding the connections to math and science. When connections were made, they seemed to be forced, superficial, indeed, inauthentic. . . . In the end, I told my colleagues that some of us would be able to engage the theme for longer periods of time than others would because certain subjects make it easier (Aschbacher, 1994).

A comprehensive assessment system has been designed by the UCLA Center for the Study of Evaluation to improve and monitor student performance. At the end of grades five, eight, and ten, students take performance exams requiring them to write interdisciplinary essays, make connections across curricular areas, link prior knowledge and experience with what they have been taught in school, and reflect on how they learn, solve problems and formulate well-substantiated conclusions. In addition, teachers use an end-of-level portfolio system to assess student progress over time.

Students, teachers, and parents have access to state-of-the-art technology in support of learning. Parents have the opportunity to take word processing classes. Teachers can videotape dramatic productions and use the Internet to download resource materials to enhance teaching. Students use computers to write their own stories, complete research on line, and access text, graphics and other resources in support of their work.

The Learning Centers emphasize the preparation of students for a transition to work or postgraduate education. Secondary students at the two sites are enrolled in an Academy of Health, Information and Technology, or Finance. They participate in specially designed courses in these career areas and before graduation complete internships in business or the public sector.

The design calls for students and teachers to use the community as an extended classroom and resource for teaching and learning. The neighborhood around the school becomes a laboratory for research. For example, the Los Angeles River is incorporated into a unit of study, including a field trip to collect biological specimens. Students interview community residents or local political leaders. The Museum of Contemporary Art brings teachers and art exhibits to the students. Parents are asked to help their children complete homework requiring library visits and the collection of information and data from magazines, books, and other materials.

Instructional practices are supported by ongoing professional development and time for planning and collaboration. There is a teacher's toolbox that provides a professional library, resource center, and meeting area. Teachers also have access to the product development center, providing access to the latest technology which teachers can use to create instructional and curriculum materials. All participants in the learning community are expected to be continual learners.

The instructional component also recognizes and focuses on the need to enable learning by addressing the health and well being of students and their families. The instructional effort addresses these needs in curriculum and practice. In addition, faculty and administrators can use the resources available to link health and social services to the school. For example, a teacher trained to notice behavior in a student suggesting he or she needs special testing or counseling may utilize the FASTNet system (Family and School Tie Network—an interactive, matching database of local health and social services) to find and obtain appropriate services for such a student. FASTNet provides a customized, detailed, and current database of school district and community health and social services and matches students and family members to available and appropriate services.

The Enabling Component

The *enabling component* provides for a comprehensive, integrated, programmatic approach to addressing barriers to learning by promoting the healthy development and well-being of students, family, and the community. The Learning Center design is predicated on a belief that such an "enabling" approach is essential to helping schools to teach and students to learn. The enabling component provides six school-based approaches to support improved learning:

- *Classroom Focused Enabling* helps teachers to prevent and handle problems.

- *Student and Family Assistance* provides for special intervention when needed.

- *Crisis Assistance and Prevention* provides resources to prevent and respond to crisis situations such as family violence or drug and alcohol abuse.

- *Support for Transitions* helps to welcome and provide social support for newcomers to the learning community, assists in dealing with changes or difficulties with the school program or community, and provides opportunities for enriched learning and recreation.

- *Home Involvement* promotes parent participation, addresses parent learning and support needs, and engages parents as problem-solvers and leaders at the Learning Center and in their communities.

- *Community Outreach/Volunteer* efforts promote greater community involvement in the Learning Center and build links between the school and local health and social service agencies, community organizations, and community leadership.

The enabling component is carried out through an array of activities. These may range from primary prevention programs or recreational efforts, to specific efforts to treat chronic problems. The work of the enabling component is integrated and coordinated with instructional and management activities at the Learning Center site.

Enabling activities are planned and implemented at a Family and Community Center on the school grounds which also serves as a site for parent activities, child care, and an access point for health and social services. A resource coordination team—which includes parents, teachers, administrators, and community representatives—plans and manages enabling activities.

For example, in cooperation with St. Francis Medical Center and California State University at Dominguez Hills, the Elizabeth Street Learning Center has opened a Medical Clinic on campus to help meet the health needs of the community.

Another key element of the enabling component is the Moving Diamond system. The moving diamond is intended to provide multiple advocates for each child's learning and development. Each student is the focus of a diamond and is linked with an adult in the school, another student, and an adult from the community. As the student moves through his or her school career, members of the diamond participate in activities designed to nurture student development and serve as advocates for student success and well-being.

The Management Component

The Learning Center design envisions the school as an autonomous, self-governed learning community focused on improving student achievement and continual learning. All participants are asked to act as full partners in the mission of educating children with decision-making responsibility and budget authority for their school community.

School governance is carried out by a site-based management council comprised of key partners in the learning community: teachers, parents, students, staff members, and administrators. Some members are elected; others are appointed because of their responsibilities at the school site. The governance structure combines collaborative, high-involvement management practices with principles of participatory democracy. The management council guides strategic planning and makes decisions regarding budgeting, curriculum, student discipline, and community relations. It may also establish committees to address specific needs or activities.

Management of the Learning Center requires participants to take on new roles and responsibilities. Administrators, particularly the principal of the Learning Center, are expected to provide leadership, support, and motivation for development and implementation of the Learning Center model. It is the responsibility of administrators to lead and support educational reform, create a safe environment for innovations, support collaborative management practices and community participation, and ensure a fair and effective distribution of resources.

Teachers at the Learning Center are the primary decision makers about the learning needs of students and exercise control over curriculum and instructional practices. Teachers are also responsible for planning their own professional development. Teachers are expected to play an active role in school governance and decision making and work collaboratively with students, parents, community members, and other adults at the Learning Center.

Students at the Learning Center play an active role in shaping their learning experience and are expected to assume a greater responsibility for their own learning. Students are engaged in Learning Center governance and a variety of school and community activities. Students participate in planning teams and committees.

The Learning Center design calls for far greater parent involvement than at many traditional schools. Parents are asked to provide active support for learning at home and share planning and decision-making responsibilities, including budget decisions, at the school site.

The Role of Technology

The three components of the design—instruction, enabling and management—all utilize technology in the implementation of the Learning Center. Technology is intended to support instruction, curriculum development, communication, collaboration, research, text and multimedia publishing, resource access, assessment, administration and management services.

Instructional efforts at the Learning Center draw upon a technology-rich environment. Teachers have the opportunity to develop the skills to use a wide variety of technologies in support of instructional efforts. Teachers and students are developing the capacity to use technologies to identify, access and manipulate information and to integrate, exchange and communicate information in support of learning. A product development center provides computers, video and audio equipment, laser discs, telecommunications capacity and other technologies in support of multiple instructional and learning needs. Teachers have access to portable computers and other technology configurations they can use daily for instruction, curriculum development, and classroom management. Technology is available across the Learning Center for classroom or community use. Students, parents, and teachers have access to technology for after-school and weekend activities. Schools are linked to the Internet through the Los Angeles Learning Community Network, a low-cost wide area telecommunications network developed by the Los Angeles Educational Partnership and the Los Angeles County Office of Education. The product development centers are also serving as training sites for other teachers across the school district.

Enabling efforts utilize technology to store and retrieve information about students and to access resources and services to address student and family needs. A client tracking system (CTS) enables school management to track a number of non-academic factors that impact student performance.

School management has access to hardware and software in support of effective school management. The design envisions the development of a Learning Center information system that maintains information required by the school district and the state, as well as information needed to support the learning community such as student profiles and electronic portfolios. An Integrated Financial System to support school-based budgeting and purchasing is being developed by the Los Angeles Unified School District.

Development of the Learning Centers

Both Elizabeth Street and Foshay elected to become LALC design sites. After presentations to the school community about the LALC design, the faculty voted and parents approved conversion of the schools to the new model. Virtually all teachers at the schools voted in favor of the conversion. Each teacher was individually counseled by representatives of United Teachers Los Angeles about whether they would prefer to remain at their school or would like to have assistance relocating to a more traditional site. Few changes were made in staff at either school.

The Los Angeles Learning Centers design working team provided a number of support services in collaboration with the schools to assist in implementation of the LALC design. These included:

- An *orientation to the design* during which faculty, staff, and parents could become more familiar with the LALC components, set their own vision for how these components could become real at their Learning Center, and develop a sense of ownership of the model.

- Faculty *site visits to other schools* in Southern California in which one or more of the LALC design components were already in place so that they could better comprehend how components such as multiage instruction or interdisciplinary, thematic teaching affects students and what it takes to implement new approaches such as those called for in the design.

- *Lead teachers* selected and assigned the responsibility of assisting individual faculty members and teams in planning new curriculum and redesigning instruction. Lead teachers were asked to coach teams, demonstrate lessons, provide sample materials, help faculty solve problems as they arose, and work to keep implementation moving forward. Two leads were selected for initial implementation activities at Elizabeth Street and four at Foshay. Currently, leads have been reduced to one at each site, supported by a pool of master practitioners (teachers with advanced levels of insight and expertise).

- A *change agent* with expertise in strategic planning and the change process assigned to work with the school community to weather the difficult stages of resistance, problem solving, and planning.

- *Technical assistance* with implementation from members of the LALC design team and consultants. For example, the LALC design team helped each school conduct communications planning to determine how communication was handled with teachers, parents, staff, and the community and how it could be improved. The LALC technology coordinator worked with individuals and teams at each school to order, install, and train in the use of computer hardware and software, video equipment, and other technologies. LALC staff helped each site through an open process for examination and reconfiguration of the school budget, a task never undertaken in an open forum at either school before. The LALC staff and a volunteer group of architects worked with the school district and each school to purchase, move, install and decorate new temporary classrooms and provide space for expanded grade levels and family service centers.

- *Training and professional development* for teachers, administrators, school staff, students, and parents. More than 20 days of paid professional development were offered to teachers and teaching assistants at the Elizabeth Street Learning Center during the first year of implementation and covered every aspect of the design. Similar professional development opportunities on a reduced schedule were offered to Foshay Learning Center.

- *Curriculum development tools* including curriculum templates to assist teams of teachers in planning instructional units and a teacher's toolbox, a room at each school which houses curriculum, instruction, and assessment resources, and provides space for teams of teachers to meet and plan collaboratively. Samples of interdisciplinary, thematic, project-based units were also provided to each Learning Center.

- A *Product Development Center* at each school with state-of-the-art technology resources used as both a training center and a place where teachers can use sophisticated computer and video tools to do research, create curricular and instructional materials, and communication products.

- *World class standards and an on-demand assessment system.* The UCLA Center for the Study of Evaluation (CSE) and the National Center for Research on Evaluation, Standards and

Student Testing (CRESST) worked with representatives from the Elizabeth Street Learning Center and Foshay Learning Center to develop a set of world class standards for student performance that matched the goals of the LALC design. They developed and tested performance assessments for grades five, eight, and ten and piloted an end-of-level portfolio system to assess student achievement.

- *Integration of health and social services* for students and their families as part of the Learning Center resources. The LALC design team assisted in developing the Elizabeth Street Learning Center Family *and* Community Center that includes a health center on campus providing an array of medical, dental, and counseling services. The Foshay Student and Family Services Center, which will be similar to Elizabeth Street, is currently under development.

- *Technology tools* including FASTNet, the Client Tracking System (CTS) and the Los Angeles Learning Community Network (LALCNet). As previously described, FASTNet is a customized database that matches the individual needs of students and their families with services offered by the school district and community service agencies. CTS enables staff to track a number of non-academic factors that can affect a student's success in school and includes a log to record referrals and outcomes, prompts of questions about different areas of student concerns, report functions, and customized questionnaires and forms. The LALCNet is a low-cost telecommunications network providing electronic access to the Internet and educational content and services from home, school, and other learning locations.

Learning Center Successes

The LALC design is understandably at different stages of implementation at the two Learning Center sites. This difference in accomplishment is due in part to the fact that the two centers started at different times. Elizabeth Street Learning Center began implementation of the design in July 1993 and Foshay Learning Center began in July 1994. Differences in implementation are also due to differences in the nature of the schools. Their school cultures are unique; the principals and school leadership at each school exhibit different styles; prior experience with risk taking and managing change varies with the sites; and the barriers to reform are somewhat different in each school. While we are finding patterns in the sequence of implementation across schools, we are also aware that how school restructuring and reform progress will be dependent upon prior knowledge of the faculty and the readiness of the school community for change.

The Learning Center design called for profound and complex changes in instruction, management and governance, and enabling (the integration of support systems for students and families with instructional practice). While the successes of the Learning Centers are not unqualified, they are substantial given the short time the participants have had to "own the design," as well as learn and incorporate new values, beliefs, approaches and skills into their repertoire of practices. The following summarizes those successes according to the components of the design—instruction, management and governance, and enabling.

The Instruction Component

The Learning Center design seeks to transform curriculum, instruction, and assessment to ensure that all students are taught in a community of learners using advanced and effective educational practices. Signs of progress are described in the areas indicated below:

Standards and Assessment. The Learning Centers defined and adopted standards for what they believe students should know and be able to do in order to live successfully in the complex world of the 21st century. As a next step toward bringing those standards to life at each Learning Center, teachers and others from both sites met to discuss student work openly and honestly. Subject area groups examined samples of work, ranked them in order of quality, and articulated characteristics that distinguish excellent work. They wrote subject area objectives for the complex thinking standards, described a relevant learning activity, and began a rubric for judging work related to the standards. Each site committed to continuing the process of expanding the standards by describing important discipline-based objectives.

New standards and high expectations for what students will understand about basic subjects of history, geography, science, mathematics, English, and the arts require new forms of assessment to match them. UCLA completed the design and development of alternative, on-demand tests (including multiple choice and essay) of student progress for grades five, eight, and ten. These tests are now being used by the centers. In addition, UCLA and the Learning Centers completed a pilot end-of-level portfolio system to assess student achievement related to the new standards. Standards and assessment have proven very difficult to develop and implement.

Curriculum and Instruction. At the start of implementation, Elizabeth Street Learning Center chose to reorganize their school into multiage classrooms with teams of teachers working and planning together. Faculty at Elizabeth Street were unfamiliar with interdisciplinary, thematic approaches to teaching prior to implementation of the design. At the end of the second year, 20 to 25 percent of their teams were teaching interdisciplinary, thematic units of instruction using themes such as the roots of racial prejudice in the United States. Teachers documented units for sharing in the Curriculum Toolbox. Faculty also introduced constructivist teaching practices including asking students to write and talk about what and how they are learning, use a variety of problem-solving strategies, and set their own learning goals.

Foshay Junior High School teachers were interested in thematic teaching and team approaches for several years and had some training in interdisciplinary instruction prior to adoption of the LALC design. But as one experienced teacher put it, "The Learning Center is pushing it further and forcing teachers to move in this direction" (Aschbacher, 1995). The new elementary school functions as a team and offers two-year multiage classes. Sixth-grade teachers work in pairs, each teaching two courses to the same students for two periods (e.g., one teacher teaches math and science, the other English and social studies). Many of the seventh- and eighth-grade teachers work in teams; although most middle school teachers were reluctant to teach multiage classes. Most of the high school classes are multi-age, but interdisciplinary instruction needs much more work. The team approach has been difficult to implement at Foshay; however, teachers are beginning to see advantages for themselves and students in the team approach.

The LALC design influenced Foshay teachers to change some teaching practices including greater use of technology with students, hands-on learning activities, instruction using a variety of approaches, learning activities outside the classroom, alternative assessments, and asking students to reflect upon their own work. Approximately one third of the teachers said they decreased their reliance on direct instruction or lecture and on selected response tests in favor of engaging students in more interaction around their own learning.

Transition to Work and Career. Elizabeth Street Learning Center established a Health Careers Academy and Foshay Learning Center organized an Academy of Finance for the integration of academics and career training of high school students. Both sites provide academic courses and internships in business for students from grades ten through twelve. In July 1995, both Learning Centers initiated Information Technology Academies for secondary students. The two Academies are linked together through telecommunications and a business-led steering committee. Through clinical experiences, the programs provide in-depth learning and practical problem-solving opportunities for students.

Technology to enhance instruction. Technology training has been successful at both Learning Centers and faculty have been enthusiastic about participation. Training modules are curriculum-based so that faculty learn how to use computer software and video equipment while they are researching and developing teaching materials. Many teachers choose to attend voluntary weekend professional development sessions in addition to basic training. A number of teachers have developed innovative, technology-rich units using Hyperstudio and other sophisticated software programs. Even though not every teacher has embraced the use of technology, its expansion in the classroom is quite evident, particularly in the lower grades.

Both Learning Centers are linked to the LALCNet so that teachers and administrators are able to access the Internet and electronic communications. The Product Development Centers are used daily and on weekends for a variety of training and project-development activities. The Product Development Centers are also used for telecommunications training, with teachers being trained to teach other teachers, both at the sites and in other schools. (More than 1,000 teachers are now using the LALCNet.) At Elizabeth Street Learning Center, parents take word processing courses and students are sometimes found coaching their parents in computer use.

Enabling Component

The enabling system and strategies at the Learning Centers support student learning and integrate school and community resources to improve the health and well-being of students and families. The following outlines the changes that have occurred.

Family Centers. Elizabeth Street Learning Center created a Family Center that coordinates family-oriented programs and student referrals. In 1994–1995 about 200 parents graduated from a Parent Institute, which taught parenting skills, how to become involved in their children's education, what requirements are needed for students to complete high school and enter college, and how to volunteer in classrooms. Some 140 adults attend English and citizenship courses on campus. Classes in sewing and aerobics are also available. The Concerned Parents group meets weekly to discuss how to help children avoid graffiti, drugs, and gangs. Youth counseling sessions are available one evening a week. The Center provides information on after-school activities for children and on health and social services available in the community.

Foshay Learning Center had an existing Parent Center which expanded its role and services during implementation of the LALC design. Six parent representatives operate the Parent Center and about 250 parents use the services each month. In addition, some 100 parents attend adult classes in English, Spanish, and reading. Planning is underway for the development of the Family and Community Center at Foshay.

Health Clinic. In partnership with St. Francis Medical Center and California State University at Dominguez Hills, Elizabeth Street Learning Center opened a medical clinic on campus that provides immunizations, medical services, and counseling nine hours a day, five days a week. Foshay Learning Center has submitted a grant application for a district-funded School-Based Health Clinic to be located on its campus. (Access to health care was the number one response from parents when surveyed about what they wanted from their school.)

Moving Diamond. The Moving Diamond is a system to provide multiple advocates for each child to support their learning and development. Its intent is to establish each student as the focus of a "diamond" linked with an adult in the school, another student, and an adult from the community. At Elizabeth Street Learning Center three fourths of the classrooms are paired with one another, older students with younger ones, for social and curricular activities. Teaching aides, staff and several adults from the community are working with students as mentors. Many more community mentors are still needed. Through referral procedures about 20 seriously at-risk students are paired with trained adults for mentoring. Foshay Learning Center is recruiting and training business partner mentors for secondary students in the Academy of Finance and the Technology Academy.

After-School Clubs and Activities. Nearly 350 Elizabeth Street students participate in on campus after-school activities including gymnastics, Scouts, science fiction club, Folklórico classes (a Mexican cultural dance), arts, computer club, and sports.

Technology Support. Elizabeth and Foshay Learning Centers use FASTNet (described previously). During the 1995–1996 school year, both sites will be able to use the Client Tracking System to facilitate record keeping, referrals, planning of follow-up with students and families, and Moving Diamond matching.

Management Component

The goal of the LALC design was to create a restructured management and governance system to engage all participants in decision making and ensure the capacity of the Learning Centers to continuously improve and evolve. Both Elizabeth Street and Foshay were schools with limited site-based management systems prior to implementation of the design. Their areas of decision making and the extent of participation in the process were narrow. The changes in governance at Elizabeth Street have been dramatic. At Foshay the changes are less visible, in part because Foshay had a stronger pre-existing system, and partly because Foshay has had a full year less to work. Highlights of progress include:

Governance. Elizabeth Street Learning Center completely re-configured its school governance and all teachers and staff now serve on a governance committee. Staff now run meetings in an effective businesslike manner and committee decisions are posted and disseminated for all on the campus to review. Committee members are assigned to all key elements of the design. Faculty and staff are included in decision making about selection of new teachers and administrators. A committee reviews the school budget in depth and recommends the allocation of resources each year to the Learning Center Site Management Council.

Prior to becoming a Learning Center, Foshay had a strong Site Management Council and a committee structure in place. The principal exercised control over the allocation of the budget. The school was initially reluctant to change any part of their structure. They decided eventually to examine parts that were not working well and added new committees for budget and technology. Campus tensions impeded progress on implementation of the design, and the Foshay staff formed a Change Team and Building Bridges Team to consider solutions. There has been some change in the informal power structure with teachers who were advocates of the design having a greater voice. The Bridges Team recommended that issues of diversity, personal esteem, and responsibility be addressed through professional development for the next school year. The Site Management Council accepted their proposal. Foshay has also drafted and approved a strategic communications plan that supports effective governance.

Management. Administrators at both sites have had to explore and adapt to new roles in support of the Learning Center design. This has proven to be one of the more difficult elements of the design as leadership has struggled to balance the goals of the design with the demands of the school system and the daily realities of providing educational services to more than 2,000 children. Because of the advantage of having more time, Elizabeth Street has made more progress in this area. Administrators at Elizabeth Street are assigned key responsibilities according to the design, play leadership roles on design committees, and now seem to be operating more effectively as a team.

Both Learning Centers have access to hardware, software, and telecommunications to enhance the efficiency and effectiveness of school management, including LALCNet, FASTNet, and Client Tracking System as described previously. In addition LALC has been exploring the feasibility of a modular student information system that allows each site to access information not normally tracked by the school district, such as discipline, attendance, and grades, without having to enter data twice in one format for the school and one for the district.

School schedules were designed at Elizabeth Street Learning Center to provide common planning time for teams of teachers to meet, discuss students they share from grades six and up, and plan curriculum together. Foshay Learning Center organized schedules so that most teams of middle school and high school-level teachers have common planning time. Coordinating student scheduling has proven more difficult.

Elizabeth Street Learning Center started its 1995–1996 school year in July with a three-day faculty meeting devoted to a self-assessment and planning process. They reviewed their progress on implementation of the LALC design, analyzed student achievement data, and made plans for renewing and strengthening their work for the coming year.

Foshay Learning Center completed a self assessment and convened a two-day Efficacy Institute in September 1995 to aid implementation of the design and to address other issues. Both sites have completed a memorandum of agreement for the steps necessary to complete implementation in 1996.

Summary

The changes required for full implementation of the Los Angeles Learning Center design by students, parents, teachers, staff and the larger school community are at a preliminary stage. Nonetheless, student attendance is up, and teacher absenteeism is down. Technology is used to enhance instruction, learning, management, and access to health and social services. Students who in the past were in need of special attention are now being identified and supported with a variety of services. Parents are much more involved as decision makers, volunteers, and learners. Teaching practices have changed with greater emphasis on developing complex conceptual knowledge and thinking skills, although not all teachers are participating at levels we had hoped for. The organization of the Learning Centers is more inclusive, more supportive of substantive decision making, and closer to our expectations for becoming a "learning organization" than the traditional approaches used before by the two participating schools.

The LALC design is a very comprehensive plan for school reform, encompassing virtually all aspects of school culture and affecting all stakeholders. Full implementation of the design to the high quality standards envisioned by the original design committee will take more time. Improvement in student achievement will take years if the literature on school reform is to be acknowledged (e.g., Fullan & Stiegelbauer, 1989) and longer than any of us would wish. Nonetheless, the participants of the Los Angeles Learning Centers are working to make the dream of success for children a reality in the near future.

LALC—Evaluation

The UCLA Center for the Study of Evaluation (CSE) conducted a two-year assessment of the Learning Center design and implementation (Aschbacher, 1994, 1995). The study included an array of data sources including surveys, interviews, focus groups, classroom observations, observations of professional development sessions and school events, school and district records and tests, and results from performance assessments created by UCLA CSE to capture the effects of high standards and changed teaching practices. Results suggest that students are more enthusiastic about learning, retention is high and absences are decreased. Teachers also report greater enthusiasm and confidence in teaching, higher expectations for students, greater interaction with colleagues, and greater use of technology for teaching and learning. Each school has clarified goals, shared in decision making, encouraged collaboration, and offered many hours of professional development. Parent participation increased significantly. Results on standardized test scores were not expected to increase during the first year at Elizabeth Street, and they did not. Data on the performance assessments and test results for the second year collected by UCLA CSE for both Learning Centers have not yet been released.

The State of California recently released scores on the California Test of Basic Skills (CTBS) for 1994–1995. Scores for Elizabeth Street Learning Center remain low.

Design Costs

The Los Angeles Learning Centers are designed to eventually run on existing school budget revenues. This requires that schools not seek to add on the design to what they are already doing, but rather to change what they currently do.

Significant costs occurred in the initial development of the design. Those costs are reflected in time for planning and professional development, and in the purchase and integration of technology. Costs were also incurred in design contracts, the development of information management systems, and standards and testing strategies.

At the initial sites, additional costs were also incurred in the development of facilities for instruction and enabling activities, and printing and distribution of information materials.

It is difficult to predict what implementation costs will be for other school jurisdictions as they will be greatly affected by the current level of funds available for planning time, professional development, faculty and staff salaries, condition and availability of facilities, quantity and quality of existing technology, the skill and knowledge level of faculty and staff, and the complexity and welfare of the community.

The Los Angeles Learning Centers are currently developing a model to provide specific information on costs, and working on methods for design implementation at affordable costs. The LALC hopes to make that information available during 1996.

LALC—Lessons Learned

Implementation of the LALC design followed a predictable path of the change process. At both Learning Center sites, participants began with enthusiasm and a little trepidation. As teachers and administrators gained a better understanding of the complexity and comprehensive nature of the entire design and its specific components, the extent of the change required of them became more clear and less desirable.

Both teachers and administrators expressed feelings of confusion and demonstrated resistance to implementation. Parent and community resistance to the design also increased, primarily in response to changes in the school configuration and the use of multi-age classrooms. Communications issues surfaced. Frustrations with the amount and difficulty of the work grew. Many felt overwhelmed.

Many felt they were asked to do "too much too soon" and the project was too ambitious. Others decided if they waited long enough that "this too will pass." Power struggles developed among teachers, between teachers and administrators, and between the LALC Design Team members and the Learning Centers' staffs. The principals were blamed for not taking enough leadership, and then, for being too directive. It's not a pretty picture of educational reform, but also not an unusual description of how the struggle to change manifests itself in schools across the country.

With time and investment came also a greater sense of ownership on the part of the Learning Center community for the design and how it would become real at their site. During the second year of implementation at Elizabeth Street Learning Center, teachers and administrators set their own priorities and developed their own training and professional development program in partnerships with a nearby university and the LALC Design Team. The majority of teachers and administrators demonstrated greater understanding, acceptance, and commitment to the design. Many staff began to appreciate the K–12 structure. Teachers felt they got to know their students better and liked seeing older students around whom they had taught before. Many noted that because their students stay with them through all of the grades, teachers will have to confront the fact that students are passed along without learning to read or attaining other important skills and knowledge.

Even though many of the feelings and reactions brought on by the change process are predictable, we have learned a great deal which suggests better strategies for implementing comprehensive changes such as those called for in the LALC design. These include the following:

Offer Blueprints, Not Mandates. It is very difficult to work with a traditional school as an outside organization for change and not be seen as one more institution telling schools what to do. At the same time, faculty and staff seek leadership and do not want to have to reinvent the proverbial reform wheel. Great care must be given to work from the very start as partners in reform while emphasizing that the real change agents are those at the Learning Center. Faculty need to be engaged from the very beginning in setting the agenda for change, planning how a design component could best be organized at their site, and testing out their ideas. The Design is a blueprint, but the Learning Center they create will inevitably be unique and molded to fit their own community's needs.

Assess the Climate for Change. Schools often believe themselves to be more ready for reform than they truly are. Special funding, technology resources, and new opportunities are attractive, and people often wish they could acquire the best of a reform package without having to change significantly. At the beginning, schools and their design partners need to assess the school's readiness for reform and how far along they already are in implementing design components. Then, should the school be ready for change, the plan for implementation should be customized to suit their level of entry into the process and capacity to move forward with integrity and speed.

Be Specific/Get Commitments/Provide Incentives/Define Consequences. Participants need to fully understand the level of changes expected and their commitment to the process. Design development requires a process for increasing understanding of design goals and the change process, and for building consensus and commitment to becoming a Learning Center. The sequence for implementation should be supported by a system of incentives and rewards with clear steps defined for addressing difficulties.

Planning Time and Professional Development Are Essential. Participants in the Learning Center will need time to plan collaboratively for implementation of the changes required by the design. This process requires changes in existing schedules and responsibilities. Participants, particularly administrators and teachers, need to develop a deeper understanding of reform strategies. Teachers need significant professional development time to increase their knowledge of content, standards and assessment strategies, and to improve their classroom skills. New scheduling needs to support educators in their role as continual learners.

Phase It In. It is possible to try to do too much too soon, even if the need for improving performance of schools is dire. Schools must be allowed to establish their own schedule for implementation while they are encouraged to embrace change.

Don't Neglect Communication. Learning Center sites need to think carefully about their communications needs and develop a plan and the capacity for effective communications. This means developing the ability to listen to and assess members of the learning community, as well as developing strategies and tools for providing key audiences with specific information. Learning Centers not only need to communicate across the school campus, but also within school systems and with parents and community members.

Think Carefully About Adding a New Level of School. The K–12 design offers wonderful opportunities for students to be part of a continuous learning community with older students sharing responsibility for younger students, and we are committed to the concept. Yet, we found that it would be best to go slowly in adding a new level of schooling to an existing school. It was painful at Elizabeth Street for the faculty to improve teaching and create curriculum in an environment with many brand new teachers, a lack of resources for the new high school students, constant building on campus to house the new classrooms and resource rooms, and all of the attendant behavior problems these things generate. Foshay closed down at the end of their school year as a junior high and five days later reopened as a pre-K through grade 10 campus. That is radical change. Our recommendation is to go slow when growing a school through the grades or instead consider creating K-12 Learning Centers across a neighborhood family of schools.

Changing Power Relationships. The LALC design calls for a realignment of power within schools. Learning Centers are open organizations engaging all stakeholders in assessment of and planning for the school community. The design asks for participants to act collaboratively; yet the nature of school systems, and urban schools in particular, is that they are grounded in hierarchical and sometimes adversarial relationships. The design asks for schools to strive for continuous improvement, implying continuous change and self-assessment. Shifting power to a wider community base and eliminating the "blame game" is a difficult task which takes continuous attention, may benefit from the expertise of an outside change agent, and requires significant time. We believe that changing school governance is critical to reforms which create schools as "learning organizations" and we have come to understand how difficult a task it is to accomplish, for all involved.

Focus On Trouble Spots. When implementing a design as complex as called for by the Learning Centers, it is easy to lose touch with the pulse of the participants about each of the changing components. For example, we have found multiage instruction to be a difficult concept for teachers to easily understand, and therefore, a difficult change for them to advocate and explain to parents. After two years of implementation, many parents and some faculty still have reservations about the benefit of cross-age and ungraded classrooms for the children. Much more work will need to be done to inform parents and demonstrate the power of multiage instruction to the entire Learning Center community.

Be Realistic About the Time Needed for Change. The Learning Center design sets very high standards for students and very high expectations for members of the Learning Center community. We have asked schools to be vehicles for change and for the professionals within them to act as change agents. At the same time, the history and traditions of schools are working in different directions. Socialization to the status quo has been their primary mission in the past. Past experience and the impact of society on schools make it extraordinarily difficult for schools to successfully reconstruct and reform themselves on short timelines. It takes time to shed the past and become centered in a new approach to our present and future. It takes a great deal of time for new practices to become a daily part of the school experience and for student test scores to reflect the benefit of using new approaches. It will not be possible for reforming urban schools to overcome the educational problems and external conditions such as drugs, violence, and homelessness without the support of parents and the wider community. Building community supports, institutionalizing changes in school culture, and waiting for those changes and supports to affect the well-being and learning of students requires patience and a zeal for continuous improvement.

Summary
Implementation of the LALC design is far from complete but also far along in growth and development. The design team and the Learning Center community members have learned a great deal about the difficulties of the change process and the complexities of reforming schools. Our next steps need to support the changes

already in place and continue to promote and encourage full implementation of the design while extending the opportunities for growing Learning Centers at new sites. The next few years are critical. One pattern found in schools in which faculty stretch themselves to take risks and attempt innovation in order to be successful with today's urban school students is for the school and the teachers to retreat to traditional practices when student achievement fails to improve and to do so quickly (McLaughlin & Talbert, 1993). The LALC will need to find ways to continuously support and encourage teachers, administrators, and parents who are struggling with the complexities of change until they can be confident of the benefits of their efforts.

Next Steps

During the 1995–1996 school year, the LALC is working to ensure full implementation of the design at its existing sites and to begin scaleup of the design at two additional K–12 families of schools in the Los Angeles Unified School District. This includes the development of a memorandum of agreement with existing sites in support of implementation and the recruitment, selection, and preparation of new participants. The LALC will also produce "how to" guidebooks in support of scaleup of the design in Los Angeles and other areas.

LALC will also use the existing Learning Centers as training sites for the advanced use of technology and telecommunications for other schools in the Los Angeles area. LALC is exploring the establishment of one of the Learning Centers as a center for urban school reform, providing training in the use of technology and the other components of the design.

References

Aschbacher, P. (1994). *First year implementation: July 1993 to June 1994: The Los Angeles Learning Centers Evaluation.* Los Angeles: University of California, Los Angeles, Center for the Study of Evaluation.

Aschbacher, P. (1995). *Interim evaluation report: Los Angeles Learning Centers, July 1994 to February 1995.* Los Angeles: University of California, Los Angeles, Center for the Study of Evaluation.

Fullan, M., with Stiegelbauer, S. (1991). *The new meaning of educational change.* New York: Teachers College Press.

McLaughlin, M,. with Talbert, J. (1993). *Contexts that matter for teaching and learning.* Stanford, CA: Stanford University, Center for Research on the Context of Secondary School Teaching.

Lessons Learned

RAND's Formative Assessment of NAS's Phase 2 Demonstration Effort

Susan Bodilly, RAND Corporation

The strong business backing provided to the New American Schools Development Corporation (NASDC) and its founding in the public debate concerning America 2000 ensured that it would be deeply concerned with public accountability.[1] NASDC was renamed New American Schools (NAS) as the designs approached Phase 3, and in this chapter, we will use the new name throughout. Since its creation, NAS attempted to track and report to the public on its program of reform (see chapter 1). As part of this effort to be responsive to public scrutiny, NAS asked the RAND Corporation to perform part of the analytic support needed to provide both internal information for making decisions and public information about progress.

This chapter summarizes the RAND findings of its formative assessment of the demonstration and test stage, Phase 2, and draws some limited lessons from it (Bodilly, 1995). Because the NAS effort will continue into Phase 3 scaleup to more schools and jurisdictions

---

[1] We do not provide a literature review of education reform implementation given the constraints on length for this chapter. However, some of the following works are very helpful: Berman and McLaughlin (1975), Cuban (1990), Elmore and McLaughlin (1988), Firestone, Furhman, and Kirst (1989), and Smith and O'Day (1990).

(see Table 11.1 for the different phases of NAS's development), the chapter is not a *final* report but may be viewed more aptly as a *progress* report. The implications for studying a demonstration phase are at least threefold in terms of the findings presented here: (a) Given the developmental nature of the effort and its short time frame, it is premature to expect significant changes in student outcomes. This assessment deals with the extent to which the design teams could demonstrate their design elements in schools, not with whether the implementation of these elements, in turn, led to improved student outcomes. (b) We are interested in understanding the function a design team plays in reform that might have application in Phase 3 or for other reform efforts. The specific experiences of any one team or sites are less important than commonality or significant differences among teams or groups of teams. (c) In addition, the emphasis is on what could be learned from the development phase that might be applied in Phase 3.

Table 11.1

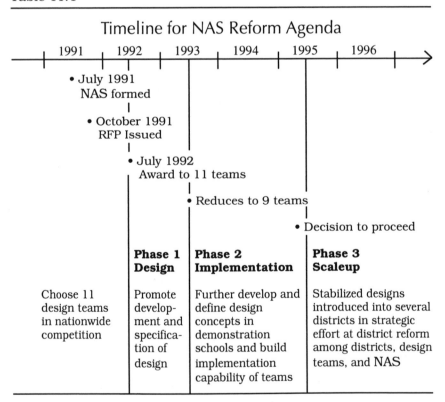

	Phase 1 Design	Phase 2 Implementation	Phase 3 Scaleup
Choose 11 design teams in nationwide competition	Promote development and specification of design	Further develop and define design concepts in demonstration schools and build implementation capability of teams	Stabilized designs introduced into several districts in strategic effort at district reform among districts, design teams, and NAS

The chapter addresses several questions:

- What were the essential differences among the designs and teams?

- How did these differences affect progress?

- As teams and schools interacted, did these efforts offer any insights into useful implementation strategies for reform?

- Given the answers to the above questions, what has been the contribution of NAS to reform so far?

The Reform Design

Methods

The methodology used was a comparative case study analysis with the design teams (listed below with their acronyms) as the unit of analysis:[2]

AC	Audrey Cohen College System of Education
AT	Authentic Teaching, Learning, and Assessment of All Students
CLC	Community Learning Centers
CON	Co-NECT
EL	Expeditionary Learning
LALC	Los Angeles Learning Center
MRSH	Modern Red Schoolhouse
NA	National Alliance for Restructuring Education
RW	Roots and Wings

An embedded case study for each design included two sites in which the team hoped to demonstrate the design by the end of Phase 2 (see Table 11.2). The definition of sites varies by design team. For some it equals a school, for others a feeder pattern, and for others a district or state. Sources of information include documents; interviews with the design teams, state and district administrators, and principals; group interviews of teachers, parents, community leaders, and students. School tours and informal classroom observations complete the picture. Each team and its sites were visited three times: in

---

[2] Our sampling and methodology pose potential problems for one team, National Alliance for Restructuring Education. We have concentrated on school-level effects of interactions between the design teams and sites. This design team intended to have major effects on other levels of governance. In addition, it has more than 81 schools. Our sample and focus might not represent all that has been accomplished by this team.

Table 11.2

Characteristics of the Sample Sites

DESIGN TEAM	SCHOOL	GRADE SPAN	ENROLL-MENT	FREE AND REDUCED LUNCH (%)	SETTING
AC					
Phoenix, Arizona[a]	Loma Linda	K–8	1,200	90	Urban
San Diego, California	Alcott	K–5	395	40[a]	Urban
	Franklin	K–5	540	72	Urban
AT					
Gorham, Maine[c,d]	Gorham High School	9–12	500	16[e]	Small city/rural
	Little Falls	K	200	16[e]	Small city/rural
	Narragansett	1–3	473	16[e]	Small city/rural
	Shaw	7–8	340	16[e]	Small city/rural
	Village	4–6	600	16[e]	Small city/rural
	White Rock	1–3	166	16[e]	Small city/rural
Prince George's County,	Adelphi[a]	PK–3	540	82	Urban
Maryland	Buck Lodge[f]	6–8	675	78	Urban
	Cool Spring[a]	PK–3	540	82	Urban
	High Point[f]	9–12	2,117	40	Urban
	Langley Park	4–6	515	92	Urban
CLC					
Cloquet, Maine[g]	Fon du Lac	PK–12	231	n/a[h]	Reservation
Duluth, Minnesota[d]	Spotted Eagle	K–6	106	n/a[h]	Small city
Minneapolis, Minnesota	Cedar-Riverside	K–6	82	90	Urban
CON					
Dorchester, Massachusetts[i]	Sarah Greenwood	K–6+	348	98	Urban
Worcester, Massachusetts[g]	ALL School	K–8	466	80	Urban

(Table 11.2 continues)

Table 11.2: Characteristics of the Sample Sites (continued)

	Location	School	Grades	Enrollment	%	Urbanicity
EL	Dubuque, Iowa	Bryan[g]	K–5	349	26[e]	Small city
		Lincoln[g]	K–5	419	26[e]	Small city
		Central	9–12	162	26[e]	Small city
	New York, New York	School for the Physical City	6–8, 10	144	38	Urban
LALC	Cudahy, California[a]	Elizabeth Street	PK–10	2,400	88	Urban
	Los Angeles	Foshay	K–10	2,700	89	Urban
MRSH	Bartholomew, Indiana	Columbus East[a]	9–12	1,234	8	Small city/rural
		Northside[a]	6–8	805	15	Small city/rural
		Taylorsville[f]	K–6	504	23	Small city/rural
	Indianapolis, Indiana[f]	Frost	K–5	293	60	Urban
NA	Louisville, Kentucky[a]	Kennedy	K–5	411	66	Urban
	Calloway County, Kentucky	Calloway Middle	6–8	727	38[j]	Rural
		Southwest Calloway	K–5	482	37[j]	Rural
	San Diego, California	Darnall[f]	K–5	407	90	Urban
		Marshall[g]	K–5	903	93	Urban
RW	St. Mary's County, Maryland	Ridge	PK–5	276	29	Rural
		Lexington Park	PK–5	474	42	Small city

[a] Data approximate as of Spring 1995.
[b] Data reported in 1994.
[c] Data reported in 1991.
[d] Grade spans and enrollment as of 1993-94 site visits.
[e] District level data, not reported by individual school.
[f] Data reported in 1992.
[g] Data reported in 1993.
[h] These schools operate under the Bureau of Indian Affairs, and meals are provided in a different manner.
[i] The design team ended its relationship with this site during the school year 1993-94.
[j] Percent reported as "low-income."

fall 1993, spring 1994, and spring 1995. Some team professional development activities or summer institutes were attended (more detailed explanation of lessons from New American Schools's demonstration phase are in Bodilly, 1995).

Elements of Design

We used elements of whole-school designs as a means to follow changes in designs and schools over time and explicate some of the differences among designs. These elements were derived primarily from a content analysis of the proposals submitted by the design teams indicating their intention of making changes to certain areas of schooling.[3] We introduce these elements here for definitional purposes and because they will be used throughout the remainder of the chapter. They act as building blocks in designs with each design choosing to use certain elements or building blocks.

- *Curriculum and Instruction* elements include what knowledge bases are learned and in what sequence and the manner in which knowledge is transmitted to the student.

- *Standards* include the skills and content areas a student is expected to master to progress through the system and the levels at which performance should be demonstrated.

- *Assessments* are means for measuring progress towards standards; they offer information about student or school progress.

- *Student Grouping* concerns the criteria or basis for assigning students to classes, groups, programs.

- *Community Involvement* refers to how parents, business, and others participate in schools and vice versa.

- *Integration of Social Services* includes how and when social services will be provided for students to be ready to learn.

- *Governance* is the distribution of authority and responsibility among education actors: states, districts, school members, and others. School-level governance changes usually increase its participatory nature, district to school governance changes

---

[3] They align well with those elements called "commonplaces" in Goodlad (1984).

usually require site-based management, and state-level changes often demand different legal responsibilities for schools and districts or different legal responsibilities among education and noneducation partners.

- *Professional Development* has several components as discussed in team documents. Staff training includes the traditional workshops and in-services provided on particular subjects or issue areas from cooperative learning to emergency procedures. These were often referred to as inservices and were highly specific and time constrained. Professional growth opportunities include opportunities to develop curriculum and instruction, to develop expertise in using standards to develop curriculum, to collaborate with others, and to enter into networks or prolonged discussions with other teachers about the profession. Several teams planned to supplement the above two types of professional development with opportunities for changed practice such as extensive on-the-job practice, coaching in the classroom, and teaming in individual classrooms as well as schoolwide forums to permanently change the ways in which teachers deliver curriculum and instruction.

- *Structure, Staffing, and Allocation of Staff Time* concerns the roles and responsibilities of different staff. Changed organizational structures and incentives encourage teachers to access both staff in-services and professional growth opportunities.

The remainder of the chapter is divided into five sections. The Second section contrasts the teams and their designs on dimensions important to the demonstration phase. The third section explains the progress made by the design teams toward accomplishing their goals at the school level in terms of the nature of the design and development approach. The fourth section then analyzes the implementation strategies of the teams and their effect on progress made as well as lessons learned as reported by both design teams and school-level staff. The fifth section discusses the implications of the analysis. The final section explores the contribution of NAS teams to the school reform effort.

Initial Differences among Designs and Teams

Content analysis of design team documents and interviews with the teams indicated numerous differences among designs and design teams at the beginning of Phase 2. At a detailed level, this included such differences as whether a design team advocated multiyear or multiage classrooms, what percent of the curriculum would become interdisciplinary, what standards would be adopted, and what type of participatory governing structure was advocated. However, experience during Phase 2 has shown that higher level differences were more important in distinguishing the teams and their performance. These more significant differences follow and can be thought of as "challenges," different for each team, that had to be overcome in Phase 2 in order to meet NAS goals.

Capacity-Building Issues Facing Design Teams

The design teams did not come to NAS equally equipped to meet the demands for rapid development, demonstration, and then scaleup. Many factors affected their readiness to undertake the NAS effort. We draw contrasts between the teams on four factors: whether the core team was newly created with new leaders working together; whether it needed to create a staff and structure to support the effort; whether the writers of the proposal were the same as the developers and implementers in Phase 2; and whether the team leaders or staff had experience in implementation of school-level reform.

We summarize the standing of the different teams at the end of Phase 1. Two teams, AC and RW, began with existing organizations, a staff with proven capability to interact effectively with schools based on past school reform experience. These two teams were presented with less of a challenge in terms of needed team building than other teams. Three other teams (CLC, CON, and NA) pre-existed NAS, had some prior experience, although not always of practical implementation in schools, but were challenged to build a staff to meet the goals of Phase 2. Four teams—AT, EL, LALC, and MRSH—faced Phase 2 with significant challenges regarding their readiness when compared to the other teams. Each was created to respond to the RFP and so had to create a staff structure and develop leadership. AT and MRSH had considerable challenges because the proposers were not the implementers of the design. And EL and MRSH did not have prior experience at school-level reform.

Number of Sites Chosen

The number of sites that each team chose to work with also emerged as important. Working with many sites could possibly impose resource constraints on a team; thus, teams with a large number of sites would be more challenged to meet NAS goals. NA distinguished itself from the other teams because it chose to demonstrate its design starting in Phase 2 in over 80 schools. By year two of Phase 2 it planned to at least double that number. It had the most ambitious number of sites. The number of sites established by the other teams ranged from 2 to 18 schools.

Differences among Teams in the Design Type

Two characteristics capture the essence of the many differences among designs: the number and type of elements (or building blocks) included in the design and the number of collaborators that the design team would need to develop the design at a site (see Fig. 11.1). Three approaches distinguish the design teams.

Core designs (AC, CON, EL, and RW) emphasize changes in elements associated with the core of schooling: curriculum, instruction, standards, assessments, student groupings, community involvement, and professional development. They focused on school-level partnerships—it is their main point of entry and continued interaction.

Comprehensive designs (AT, CLC, LALC, MRSH) emphasize more elements, including integrated social services, governance changes, and organization and staffing changes as fundamental to the design. While these teams believe that they need to construct complex collaborative efforts with groups outside of schools to

Figure 11.1

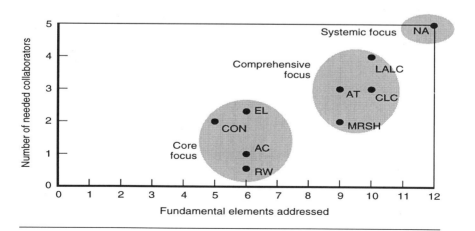

Design Types and Collaborators Needed

accomplish these goals, their main interventions are still at the school-building level.

The sole *systemic* design (NA) emphasizes changes to all elements and the need for collaboration among many partners. Rather than focus only on the school as the intervention point, this design focuses on changing the systems that surround schools including the central office, state legislation, professional development providers, social services providers, and the community to better support schools.

Potentially, all else equal, the comprehensive designs and the single systemic one would face greater challenges in meeting NAS Phase 2 goals than the core designs in that they pursue change in more elements of design or building blocks of the school, need to influence policies of more actors both internal and external to the schools, and intend to make changes that reform both schools and, for some, the social system surrounding schools.

The horizontal axis of Fig. 11.1 deserves some further elaboration. Content analysis of the original design proposals, including updated design documents in 1994, and interviews with the teams, showed that the teams differed in the inclusion or exclusion of desired changes reflected in the relative emphasis they put on specific elements of the design. The results, which indicate elements included in the design at the beginning of Phase 2 based on a document review and discussions with the design teams, are shown in Fig. 11.2. If a team strongly emphasized an element, that is the team said they intended to make significant changes in that building block of a "whole" school, we indicated this by using a light gray shading to show that the team is challenged to demonstrate changes in this element in the Phase 2 schools. If the team intended to demonstrate only modest changes in an element compared to that demanded by other designs, we indicate so with black. If the design did not address that element, the category is cross-hatched.

Curriculum and Instruction. All design teams intended to make significant changes relative to existing schools' curriculum and instruction. There is a general move by all teams toward interdisciplinary, project-based curriculum. Several include service to the community and internships as part of a required curriculum. However, the details of these changes indicated a great deal of variation among teams. Nevertheless, all teams felt that changes in these two elements were fundamental.

Standards. Seven teams intended to create new standards, of one type or another. Two designs (CLC and RW) intend to bring all

Figure 11.2

Level of Initial Challenge to Design Teams Keyed to Number of Elements Included

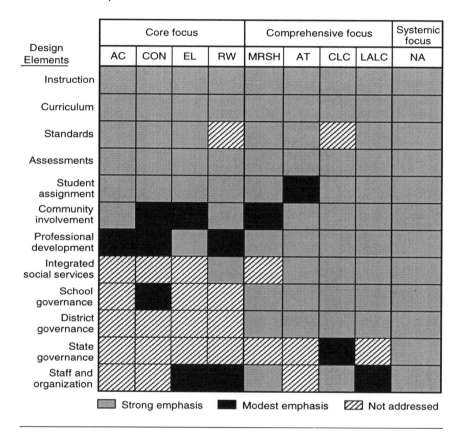

students to existing state standards. Two teams (AC and MRSH) intended to create their own unique standards, and others wanted to combine existing standards and particular skills to emphasize the concerns of their teams.

Assessments. All teams intended to develop at least performance-based student-level assessments keyed to their standards, curriculum, and instruction. Several talked about systems of assessments. The designs did not distinguish themselves further.

Student Assignment. Seven teams emphasized changes in the assignment of students within schools such as multi-age grouping, multi-year groupings, cooperative learning, and project-based learning in groups. The exceptions were AC and AT. However, although not explicitly specified by the latter teams, some form of assignment change was implied by their curriculum and instructional methods.

Community Involvement. Six teams emphasized the need for greater community involvement in the school or greater school involvement in the community as a key thrust of the design. For the three others (CON, EL, MRSH) some degree of community involvement was noted, but was not a major emphasis.

Professional Development. Six teams stated that they intended to make fundamental changes to the professional development process for teachers as part of their designs, oftentimes including changes to the role of teachers and to teacher education. Two other teams (AC and RW) did not indicate fundamental changes to the process; rather, they indicated that professional development would change to emphasize significant training in their particular methods.

Integrated Social Services. Five teams emphasized the provision of integrated social services in schools (AT, CLC, LALC, NA, and RW). AT, CLC, LALC, and NA viewed the school as the focus of provision, integrating education and social services. RW included a family support coordinator at the school but did not require the school to provide integrated social services.

School-Level Governance. Five teams (AT, CLC, LALC, MRSH, and NA) required formal changes to school-level governance usually the setting up of governance committees with participation of teachers and others. CON promoted the creation of two committees as desirable, but this was not required. Others encouraged these types of changes but did not require them.

District–School Governance. Five teams required formal and very significant changes to the relationship between the school and district (AT, CLC, LALC, MRSH, and NA). These changes dictated school-level control over resources, budgeting, and staffing. The other teams promoted and encouraged such control but did not require it.

State Governance. One team (NA) sought changes at the state level to promote reform, including formal changes to the responsibilities of the education and social service agencies. CLC implied state-level support for charter schools, but this was not a prerequisite for noncharter school districts in its sample.

Staff and Organization. Three teams emphasized the need for significant, permanent changes to the staff structure, and in fact based their designs on these changes (CLC, MRSH, and NA). Three others saw this as a possibility but did not require it, or they asked for the addition of a single facilitator (EL, LALC, and RW).

Differences Among Teams in Approaches to the Choice Between Further Team or Site-Level Development

Interviews with the design teams and a review of the proposals indicated that all had given thought to the dilemma faced concerning the relative responsibility of the team and the sites in further specification and development of the design. All teams talked in terms of organizational change being more likely if a flexible, mutual adjustment process was used. They avoided highly prescribed designs or mandatory styles of implementation. All teams used at least some aspects of a prototype development where the design was expected to evolve as the schools and design teams responded to each other and moved together toward improved levels of performance. Each team talked of its design unfolding or evolving with practical experience.

Although a common approach was apparent, at least when compared to some past top-down reform efforts, the teams tended to cluster around three, not sharply distinct, development strategies that determined the relationships between teams and sites.

Team-Developed Designs. One group of teams (AC and RW) relied on the capabilities of the design teams to develop further the design. Although they work with schools in this process through feedback, these teams intended to take major responsibility for providing the curriculum frameworks, models of lessons plans, list of resources, and models for student assignment and assessments in keeping with the specific elements of the design.

Extensive Site-Based Development. In contrast, another set of teams (AT, CLC, and NA) provided only a few specifics and general guidelines or processes of change to the schools. The schools then develop their own local designs in keeping with general guidelines. The schools develop a vision of what they will become, develop their own curriculum, and choose what kind of student groupings are appropriate. Whereas AT specified a governance structure to be followed and NA specified standards and assessments to be met and used, CLC relied most heavily on site-based development.

More Limited Site-Based Development. A final group of teams (CON, EL, LALC, and MRSH) took major responsibility in specifying the design, but relied on the sites to further develop some elements, at least in Phase 2. In common, each relied on the sites to develop curriculum and instructional models following team developed standards, and to implement student assignment models specified by the team.

Local variation should be expected in all designs, but all else equal, the designs with greater reliance on site-based development faced potentially more challenges for Phase 2. Greater reliance on sites for local development put the ability of the teams to demonstrate progress under the direct influence of sites and site-level capability, especially in the areas of curriculum and instruction development. Sites that did not promote the designs and assign time and resources to development did not show as much progress as those associated with team-developed designs. On the other hand, team-developed designs might be subject to some set-backs if the sites did not like the developed design provided to them.

Implication of Combining Challenges Faced by Teams

The capacity-building challenges, numbers of sites, type of design, and demonstration approach combined into four groupings that distinguished the designs and teams at the beginning of Phase 2 and implied unique sets of challenges in meeting NAS goals:

- AC and RW were both core designs with team development approaches. Neither team faced significant team capacity-building or site challenges when compared to others.

- CON and EL were also both core designs, but required shared development between the team and sites. Although CON had some team capacity issues to address, EL had significantly more than most other teams, being newly created and having significantly less experience as a team in school-level reform.

- AT, CLC, LALC, and MRSH were comprehensive designs requiring some team and site-based development. AT and CLC required more site development than most other teams. In addition, AT,

LALC, and MRSH faced significant challenges to team building in Phase 2.

• Alone, NA was a systemic design requiring significant site-level development. While having a few challenges to team building, its greatest challenge was to produce significant change in over 80 schools and their associated districts and states.

Differences in Progress among Designs and Teams

Over the two-year period of Phase 2, RAND tracked the progress made by the teams toward their uniquely stated goals within each element. The criteria for progress and the tracking system are described in Bodilly (1995) and are derived from NAS goals for having a full demonstration of the design in two schools by the end of Phase 2. Review of documents, unobtrusive observation, interviews with design teams and site-level actors, including group interviews of approximately 75 percent of the teachers at each school were used to gauge progress and also construct possible cause and effect relationships between factors, as seen through the eyes of the participants. These findings are summarized in Figure 11.3 and discussed below.

Manifestations of Progress

By the end of Phase 2, NAS expected no less than the creation of design teams, full demonstration of the envisioned changes in elements in at least two schools, and the building of team capability for expansion in Phase 3. As we use the term, *substantial progress* equates to full demonstration of the design with the majority of students and teachers adopting the behaviors described by the design document. Failure to meet the NAS goal of substantial progress cannot be interpreted as failure to reform or failure of the efforts of the design team or associated schools, but only failure to fully comply with NAS expectations. A highly successful effort by other standards may not meet the NAS goals.[4]

---

[4] Other school-level transformation activities allow schools a longer period to demonstrate changes. Levin (1993) stated, "It takes about six years to fully transform a conventional school to accelerated status." Prestine and Bowen (1993) in writing on the Coalition of Essential Schools state, "a minimum of five years was recommended for the entire process" (p. 302) or "between two and seven years" (p. 305).

A white block in Fig. 11.3 indicates that the team did not address this element in its original proposal; therefore, it did not have the challenge to demonstrate changes in the element.

Hatching in Fig. 11.3 indicates that a team did include this element, but showed a comparatively low level of progress toward full demonstration of the concepts in the design. Demonstration was at the beginning stages with the team in the process of specifying concepts, developing models, introducing the site to the ideas through training, and establishing or running pilots. Teachers might be busily working on curriculum units, but these units had not been fully developed, reviewed for quality, or put into a scope and sequence. Outreach to external actors might be tentative at this point—establishing contact and getting regular meetings underway with actors such as social services or professional education schools. Participatory governance committees might be formed, but are not yet working smoothly.

Light gray indicates that the team intended changes in this element and that progress toward full demonstration was moderate. The schools were moving away from pilots with limited participation toward increased involvement of teachers and students. Training switched from introductory sessions to address more substantial issues of change. Quality control was initiated by reviewing curriculum units against standards and deleting or improving units to fit into an agreed upon scope and sequence, for learning across the

Figure 11.3

Progress toward Goals Indicated by Design

Elements of Designs	Core/Team Dev		Core/Site Dev		Comprehensive/Site Dev				Systemic Site Dev/
	AC	RW	CON	EL	AT	CLC	LALC	MRSH	NA
Instruction					▨		▨		▨
Curriculum	■				▨		▨	■	▨
Standards	■		■	▨					
Assessments		■		▨	▨				
Student Assignment	■	■		▨	▨		▨		▨
Community	■			▨			▨	▨	
Professional	■	■							
Integrated Social Services	■				▨		▨		▨
School Governance						■		■	■
District Governance							▨		■
State Governance									■
Staff Changes	■	■		▨			▨	▨	

■ = substantial   ☐ = moderate   ▨ = beginning   ☐ = not emphasized school as a whole. Teams and sites were refining the models and materials used. Links to outside actors were beginning to be strengthened with actual changes being made in service delivery. Participatory governance was affecting school decisions and autonomy was moving from waiver-based toward grants of independence based on performance.

Dark gray shows that consistent with the final goal for Phase 2, there was full demonstration of the concept in at least two schools, and consistency across sites associated with the design. Most students and teachers were affected within the schools. The infrastructure of the school was changing to support the new design on a permanent basis and quality control was automatic through teacher evaluation, new assessments, and others.

We note that in all cases (a) progress in middle schools and high schools was less than progress in elementary schools,[5] and (b) the design teams' sites and our sample were more heavily weighted toward elementary schools. Therefore, a design team can be marked as having substantial progress when, in fact, most of that progress was evident in elementary schools, and progress in associated high schools lagged.

Basic Patterns of Progress

As may be seen in Fig. 11.3, the two teams (AC, RW) regarded as most ready at the beginning of Phase 2 and with core designs (fewer elements) that relied heavily on team development demonstrated most of their elements at the substantial level. The two other core designs, but with site development (CON and EL), did not demonstrate their design elements to the same extent. Of these two, EL had the greatest challenges in terms of team capacity and demonstrated less of its design than the other core designs.

In general, the comprehensive and systemic designs showed the lowest levels of demonstration across their many elements. They did not accomplish the extent of progress exhibited by the core designs in the elements of curriculum instruction, standards, assessment, professional development, and community involvement. The exception appears to be MRSH. Aside from participatory governance, these teams at best achieved only moderate

---

[5] In several cases this was deliberate. For example, both AC and MRSH focused their initial efforts in elementary schools and delayed design development and implementation in high schools. This was understood in the contract between NAS and the teams.

demonstration of the elements peculiar to their designs: governance, integrated social services, and staffing and organizational changes.

Finally, among the group of comprehensive and systemic designs with shared development, those that we identified as having significant challenges in terms of team building or number of sites (AT, LALC, NA) tended to have demonstrated fewer elements than the teams without those challenges. The exception appears to be MSRH.

Effects of Team Capacity-Building Challenges

The progress results indicate a general association between the identified team capacity-building challenges evident in Phase 1 and the level of demonstration observed in Phase 2. The two design teams that had fewer evident challenges (AC, RW) tended to make the most progress. Three of the four teams we identified as facing greater challenges in terms of initial capacity accomplished a lower level of demonstration (AT, EL, LALC). Interviews with the teams and the sites indicated that the capacity of the team was a key factor in producing or not producing the full demonstration results NAS wanted.

The AC and RW teams entered the sites in Phase 1, one year earlier than the other teams. Because the sites had a longer period of time to demonstrate the design, they naturally appeared more mature in terms of demonstration. The sites associated this early entry with the existence of fairly well developed models for standards, curriculum and instruction already existing in the teams' repertoires. For example, RW used the existing Maryland state standards and state assessments, and its' previously developed Success for All reading component.

In contrast to RW and AC, three of the four comparatively less ready teams (AT, EL, and LALC) were affected heavily by the need to develop the design at the same time they were building team capability and capacity. These teams suffered to differing degrees from the following:

- Struggles to combine existing organizations with strong cultures into a new partnership (AT and LALC).

- Difficulties in translating abstract notions into implementable actions and specified design concepts (AT, EL, and LALC).

- Difficulties in quickly building the staff needed to fully develop the design and address fundamental issues (AT, EL, and LALC).

- Entry into the school before the design was adequately developed resulting in confusion by the site in the first year (AT, EL, and LALC).

Effects of Number of Sites

The number of sites selected tended to adversely affect only one team, NA. This team, which took on significantly more sites than did other teams, showed lower demonstration levels across all elements at the sites observed. NA began its efforts in seven states, 25 districts, and more than 80 schools. Team interviews in fall 1993 indicated that the team had difficulty growing fast enough to meet the demands placed upon it by so many sites. Instead, NA provided for a small group of "lead" teachers from each school to attend conferences and bring back reform ideas to the schools. Teachers did not credit this team with strong support and specifically criticized the lead teacher model. The team had a very ambitious schedule for scaleup to more sites by year two of Phase 2, but abandoned that in the face of slow across-the-board progress. In response to its Phase 2 experiences, NA will concentrate during Phase 3 on its existing jurisdictions and build its capacity to facilitate change at the jurisdiction and state levels.

Other teams might have been affected by the number of sites, but we could not distinguish these effects from other factors. In several instances designs that started out with fewer sites added sites during the second year of Phase 2. For example, CON started with two sites (actually K–9 schools). One in Boston was dropped by the second year, but several schools were added in two jurisdictions: Hammond, Indiana and Juneau, Alaska. AC also added several new schools in Dade County, Florida. Four additional elementary schools adopted the RW model in St. Mary's County, Maryland, and several schools were added to EL in Dubuque, Iowa.

Effects of Design Type

The level of demonstration also appears to be associated with the type of design. Three (AC, RW, CON) of the four core designs showed substantial progress in over half of the elements included in the design. Only one (MRSH) of the five comprehensive or systemic designs showed comparable progress. The others tended to show low to moderate progress across almost all their elements including their distinguishing elements: governance, integrated social services, and staffing changes.

The lower levels of progress toward full demonstration by the comprehensive and systemic designs does not mean they accomplished less than the core designs. It may be interpreted to mean that they attempted more and made broad progress across the board.

Progress in Core Elements. Four teams (AC, CON, MRSH, RW) stand out as having made significant progress in the elements that represent the core focus of schooling, especially curriculum, instruction, standards, and student assignment. These teams exhibited some commonality that explains this level of progress: an unrelenting emphasis with a clear focus on producing results in these elements and their early development and introduction of concrete models and materials to accomplish these tasks. In contrast, other teams, whether core or other types of designs, had less initial focus or did not have the "core" of solid design models to produce results quickly.

Participatory Governance. Most of the design teams (AT, CLC, LALC, MRSH, NA) attempting to establish participatory governance changes did in fact accomplish, at least superficially, what they intended. Design documents tended to describe committee structures within schools that were intended to increase teachers' input into decision making at the school level or increase the diversity of representation in general—adding parents, community members, and business people to those heard. By the end of Phase 2 these committee structures had been set up and were functioning. The committees were more representative, including teachers, parents, business representatives, and sometimes students, than in the past. Meetings were being held on a routine basis.

Respondents noted that the function or focus of the committees was as important as the level of participation. Two teams received particularly positive comments from school personnel in this regard: MRSH and NA. Both imposed a committee structure on the schools that corresponded to tasks each design team thought were most important. The immediate effect was to reduce the number of committees within the school to a reasonable number and to focus the school decision-making bodies on the design and its school transformation goals. Respondents said these committees enabled the design to become the center of school attention cleverly marrying the design to its implementation.

School–District Relationships. School autonomy from districts proved more elusive. The exceptions to the following discussion lie with a few sites that had pre-existing autonomy[6] and with design teams that asked for relatively small concessions.[7]

The needed school-level autonomy tended to lie in three areas (see Turnbull, 1985): control over the entire school budget, not just discretionary funds; control over hiring, firing, and transfer, as well as staff positions; and control over assessments and accountability measures used. In general, interviews at sites associated with comprehensive and systemic teams attempting change in the area of school level autonomy indicated:

- Most schools have the ability to innovate in terms of curriculum and instruction or can easily obtain waivers to do so, except when these innovations come in conflict with required testing regimes. All teams experienced instances in which testing regimes conflicted with desired curriculum and instruction. In these instances, the teachers usually went outside the design in order to meet testing requirements.

- The team often lacked the political clout as outsiders to affect the system of rules and regulations sufficiently to promote autonomy over budget, personnel and staffing, or assessments within the time frame of Phase 2. But, in that time frame, the team could build upon small successes to encourage an open dialog or negotiation between the school and the district for increased autonomy.

- While the teams often lacked the local presence needed to build political influence, existing expertise by the team could substitute for this and in several instances worked to relieve schools of misinterpretations of existing laws that stood in the way of improvements[8] (footnote 8 on p. 310).

---

[6] For example, the NA sites in Kentucky had existing autonomy granted through the Kentucky Education Reform Act. A San Diego site for NA is a charter school under the California charter law. And, several schools associated with CLC are charter schools, contract schools, or reservation schools. In each of these cases the autonomy available to the schools preceded to a large extent the relationship with the design team.

[7] AC and RW are designated as core teams and yet have been marked as accomplishing changes in this area. However, these were very limited changes requiring the funding of one additional staff person as a school-level facilitator. This was approved in all cases. But, this concession to staffing does not match the comprehensive and systemic designs ambitious requirements for full school-level autonomy over staffing decisions.

- School staff lacked the ability to effectively use power granted in these areas because they had not been trained to do so. This was most especially felt to be the case in the area of budgeting.

- District representatives often said that many schools had been granted autonomy in these areas, but did not choose to use it because of tradition or because of lack of competence.

- Districts were willing to grant additional school-level powers if and when schools demonstrated they could effectively use their existing powers.

The successes we observed in terms of completing goals of site autonomy tended to be restricted to obtaining waivers, acting more forcefully in making school-level choices, and proper interpretation of existing regulations in favor of design teams principles. Significant restructuring and site-based management were not obtained by the design teams, but were built on pre-existing changes.[9] Design teams concluded, and district officials appeared to agree, that the move toward autonomy was a process, not an event, and that the school-level autonomy needed for some of the designs would develop over time (for discussion of this issue, see Bimber, 1994; Liberman, 1991; Policy Studies Associates, Inc., 1994; and Summers & Johnson, 1994). As more schools reformed, the demand for specific powers necessary to promote the design would grow and the district would begin to remove more barriers.

Social Services. Teams pursuing this goal showed us local models that demonstrated the concepts in their proposals. For example, the Challenger campus associated with Prince George's County mirrors the integrated social services element described by AT. The same could be said for the JFK School Family Support

---

[8] The clearest example actually comes from a core design, RW, which has on its staff nationally recognized experts on the use of federal funds. These experts could argue with mid-level state and district bureaucrats for proper interpretation of federal rules based on their strong experiences in other schools. The same could be said of CLC's expertise in charter and contract schools.

[9] Difficulties associated with restructuring and the lack of political clout of any one actor to ensure this have been described by Tyack (1990). He notes that restructuring flies in the face of a century of the buildup of central office power over individual schools.

Center in Kentucky and the Crawford Cluster in San Diego, both associated with NA. Neither team is responsible for these changes; they predate the presence of both teams. However, it could be said that the teams did reinforce these changes and encouraged the schools to be more supportive of them, and that these centers stand as examples of what the team is trying to accomplish.

Teams attempting to provide integrated services at the school report that the team and schools did not have the necessary contacts with social services and were not strong political players in social service provision. They were the outsiders stepping in and as such had little standing in the community of social service agencies (see Smrekar, 1994).

In addition, teachers noted that when they were called upon to perform social services outreach, they did not know how to go about it and did not have the time needed to undertake it. As a result they tended to follow familiar paths toward improvement with marginal changes to the existing system, for example, advocating a school nurse position or building a stronger teacher referral system for students in need of services.

Number of Elements. In addition to problems associated with progress in certain elements, the sheer number of elements to cover posed problems for the comprehensive and systemic teams. More than the core teams, the comprehensive and systemic teams were taxed to meet their stringent NAS goals in all elements by the end of Phase 2 and teachers reported they felt drawn into areas where they had little expertise and little time to address overwhelming problems.

Effect of Site Development Approaches

The approach to development of the design, whether assumed by the design team or the site, was also associated with different levels of progress among teams. The two teams that provided the greatest amount of team specification and development (AC and RW) showed the most substantial progress toward demonstration. Three teams (AT, CLC, NA) intended that each site be responsible for site development. Of these teams, AT and NA showed relatively low levels of progress. The LALC team intended to take a greater role in development, but experienced difficulties in developing team capability. This resulted in school staff taking on the role of developing the design. This design team showed progress like that of AT and NA.

The reasons for slower progress demonstrated by teams relying on substantial site-based development are straightforward. Imagine the challenge to site capacity (time, expertise, and resources of staff) when a design team asks a site to simultaneously develop an interdisciplinary curriculum, a new governance structure with all teachers participating, a plan for integrated social services, and student assignment plans, while providing the site with access to experts in each of these areas and perhaps days for professional development. This was the approach of AT, CLC, and NA (and, to a lesser extent LALC because it relied on consultants to develop some elements).[10] AT also asked sites to develop their own sets of standards. The site-development approach during the demonstration phase when combined with a comprehensive or a systemic design often resulted in reform exhaustion—teachers and staff so overextended that they were exhausted at the end of the two-year period.

Changes to Designs

The experiences of Phase 2, just noted, led teams to reconfigure themselves. Even though the core designs did not originally say they intended to change school autonomy or social services, by the end of Phase 2 they found the designs could not be maintained in schools that did not have autonomy over some budget and personnel decisions and did not seek out ways to better prepare children for learning. By the end of Phase 2, core designs teams were beginning to consider the elements that had once distinguished the comprehensive and systemic designs.

What seems clear from all this is that whether the issues of governance, staffing, and social services are treated as a starting point in the design or as a bridge to cross when necessary, all designs had to face issues concerning these elements as they tried to move from initiation to institutionalization of the design. Each team developed approaches to dealing with these systemic barriers to school improvement. Some are direct, others more opportunistic.

The teams, as they finished Phase 2, began to change their approaches to development and implementation as well. CON, EL, LALC, and MRSH had intended from the beginning that their designs become less dependent on site development over time as the team benefited from materials and models or curriculum developed by sites in Phase 2. As the Phase 2 sites developed more materials and tried different combinations of student assignment or instructional

---

[10] This approach by AT is similar to that of CES, one of its principal organizations. The literature evaluating CES has found problems related to reliance on sites for development without providing clear models or materials (see Herman & Stringfield, 1995).

strategies, these teams intended to cull the lessons and provide firmer models to future sites. Importantly, CON, EL, and MRSH still believe that a significant amount of curriculum must be developed by teachers at new sites so that teachers can go through the process of learning how to use standards, curriculum, instruction, assessments, and student assignments in a coherent way. However, new schools will benefit from lessons learned and from already developed materials and examples of units developed in Phase 2; thus, some of the difficulties of Phase 2 in regard to site-based development and issues raised as to site capability might be reduced.

AT, CLC, and NA do not intend to change their approach to site-based development. Significant site capability for development will be required as the teams act as assisters in a fundamentally school-level process of learning and growth. However, even at this extreme, the clearer processes and materials developed during Phase 2 promise to expedite this effort when compared to the experiences of Phase 2 sites using undeveloped designs. For example, standards and assessments by NA should enable smoother progress.

A final evolution by the teams was that several had learned more about which elements to introduce first and which to implement later. A general consensus, with the exception of AT and NA, is to move quickly to institute change in curriculum and instruction. For four teams (AC, CON, MRSH, RW) such changes would be accompanied by significant revisions in student assignments such as the use of multiyear or multiage approaches and "neverstreaming." AT, CLC, MRSH, and NA would focus on setting up the internal governance structure and school improvement planning process as fundamental in bringing about other changes, but they would not force school-level autonomy, staffing changes, or integrated social services. These elements would be fixed goals that would unfold in an opportunistic manner geared to site-level conditions. At the end of Phase 2, none of the teams was still pushing toward implementation of all elements simultaneously.

Implementation Strategies and their Effect on Progress

In order to meet NAS goals, it was not enough to have a well-crafted design. Our findings support a long held position in education reform: A strong implementation strategy that matched the design was important to successfully meeting NAS's goals for Phase 2.

Achieving Initial Buy-In from Sites

The published baseline report on the fall 1993 site visits for this study described the initial site selection process for Phase 2 and how teams initiated their relationships with potential sites. We found the following:

- Several designs chose potential sites based on previous personal contacts between the site and teams, oftentimes with the district rather than the design team choosing the site (AC, CON, AT, NA, RW). The district control was due to the hurried nature of initiation imposed by NAS deadlines. Some did try to institute a more formal application process with deliberate selection (EL, CLC, LALC, MRSH), but did not appear to consistently accomplish it.

- Most teams intended to ensure early teacher buy-in by encouraging majority votes and the ability of teachers not interested in the design to transfer to another school. But, these ideas were applied irregularly across sites within teams. Huberman and Miles (1984) cited an example of how teachers often chose to adopt reform as "The principal wanted it; we got the message," (p. 40). This was very similar to what we heard at the majority of sites that took formal votes.

- Sites reported that they chose to work with design teams because they wanted: additional resources, especially new technology; access to professional development or the legitimacy gained from association with reputable reformers; and the design (as they understood it) matched where they were headed. The idea that there would be multiple different reasons for adoption of a design or a reform is discussed in Huberman and Miles (1984). Because most designs were still rather hazy at that point in time, the understanding was at the general level. Principals and teachers did not talk of the resources they would have to expend or the work they would have to do. In short, sites entered into the arrangement looking for gain, not recognizing the effort needed to reform, even for those who went through the more stringent application process.

In general, design teams were dissatisfied with this selection or initiation process thinking that it could be done in a much more organized and fruitful way in Phase 3.

In the final set of interviews with design teams and sites we asked "What worked well to promote the required changes in the school and what did not work well?" When specifically addressing the initial matching of teams to schools, general consensus was clear:

1. Obviously a *more fully developed design, documented in easily readable form*, would be helpful. During Phase 2 some teams were still specifying and developing their designs as they entered schools. The less developed the design, the more confusion at the sites in terms of what staff was supposed to do. Sites simply reflected the confusion of some of the teams. As a partial solution, for Phase 3 NAS required all teams to develop 2-page, 10-page, and 50-page descriptions of their designs. Several developed other materials such as descriptive videotapes. These were delivered in June 1995.

2. Teams and sites agreed that the *team should present the design to the whole school*. Both believed that this procedure would help avoid problems of misinterpretation and "selling" by principals or assignment by districts that plagued several teams and schools. In interviews at more than one site associated with more than one team, teachers told us that they did approve the design after the principal framed the premise as, "Agree to do this and get discretionary funds or don't agree and get no discretionary funds."

3. *Teachers should be involved in the decision to accept a design*. Some teams now require a formal, anonymous vote by teachers. For example, AC and RW require an 80 percent vote and transfer of teachers where possible who are not willing to implement. Others are less specific, not requiring a formal vote, but requiring a "getting to know you period" where teachers are introduced to the design and debate undertaking it (for example, AT).

4. In making a choice, the design teams preferred that *schools* enter into a *search for a design suitable to their needs*. NAS, therefore, arranged to have "fairs" in potential Phase 3 districts where schools could hear presentations of several designs and follow through with invitations to teams they were interested in visiting their schools.

Required Interactions and Supports for Teachers in Reforming Schools

In focus groups at the sites we asked teachers what interactions and supports they thought they needed to undertake their design tasks, what actions or activities were provided by the team or school, and what was lacking. The results of the group interviews were straightforward. Teachers were fairly consistent across all sites in what they felt was needed to promote change, regardless of the design (see Gitlin & Magonis, 1995; Muncey, 1994; Muncey & McQuillian, 1993; Prestine & Bowen, 1993; and Rosenholtz, 1989):

- An introduction to the design by the team that was compelling or at least clear and that was provided to *all* teachers.

- Relevant training provided to *all* administrators and teachers at the school with behavioral changes or new processes modeled.

- Concrete materials and models to use in classrooms, committees, or other forums for reform.

- Presence of the design team members to help them or presence of a facilitator to aid in their understanding on a day-to-day basis.

- Teacher teaming to work on design issues or curriculum development.

- Participatory governance to ensure continued support by teachers to the design.

- Teacher time for curriculum development, teacher-to-teacher interactions, and becoming adept at new behaviors (time for practice at the individual and school level).

- Exposure to new ideas.

However, teachers and design teams did indicate that the above components of an implementation strategy can substitute for each other. For example, strong documentation of a design can substitute at least on the margins for training and facilitators at the site. In addition, some implementation components might be more important for some type of designs. For example, teacher time was significantly more important for sites working to develop their own curriculum with a design team that used a site-based development approach than it was for a team that supplied curriculum units.

Effects of Different Team
Approaches to Implementation

Initial content analysis of the design documents in the fall of 1993 indicated a disturbing lack of attention in the proposals to implementation strategies. Much more emphasis had been given to the design itself. The teams had given little thought to how to get a design into a school aside from the large distinction between the team-development approach and the site-development approaches.

As Phase 2 continued, implementation strategies evolved and the teams began to distinguish themselves from each other. Design teams differed dramatically in their interactions with the sites and their role or their associated school's ability to provide the support teachers indicated was helpful. The results of the teachers' feedback on what they received from design teams is presented in Fig. 11.4.[11] The following sums up the implications:

- AC and RW, teams we indicated made substantial progress toward their goals, were also associated in teachers' minds with having many components of a strong implementation strategy.

- CON, CLC and MRSH used strong strategies, improved them over time, and made greater progress toward design goals as indicated previously with more moderate to substantial progress on elements.

- Teachers indicated that the EL strategy was very strong for getting underway, but that it did not provide aid in all areas. This team was associated with lower levels of progress by the end of Phase 2.

- Teachers indicated that LALC, AT, and NA did not provide them the needed assistance in the first year, but these teams improved by the second. Teachers associated this slow progress with initial poor implementation strategies.

Implications for Phase 3 and Reform

Our assessment indicated that the team capability at the beginning of the effort, the number of sites chosen, the type of design and the approach to demonstration, and the implementation strategies had strong effects on progress in Phase 2. Some of these differences will likely be less important in Phase 3.

---

[11] Consensus among the teachers we spoke with appeared to be very strong, so that we suspect that a survey using similar questions would reproduce our results with high reliability. AT, LALC, and NA admit that their implementation strategies have not produced the results they desired and are in the process of restructuring them.

Figure 11.4

Implementation Strategies by Design

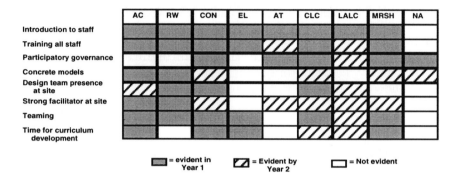

progress during Phase 2, they are not likely to be as important in Phase 3. The exclusion of LALC from initial Phase 3 sites, the reorganization of AT, and the more recent progress of EL, indicate that the more severe issues of lack of team capacity or capability should dissipate by Phase 3.

The issue of team capability, that is, what skills and capabilities are needed, holds some implications for other reform efforts. The organizations that develop designs and assist schools to transform require a conglomeration of visionaries to drive the design toward ambitious undertakings; expertise in development in many elements, such as standards assessment and curriculum development to ensure a quality product; "people" people who can interact with school staff and train them; communicators who can write documents designed to convey visionary and concrete changes to be made; political negotiators for those designs that take on changes in the system governed outside of the school; and strong administrators who can count the beans and hand in deliverables to NAS. These different skills and talents are normally rather dispersed through the education domain and do not come neatly packaged in existing teams. Organizations like those that NAS is trying to create are few and far between and require deliberate development.

The need for these many capabilities when combined with the experiences of NA in serving many sites indicates the possible difficulties that will be faced by teams in Phase 3. The capabilities that had to be gathered to create a team indicate the enormity of the undertaking involved in educational reform—often overlooked in the general press as a matter of simply changing curriculum in superficial ways. Phase 3 requires that the teams now build capacity to affect more sites. NA had difficulty beginning at a high level of sites. On the other hand, some of the teams have shown the capability to grow to more sites, even as they were developing capacity. While the evidence is unclear on this point, there is some indication that the Phase 3 scaleup requiring teams to add more schools or sites is a "doable" approach to reform.[12]

Differences between design types, specifically core, comprehensive and systemic designs, will remain somewhat during Phase 3. Changes in governance, staffing and social services promise to take a long time and might be beyond the capability of most teams without a predisposed jurisdiction and community. Thus, comprehensive and systemic designs will always take longer and their success will be more susceptible to site capability than core designs. However, by taking on these issues they hope to ensure more permanency than the other approach. If core design teams do not adequately address social services, autonomy and staffing issues, then permanency of the changes accomplished in individual schools might be at risk.

Significant differences will continue to exist between designs in the demands they make upon schools for time and resources, especially in the area of curriculum development. This should be understood by new sites entering into agreements with teams. Important to reform in general, no firm agreement exists as to a best approach to helping teachers effectively use new curriculum. NAS teams took different approaches and, at least from Phase 2 evidence, several contrasting ones appear to have been useful in getting teachers to use them. Whether teachers or a team develop the curriculum appears to be less important than that the teacher's burden is reduced by the provision of standards, curriculum frameworks, and solid materials for development (Gitlin & Margonis, 1995; McLaughlin, 1990). If the team chooses to develop the curriculum, then it should value teachers for their ability to improve on experts' products.

---

[12] Other reform organizations have had rapid increases in the number of sites in which they work. For example, Henry Levin's Accelerated Schools began at two pilot sites in 1987-1988. By 1990 it was in 54 sites and by 1994-1995 it was in over 700 sites. Doing so required the development of regional centers in fall 1990. The Coalition of Essential Schools under Ted Sizer started with 10 schools in 1984-1985. When it linked to Re: Learning in 1988 it had grown to 99. In 1993-1994 it had grown to over 820 schools.

The findings indicate that typical schools cannot muster the capacity to enact the many reforms advanced by teams within the limited period of time provided and to the extent demanded by NAS's Phase 2 goals. This is more the case the more reformers rely on teachers to specify, develop, and implement the reforms. Attempting major changes across many elements is draining. Thus, teams with ambitious designs might be forced into slower progress as they are limited by teacher time and the capacity of teachers to absorb multiple changes at once.

A general lesson for all school reform is that teachers cannot operate effectively to change classroom behaviors without concrete supports to guide their efforts, and time to learn and assimilate new behaviors. Schools cannot hope to accomplish the changes envisioned by the designs, unless the implementation strategy supports all the staff and enables them to effectively work together toward reform. In addition, the experiences of the schools we sampled indicated that initial buy-in to a design was fleeting. Long-term commitment by teachers was developed over time in a working relationship where a team and a school staff interacted with each other toward common goals. Strong assistance toward change, concrete models, coaching, and time produced change and, therefore, more commitment.

We think this issue ties back to the notion of the many competencies required by design teams. As the number of elements and sites grows, the teams will be increasingly challenged to develop new and more extensive competencies in many areas of reform.

Accomplishment of NAS As a Whole

NAS has encouraged the creation of nine design teams, seven of which it has chosen to go on to Phase 3. Some of the teams have been more successful than others at meeting NAS deadlines and goals, but all have had some important success in enabling schools to begin the process of transformation. These teams, learning from a development period, appear to be transforming themselves from fledgling enterprises to more solid organizations that can help schools make fundamental changes in the way they deliver curriculum and instruction to students and the manner in which they are structured. The teams have interacted with over 140 sites which have accomplished different levels and different types of reforms. Significant input and process changes have taken place in the majority of the schools associated with NAS designs. This by itself is no small accomplishment. It remains to be seen if these changes result in improved student outcomes in all cases and if they can be reproduced in multiple sites during Phase 3. RAND analysis in Phase 3 will focus on changes over time in school-level student outcomes and factors that have contributed to them.

In a broader sense, the distinctive contribution of NAS has been to help capitalize, support, and legitimize a new mechanism for the building of school-level capability for transformation: a design-based assistance organization. In this sense NAS's efforts can be seen as an attempt at capacity building (see McDonnell & Grubb, 1995). Lessons from the Phase 2 effort indicate that to be effective in helping transform schools a design-based assistance organization should have the following:

- A capable design team that can provide design-related assistance to multiple sites.

- A fully developed design that communicates effectively the vision and specific tasks of school reform advocated by the team. This design should include a regular self-assessment by the school to feed back information useful in measuring the school's progress toward reform and to provide guidance for areas of improvement.

- A proven implementation strategy that allows the schools to become adept at quality control of the curriculum and instruction within the school and that aids schools in changing the structure of professional development, scheduling, and governance to support student education goals.

- The existence of demonstration sites to act as further laboratories of reform and to provide hands-on evidence of success.

In addition, this type of organization must be supported by reasonable expectations on the part of its partner districts and schools. Time and resources must be provided to allow the unfolding of all the elements. Parties to the reform must understand that some elements will take longer to develop and will require significant contributions of time and effort by the schools and districts involved.

Limited Influence of NAS on School Reform

If fully developed over the next few years, this combination of design and of assistance in transforming schools might prove to be a powerful impetus toward improved student outcomes in many schools. However, it does not present the only intervention or a complete picture of needed reforms. The NAS approach of design teams is only part of a strategy aimed at wide-scale improvement.

The usefulness of the design-based assistance organization appears limited to school- and perhaps district-level changes. NAS's approach to Phase 3, concentrating on systemic, district-level changes to the operating environment in conjunction with the assistance by design teams of particular schools is intended to marry bottom-up school reform with a limited set of mid-level systemic reforms. The ability of NAS to influence change at this middle level will be put to the test in Phase 3 as it enters into agreements with a small group of jurisdictions to work toward school-level transformation for more than 30 percent of the district's schools within a five-year period.

However, important actors with strong systemic influence on states, districts, and schools remain outside these teams' and NAS's ability to influence. These are quasigovernmental bodies, higher level governmental bodies, assessment organizations, teachers' colleges, schools of higher education, and the more general public. These groups and their systemic influence will have to be addressed by other interventions, outside NAS's range. For restructuring to succeed, effective ways must be found to incorporate these other actors or groups into the effort. This will remain a major challenge for NAS and other like institutions in the coming years.

Acknowledgments and Notes

This research was produced with the support of NAS and the Ford Foundation. Although the author took responsibility for the writing of this chapter, the research is the product of efforts by Tom Glennan, Sarah Keith, Karen Mitchell, Susanna Purnell, Kim Ramsey, and Christina Smith. Further details can be found in two published RAND reports: Bodilly, Purnell, Ramsey, and Smith (1995) and Bodilly (1995).

References

Berman, P., & McLaughlin, M.W. (1975). *Federal programs supporting educational change, the findings in review*. (R-1589/4-HEW). Santa Monica, CA: RAND.

Bimber, B. (1994). *The decentralization mirage, comparing decisionmaking arrangements in four high schools*. (MR-459-GGF/LE). Santa Monica, CA: RAND.

Bodilly, S. (1995). *Lessons from New American Schools Development Corporation's demonstration phase.* (DRU-1175-NASDC). Santa Monica, CA: RAND.

Bodilly, S., Purnell, S., Ramsey, K., & Smith, C. (1995). *Designing New American Schools, baseline observations on nine design teams* (MR-598-NASDC). Santa Monica, CA: RAND.

Cuban, L. (1990). Reforming again, again, and again. *Educational Researcher, 19* (1), 3–13.

Elmore, R., & McLaughlin, M. (1988). *Steady work: policy, practice, and the reform of American education.* (R-357-NIE/RC). Santa Monica, CA: RAND.

Firestone, W., Fuhrman, S. & Kirst, M. (1989). *The progress of reform: An appraisal of state education initiatives.* New Brunswick, NJ: Rutgers University, Center for Policy Research in Education.

Gitlin, A., & Margonis, F. (1995, August). The political aspect of reform: Teacher resistance as good sense. *American Journal of Education, 103,* 377–405.

Goodlad, J. (1984). *A place called school.* New York: McGraw-Hill.

Huberman, A. M., & Miles, M. (1984). Rethinking the quest for school improvement: Some findings from the DESSI Study." *Teachers College Record, 86* (1), 34–54.

Herman, R., & Stringfield, S. (1995, April). *Ten promising programs for educating disadvantaged students: Evidence of impact.* Paper presented at the American Education Research Association meeting, San Francisco.

Levin, H. (1993). Learning from accelerated schools. Unpublished manuscript, Stanford University, Stanford, CA.

Lieberman, A. (1991). *Early lessons in restructuring schools: National Center for Restructuring Education, Schools, and Teaching (NCREST).* Unpublished manuscript, Columbia University Teachers College, New York.

McDonnell, L. & Grubb, N. (1995). *Education and training for work: The policy instruments and the institutions* (R-4026-NCRVE/UCB). Santa Monica, CA: RAND.

324

McLaughlin, M. (1990). The RAND Change Agent Study revisited: Macro perspectives and micro realities. *Educational Researcher, 19* (9), 11–16.

Muncey, D. (1994). *Individual and schoolwide change in eight coalition schools: findings from a longitudinal ethnography study.* Paper presented at the annual meeting of the American Education Research Association, New Orleans.

Muncey, D. & McQuillian, P. (1994). Preliminary findings from a five year study of the Coalition of Essential Schools. *Phi Delta Kappan, 74* (6), 486–489.

New American Schools Development Corporation. (1991). *Designs for a new generation of American schools: Request for proposal.* Arlington, VA: Author.

Policy Studies Associates, Inc. (1994). *School reform for youth at risk: an analysis of six change models, vol. I. Summary analysis.* Washington, DC: US Department of Education.

Prestine, N., & Bowen, C. (1993). Benchmarks of change: assessing essential school restructuring efforts. *Educational Evaluation and Policy Analysis, 15* (3), 298–318.

Rosenholtz, S. (1989). *Teacher's workplace, the social organization of schools.* New York: Longman.

Smith, M., & O'Day, J. (1990). Systemic school reform. *Politics of Education Association Yearbook.* (233–267). Taylor & Francis, Ltd.

Smrekar, C. (1994). The missing link in school-linked services. *Educational Evaluation and Policy Analysis, 16* (4), 422–433.

Summers, A., & Johnson, A. (1994, October). *A review of the evidence on the effects of school-related management plans.* Paper presented at the conference on Improving the Performance of America's Schools: Economic choices, National Research Council, National Academy of Science, Washington, DC.

Turnbull, B. (1985). Using governance and support systems to advance school improvement. *The Elementary School Journal, 85* (3), 1985, 337–351.

Tyack, D. (1990). Restructuring in historical perspective: tinkering toward utopia. *Teachers College Record, 92* (2), 169–191.

Appendix

ATLAS Communities   (617) 969-7100
55 Chapel Street
Newton, MA 02158

Audrey Cohen College   (212) 343-1234
345 Hudson Street
New York, NY 10014

Community Learning Centers   (612) 645-0200
2550 University Avenue, Suite 347N
St. Paul, Minnesota 55114

Co-NECT Schools   (617) 873-3000
BBN Corporation
150 Cambridge Park Drive
Cambridge, MA 02138

Expeditionary Learning Outward Bound   (617) 576-1260
122 Mount Auburn Street
Cambridge, MA 02138

Los Angeles Learning Centers   (212) 622-5237
Los Angeles Educational Partnership
315 W. 9th Street #1110
Los Angeles, CA 90015

Modern Red Schoolhouse   (317) 545-1000
Hudson Institute
5395 Emerson Way
Indianapolis, IN 46226

National Alliance   (716) 546-7620
    for Restructuring Education
39 State Street, Suite 500
Rochester, NY 14614

New American Schools   (703) 908-9500
1000 Wilson Boulevard, Suite 2710
Arlington, VA 22209

Roots and Wings   (410) 516-8800
CRESPAR
3505 N. Charles Street
Baltimore, MD 21218

Index